CAMPUS POLICING

The Nature of University Police Work

Diane C. Bordner
Professional Research Services, Inc.

David M. Petersen
Georgia State University

UNIVERSITY
PRESS OF
AMERICA

LANHAM • NEW YORK • LONDON

For Our Mothers

Ronie Campbell Bordner

and

Betty Jean Muir

ACKNOWLEDGEMENTS

We are grateful to the many persons connected with the research setting who aided us in this project. Our prime debt is to those university police officers about whom this book is written. Without their cooperation and generosity this investigation would not have been possible. Our appreciation is extended to the many individual officers whose willingness to talk freely enriched these pages and made a significant contribution to knowledge.

We wish to thank (with the customary disclaimers) our colleagues Bill Amis, Phil Davis, Jim Inciardi, and Harv Voss for their general criticisms and specific suggestions on earlier drafts of this book. Those comments we were able to address led to a significant improvement in the book; as for the others, they pose important challenges to our future research efforts in this area.

vi

CONTENTS

\

PREFACE

Despite the fact that the first generally recognized "campus police department" was established in 1894 when two commissioned New Haven police officers were employed full time by Yale University, there was little need for campus law enforcement organizations per se during the early 1900s. During this time educational institutions handled most campus disciplinary problems internally and depended upon local police agencies' assistance only in criminal violations.

The beginning of the modern campus police force derives from many sources ranging from custodial workers to high-ranking administrative officials of educational institutions:

> In different eras and on different campuses his forerunner was the janitor, or the watchman, or the faculty chairman of the grounds committee, or in some cases the lineage can be traced directly to the president of the institution. Neil (1980:28)

Typically most people think of the watchman as the direct lineal predecessor of the campus police officer. It was not until the 1920s that the campus watchman or guard came into prominence in educational institutions. Historically these watchmen, who were usually older retired men and employed only at night and on weekends, were attached to the maintenance or physical plant department, and their main concern was with the protection of college property. The watchmen were given no training as law enforcement officers and were not expected to perform as such. Their chief functions were to determine the security of buildings at night and on weekends (e.g., closing windows, locking and unlocking doors, and other duties to protect property) and "patrol" the campus in order to detect fire hazards, check boilers, detect leaky pipes and otherwise perform preventive maintenance duties. With the repeal of prohibition in the early 1930s the watchmen-guards gradually began to take on other functions dealing with the enforcement of rules and regulations governing student conduct. For example, they became responsible for detecting violations of curfew rules and reporting infractions of the ban on drinking on campus, in addition to their security and preventive maintenance duties.

Watchmen-type operations were predominate until the 1950s. During this decade university administrators began to recognize the need for a more organized protective force on campus brought on by the problems created by the increasing growth and, consequent, complexity of the campus. Increases in enrollment and, thus, potential increases in behavioral incidents, expansion of the physical plant, increases in motor traffic, and problems incident to parking led to an awareness of the need for some semblance of police presence on campus. Consequently, at the beginning of the 1950s retired law enforcement officials were hired as upper level administrators of departments and they tended to model their campus departments after the model most familiar to them--urban police departments. Despite structural reorganization, concomitant switches in officer titles from watchmen to security officers, and increases in department size, most campus "enforcement" organizations remained little more than the watchmen-guard type operations that preceded them in terms of function and caliber of personnel. Like their watchmen predecessors, line security officers were generally older males, poorly educated, poorly paid, and untrained (Steinberg, 1972); they continued to perform the same security functions (i.e., protection of university property and equipment, and preventive maintenance). Additionally, like their watchmen predecessors, security officers of the fifties were limited in enforcement to a pseudo police function. Generally lacking in police authority, campus officers had no more power to control the behavior of others than the ordinary citizen. Consequently, upon detection of a crime the security officer's major responsibilities included protection of evidence at the crime scene, detention of the suspect, if known, and notification of the local police. Stated differently, in their enforcement role campus officers were limited to detection, detention (if possible) and reporting rather than apprehension and arrest. Moreover, like their watchmen predecessors, campus officers continued to operate under the doctrine of in loco parentis which had prevailed in educational institutions for many years. This doctrine, in effect, limited the officers' enforcement function by

establishing a double standard on campus which called
for the detention of "outsiders" for arrest but referred student law breakers to the dean's office for
discipline. Additionally, officers were often expected to take no action with regard to faculty,
staff and other employees when a law violation
occurred.

The transition from the silent generation of the
fifties to the active generation of the sixties and
early seventies left many colleges and universities
totally unprepared to cope with the new threats to
the tranquility of the campus (Skolnick, 1969;
Becker, 1970; Kobetz and Hamm, 1970; President's Commission on Campus Unrest, 1971; Powell, 1981). With
the advent of the era of student dissent, campus protest demonstrations, disruptive student activities,
violence and increases in reported crime and fear of
crime, an increasing number of educational institutions began replacing their line security officers
with more educated and better trained police officers
with police powers of arrest and duties to enforce
state statutes on campus. The decision to professionalize the campus police was, in part, a direct
result of the negative experiences with intervention
of local police and national guardsmen on campus.
During the era of student dissent, Kent State offers
a vivid example. It was also recognized that if the
university did not govern itself it would be governed
by others who might be less responsive to the campus
community. Thus, professional police departments began to emerge on college campuses during the 1960s
and early 1970s, and law enforcement activities became part of the ever expanding role of the university officer.

In short, in the post World War II era, the major change on the campus was the divestment of the
campus watchman-type organization and the formation
of a formal police organizational structure. The
formalization of police structure was largely the result of factors such as the presence of larger student bodies, more vehicles on campus, the expansion
of the physical plant (i.e., more buildings to patrol), a rise in the individual crime rate and fear
of crime, and the potential for disorder arising from
student demonstrations. With the formalization of
campus police departments during the 1960s and early
1970s there was an expansion in the functional scope
of university policing to include enforcement of the

law, in addition to the more traditional functions of plant protection, preventive maintenance and regulation of student conduct. Concurrent with formalization and functional expansion was a change in the nature of campus protection personnel: the new campus officers were generally younger, better educated and trained, and more professional (Powell, 1967; Kassinger, 1971; Holloman, 1972; Abramson, 1974; Webb, 1975).

At present, there is a tremendous diversity to be found in university and college police forces. At least three types can be identified (Powell, 1971a, 1981; Gelber, 1972; Holloman, 1972; Sims, 1972; Post, 1977; Neil, 1980; Ricks et al., 1981). At one extreme there still exist watchmen or guards who are typically untrained and whose duties consist of locking/unlocking doors, detecting vandalism, and handling other maintenance problems. In the middle of the continuum are modern security forces in which the watchman function has been extended to include pseudo-police functions and are generally involved to some degree with regulation of student conduct. At the other end of the pole are sophisticated police forces, often headed by former police officers and organized like municipal departments, whose officers have full peace officer authority, project a strong police image in their uniforms and equipment and are concerned with the straightforward application of the law in the academic community, that is, they are not concerned with the academic status of law violators nor do they have anything to do with regulation of student conduct.

Local law enforcement agencies, such as county and municipal agencies, simply are not in an adequate position to provide police protection for the nation's college and university campuses. Their other responsibilities preclude them from giving institutions of higher education the special attention they need. There are over 3,000 colleges, universities and branch campuses in the United States today. They serve approximately 11.5 million students, employ approximately two million people, and represent more than 78 billion dollars of investment in property, facilities and equipment (National Center for Educational Statistics, 1981). On any given campus, campus police are responsible for the safety and security of thousands of people and a multi-million dollar investment in plant and equipment in their

daily work. They complement local police by providing a greater degree of protection and enforcement in
an area largely overlooked by local police. Given
the masses of humanity either passing through or
economically dependent upon educational institutions,
the sizeable investment in physical plant, and increases in crime, the campus police occupy a more
pivotal position today than was the case in the past.

CHAPTER I

INTRODUCTION

The police are perhaps the most visible and active institution of social control in American society. Throughout the last century increasing urbanization, modernization and heterogeneity within the United States have combined with climactic social upheavals and increases in crime to thrust the police progressively into the center of the public arena where their vital significance cannot be ignored. Because their role and function is far too important to be taken for granted, the police deserve intensive and continual study. Recognition of the importance of conducting research on the activities of rule enforcers (agents of social control) as well as rule breakers (criminals) was evident in sociology and criminology almost two decades ago (Erikson, 1962; Kitsuse, 1962; Becker; 1963; Quinney, 1964). Since that time police practices have become a major subject of scholarly interest and numerous systematic studies have been conducted of police in major metropolitan areas using a variety of methods (see, for example, Banton, 1964; Skolnick, 1966; Niederhoffer, 1967; Wilson, 1968; Alex, 1969; Bayley and Mendelsohn, 1969; Westley, 1970; Cohen and Chaiken, 1973; Webster, 1973; Manning, 1977). This research has amply demonstrated that while policing is an occupation which is universally practiced, it varies by location as well as by specialty. This feature of American policing warns scholars of the danger of overgeneralization; at the same time it points to the need for the study of policing in a variety of settings and contexts.

While there has been a voluminous amount of research on and scholarly interest in municipal police organizations and the work behavior of their members over the last several decades, other types of policing have been largely neglected. One type of policing that has received little attention is campus policing. The present research is a study of the nature of police work in the university setting. It is an investigation of the organization and reality of everyday campus policing. The focus is on the

1

ways in which campus police actually go about their
work and how they conceive of that work.

What is campus police work? What is known
regarding the essence and variety of campus police
procedures and practices? How does campus police
work differ from municipal policing? In the next
several pages we will look at what others have concluded about the work world of both campus and
municipal police in order to place the current
research in perspective.

Campus Police Forces:[1] Organizational Structure and Function

Even though the student protests and unrest of
the 1960s and early 1970s spawned considerable
interest in campus disorder, little serious attention
was directed specifically to the campus police. In
other words, the literature on student protest and
disorder reflects an emphasis on the role of outside
police interventions on campus to the exclusion of
consideration of the role of the campus police. If
campus police are mentioned, they are referred to
only in an incidental manner (see, for example,
Stark, 1972; Dynes et al., 1974). In fact, somewhat
surprisingly, much of the protest literature does not
even mention the campus officer[2] (see, for example,
Flicker, 1969; Holmes, 1969; Skolnick, 1969; Becker,
1970). Despite the lack of direct attention to
campus police in the protest literature, the campus
disorders themselves spawned a residual interest in
campus police and increased attention to them in professional police and security magazines, as well as
book length publications in the 1970s.

There are several general features of the current
literature on campus police worthy of note. First,
much of the literature that does exist is not sub-
stantiated by research. To a considerable degree,
the literature reflects the authors' opinions as
formulated on the basis of personal experiences or
haphazard observations, rather than any rigorous
scientific analysis. For example, much of the literature providing an overview of the organization,
administration and operations of campus police offers
no supporting evidence for the statements made and
the conclusions reached (see, for example,
Iannarelli, 1968; Kobetz and Hamm, 1970; Nielsen,

2

1971; Sims, 1971 and 1972; Kimble, 1978; Kassinger, 1980; and Powell, 1981). Second, much of the literature on campus police reflects the same issues and concerns found in the literature on urban police. These issues and debates translated to the campus setting include the role of campus police (Powell, 1971b; Gunson, 1979), the hazards of using official statistics (Bielec, 1981), the need for increased training and professionalism (Powell, 1967; Kassinger, 1971; Holloman, 1972; Webb, 1975), the carrying and use of weapons on campus (Morgan, 1979), the theoretical classification of campus agencies as police or security (Calder, 1974; Kirkley, 1978), and the autonomy of the campus law enforcement agency (Cox, 1977). The final characteristic of the existing literature is that it often deals with rather narrow and specific solutions to immediate problems in particular university settings. In other words, the literature is highly descriptive and deals with such things as the use of mounted patrol on a sprawling park-like campus (Nielsen, 1974), the use of student aides in patrolling residence halls (Peabody, 1977), the use of scooters on urban campuses (McDaniel, 1970), solutions to campus shoplifting (Mapes, 1968) and bicycle theft (Peabody, 1975), standardization of officer performance evaluations (Williams, 1979), and so forth.

There have been only a limited number of scholarly investigations of campus police. These studies have focused largely on departmental characteristics and functions and have utilized data obtained largely from questionnaires mailed to department administrators (see, for example, Csanyi, 1958; Bartram and Smith, 1969; Adams and Rogers, 1971; Gelber, 1972; Abramson, 1974; Scott, 1976; and Cox and Sutherland, 1979). This research demonstrates that campus police departments vary in size, organizational structure and range of function due to type of institutional control (public or private), type of institution (university or college), source of authority (legislation, deputization, contract guard), size of enrollment, setting (urban, rural, suburban), and academic level (junior, senior, graduate). More specifically, for example, research has shown that most American universities with an enrollment of 10,000 or more students tend to operate police departments which provide the entire spectrum of police services, and those with fewer students tend to operate a night watchman or guard system that

3

is responsible for the physical plant and university facilities, but not law enforcement (Bartram and Smith, 1969; Nielsen, 1971). Large urban schools tend to place more emphasis upon specially trained, experienced and fully qualified officers (Bartram and Smith, 1969; Adams and Rogers, 1971). There has been a dramatic increase in the use of females in campus police work in recent years, especially in large urban public schools (Drapeau and Cudmore, 1979). Most campus police departments have a proprietary relationship with the institution in which they are located rather than a contractural relation, though the likelihood of a contractural relation with private security agencies increases if the institution is a private, small college (Cox and Sutherland, 1979).

There have been only three major studies of campus police (Etheridge, 1958; Gelber, 1972; Scott, 1976). A brief description of each of these works in terms of purpose, methods and findings will enable the reader to assess more fully the existing state of knowledge with respect to campus police. In order to analyze the organization and administration of campus protective and enforcement programs and determine their objectives and functions, Etheridge (1958) studied nine major mid-eastern universities similar in size, educational objectives, student bodies and administrative organization. His methodology included structured interviews with the Chief Campus Security Officer and the Dean of Student Personnel Affairs at each of these institutions, personal observations based on campus visitation, and an examination of published materials such as student codes and traffic regulations. Among Etheridge's more significant findings were: (1) the predominant pattern of departmental location within the institution was under the physical plant department; (2) the universal problems of the campus protective and enforcement agencies were the situations created by motor vehicles; (3) the most common reason for persons leaving campus policing were not those related to prestige or status factors, but rather were objections to the physical conditions under which officers had to work (e.g., having to climb stairs, walking great distances, being involved in night work); (4) suppressive tactics generally were not used to control student groups; and (5) since World War II campus protective and enforcement agencies have increased both in size and scope of activities changing from a primary emphasis on providing watch services to providing a wide range of services in traffic regulation, investigation and other areas of normal police service.

Gelber (1972) describes the role of the campus security officer in terms of historical origins, legal structures and operational functions and, in addition, provides an appraisal of the campus security officer by four components of the educational institution (i.e., security director, student, faculty and administrator). Data on characteristics and operational functions of the campus security office were obtained by a mailed questionnaire distributed to the campus security director of the 245 member schools (210 responded) of the International Association of College and University Security Directors (IACUSD). Data appraising the role of the campus security function and the perception of it were obtained by mailed questionnaires submitted to each of the following on the campuses of the membership of the IACUSD: campus security director, department chairman in both political science and sociology (if both were returned, only one was utilized), editor of the campus newspaper and president of the student government (if both were returned, only one was utilized), and the dean for student personnel affairs. From the analysis of his data Gelber draws three important conclusions. First, variables such as size of enrollment, type of institutional control and academic level influence the operational functions and duties assigned to the security office. Second, campus security officers perform a wide variety of duties and the extent to which they perform non-police duties suggests more emphasis on service than on law enforcement. Finally, campus security officers have long been cast in menial roles with minimal responsibilities and have never attained professional recognition or legitimacy within the university community. Hence, the campus security officer continues to exercise an uncertain authority amidst a questioning constituency.

Focusing on campus police agencies possessing powers of arrest and providing at least one direct police service (i.e., patrol, traffic control or criminal investigation), Scott (1976) conducted a mailed survey of agencies on 108 campuses representing 28 states and 60 standard metropolitan statistical areas. His major purpose was to examine patterns of college and university police training, personnel practices and compensation and to highlight differences in service provision among departments according to geographic location, size and form of institutional control. His major findings were: (1) public institutions tend to have larger police agencies; (2) an overwhelming majority (82%) of the agencies required entry level training of officers; (3) larger departments were more likely to require training; (4) an overwhelming majority (87%) of the agencies required officers to hold at least a high school diploma or its equivalent; (5) salary levels increased with departmental size; (6) average salaries of officers lagged behind those offered by municipal departments; (7) most campus agencies considered patrol their primary function; (8) larger departments were more likely to investigate crimes; and (9) campus agencies of all sizes had a higher density of patrol than municipal agencies in that they deploy considerably more officers per 1,000 population than do municipal agencies.

To summarize, much of the existing literature on campus police may be generally characterized as highly descriptive and particularistic, concerned with specific issues and statements of opinion, and lacking in supportive research evidence. Most studies to date have employed a quantitative survey methodology to discover the characteristic features of campus police agencies (e.g., function, size, type of personnel, administrative style, and so on). While the existing research provides data on the nature of campus police departments, it offers little, if any, insight into the nature of campus policing.

Municipal Police and Policing in Urban Society

Given the relative dearth of research on campus policing, a review of the literature on urban police was undertaken to discover major recurrent themes and, thus, to provide guidance for the present study. Scholarly and applied interests in urban police are so diverse and the potentially relevant literature so vast that no brief review can do them justice. The works cited were selected because of their more sociological cast and because they introduce the reader to a range of relevant material.

6

Police Organization

Police departments share several important features with other large-scale formal organizations. In the first place, like other organizations, police systems are essentially "open systems"; police systems are institutions in interaction with the rest of the social structure. Not only do the police have a direct influence on elements of the external environment but the external condition has consequences for the character of police organization and operations (Niederhoffer, 1967; Reiss and Bordua, 1967; Clark and Sykes, 1974). Niederhoffer (1967) notes, for example, that the power structure and ideology of the community direct and set boundaries to the sphere of police action as evidenced by selective enforcement practices. Clark and Sykes (1974) argue that the external influences which determine the major tasks, organization and operation of the police include population ecology and demography, culture, law, politics, economy and technology. The importance of the environment in shaping police organization and operations is developed in Wilson's (1968) work on the influence of community context on styles of policing. He identified three styles of policing--watch, legalistic and service--and suggests that the primary differences in them result from differences in the communities and citizens served by the departments. In communities in which the residents share a common life style, set of values and level of affluence policing is generally service oriented and emphasizes counseling and referral rather than arrest. In communities in which residents share little in common with each other, policing is either watch or legalistic in orientation depending upon the orientation of upper-level municipal and police administrators. In cities where officials are part of the political machine policing tends to be watch oriented and emphasizes informal processing, that is, "street justice." In cities where officials are reform oriented policing is legalistically oriented and stresses the formal processing of nearly all criminal incidents. Because of the importance of the environment for police organization and operations, considerable attention is devoted to police community relations in the literature.[3]

A second feature the police share with other formal organizations is that they operate in a complex and contradictory normative environment. These contradictions place police in a dilemma, generate tension and may lead to improper police action. On the one hand, police organizations are independent and autonomous agencies operating in an unbiased manner in the interest of all people. On the other hand, police organizations are obligated to their funding source for survival and, hence, must operate realistically in the interests of the power structure. When the general interests come in conflict with the interests of the power elite, the latter usually prevail over the former. The result is biased policing in terms of differential enforcement, selective enforcement, manipulation of crime statistics to arrive at an "acceptable" crime rate, and so forth (Skolnick, 1966; Wilson, 1968; Sherman, 1974; Manning, 1977).

Perhaps the greatest contradiction in the normative environment surrounding police organization is the inherent contradiction between the two socially defined functions of police--law and order. It is generally noted in the literature that the legal regulation of public conduct is inconsistent with the protection of civil liberties (Skolnick, 1966; Niederhoffer, 1967; Wilson, 1968; Westley, 1970).4 On a practical level police are expected to maintain order but to do so under the rule of law by adhering to ideally formulated legal principles. In other words, police are expected to protect society against crime and other threats to order while, at the same time, they are expected to extend procedural safeguards to persons responsible for crime and disorder. These contradictory expectations place a tremendous burden on the police. Skolnick (1966:6) describes the situation as follows:

> The police in democratic society are required to maintain order and to do so under the rule of law. As functionaries charged with maintaining order, they are part of the bureaucracy. The ideology of democratic bureaucracy emphasizes initiative rather than disciplined adherence to rules and regulations. By contrast, the rule of law emphasizes the rights of individual citizens and constraints upon the initiative of legal officials. This tension between the operational consequences of ideals of order, efficiency, and initiative, on the

one hand, and legality, on the other hand, constitutes the principle problem of police as a democratic legal organization.

Because officers believe that due process protections make it more difficult for police to control crime effectively, they may minimize the importance of due process to get their job done.

The final major feature police organizations share with other formal organizations is a bureaucratic structure. To date, there has been a great deal of systematic sociological work done on the internal organization and task differentiation of police agencies (Banton, 1964; Skolnick, 1966; Buckner, 1967; Skolnick and Woodworth, 1967; Wilson, 1968; Westley, 1970; Manning, 1977). It is to a general discussion of this literature that we now turn.

Bureaucratic structure

Much of the literature typically portrays large urban departments as formally resembling bureaucracies.[5] Among Weber's (1946) characteristics of an ideal bureaucracy which police departments generally display are: (1) a labyrinth of hierarchy and channels of communication; (2) a clear division of labor with functional specialization and task differentiation; (3) selection by fixed criteria of merit; (4) promotions based on competitive exams, competence and seniority; (5) job security in the form of salaries, tenure and retirement; (6) red tape, written documents and massive permanent files; (7) work as the primary occupation; (8) impersonality and authority in one's office rather than in his person; and (9) emphasis on rules and regulations in guiding and controlling the activities and actions of members.

In recent years, scholars have noted several major ways in which police organizations deviate in reality from the ideal model of bureaucracy. Many scholars have noted, for example, that the assumption that activities are guided by rules and regulations simply does not work in practice (see, Skolnick, 1966; Wilson, 1968; Reiss, 1971; Manning, 1977). There are essentially two reasons for this espoused in the literature. First, many of the rules that

9

exist in police organizations are essentially use-less. While bureaucracy requires the standardization of rules by a central authority in the expectation that universalism will prevail in the application of those rules, rules cannot be written to comprehend every situation and cover all contingencies. Existing departmental rules can tell an officer what should be done, but what is actually done depends on the contingencies of the situation. Moreover, all rules cannot be enforced. Hence, variability and discretion rather than standardization characterize police behavior (Banton, 1964; LaFave, 1965; Skolnick, 1966; Black and Reiss, 1967; Petersen, 1968; Wilson, 1968; Reiss, 1971). On a practical level, interventions are a matter of discretion. Consequently, Manning (1977) argues that police actions are "situationally justified actions" rather than bureaucratic actions, that is, actions are rationalized and justified after the fact rather than undertaken because certain rules prescribe certain responses. Second, the rules that exist are essentially unenforceable. In police organizations, operations are atomized at the level of patrol, and street-level officers possess a great deal of latitude in their work. Police supervisors at head-quarters have no reliable way to determine what an officer in the field is doing during his/her eight hours of patrol; supervisors are not in a position to determine whether rules and regulations are being followed. Police command is precarious, and to a great extent the work of patrol is unsupervised and unsupervisable.6 Because departments lack internal control over their members in the field, they cannot control discretion. In general, the lack of internal control and the opportunity for the exercise of dis-cretion in the field led Manning (1977) to argue that the model of police organization as a bureaucracy involves more symbolism than reality. In other words, the organizational form surrounding police may be thought of as a symbolic bureaucracy.

Another major way in which police organization does not quite fit the model of an ideal bureaucracy is in the area of personnel relations. In the ideal bureaucracy these relations are impersonal, but impersonality is not a characteristic of relations among role incumbents in police organizations, especially among patrolmen themselves and between patrolmen and their immediate supervisors. Many scholars have commented on the degree to which

10

officers display a sense of in-group solidarity and a high degree of cohesiveness which extends to off-duty relationships, as evidenced by the fact that officers frequently socialize with one another (Banton, 1964; Skolnick, 1966; Buckner, 1967; Petersen, 1968; Wilson, 1968; Westley, 1970). More specifically Rubinstein (1973), for example, notes that in terms of internal relations sergeants and lieutenants seek to minimize the distance between themselves and patrolmen because the latter are needed to make the former look good. Techniques of minimizing this distance and consequently enhancing personability include disdaining of formal respect, the use of dirty language, and strategic leniency in super- vision, that is, ignoring minor violations of depart- mental regulations in exchange for a modicum of loyalty from officers. Rubinstein concludes that police are not really organized into a formal hier- archy with each man responding to the authority of rank, but rather they respond to the person. Lundman (1980:55) argues that impersonality between subordi- nates and superiors in police organizations is blunted by two features of police organization: (1) a shared, common street experience as virtually all promotions come from within the department, and (2) a shared sense of defensiveness, that is, a sus- picion of outsiders and a feeling that they cannot be trusted. In short, it would appear from the litera- ture that internal relations within a police organi- zation are not nearly as impersonal as the ideal model of bureaucracy suggests.

Despite the fact that in practice police organi- zations do not conform totally to the criteria of an ideal bureaucracy as set forth by Weber, it is clear that they do exhibit many of the features of a bureaucracy and in many ways are similar to other formal organizations. While the consequences of this organizational structure for police and policing are numerous, two themes appear to be prominent in the literature. First, the bureaucratic emphasis upon efficiency and the impossibility of achieving the organizational goals of crime prevention, apprehen- sion of violators and order maintenance result in the deceptive manipulation of criteria to assess police efficiency in order to give the appearance of meeting organizational goals efficiently. In police organi- zations there is a reliance on statistical records to assess police efficiency. These records oftentimes become ends in themselves and are altered to give the appearance of efficiency. Skolnick (1966), for example, found that detectives will "unfound" a case (i.e., say an incident previously thought to occur did not occur) to make the department look better. More generally Manning (1977) argues that police claim and legitimate themselves through crime control, but in reality they cannot control crime so they use various presentational strategies (e.g., professionalism, bureaucratic ideology, secrecy, crime statistics, and so forth) to maintain credibility with the public and create the appearance of control. Lundman (1980:68) concludes that largely because of its bureaucratic structure, policing is rich in "little lies" intended to give outsiders the appearance of effective policing. In short, in bureaucratic police organizations, concern with presenting the appearance of efficient attainment of organizational goals has displaced actual attainment of goals.

A second prominent theme with respect to the consequences of current police organization is that the formal bureaucratic structure undermines and acts as a barrier to professionalism.7 For example, Reiss (1971) notes that while the key element in professionalism is the exercise of discretion, the command organization of the police threatens professional status because it expects men to follow orders and obey rules regardless of their judgment.8 Myren (1960) notes, in addition to the nature of police work itself, the important role of organizational structure in turnover of personnel, especially among college educated officers. That college educated officers leave police work is seen as thwarting efforts to upgrade personnel and, hence, professionalization of the police. In his discussion of turnover Myren (1960:604) comments:

> When the college-trained policeman does take
> his place on the force, he finds that he may
> be doing any one of a number of tasks only
> remotely connected with true policing...many
> of these tasks are menial in nature. This
> makes it impossible to develop pride in
> being a policeman. It also limits job sat-
> isfaction. Chances are that his specialized
> education is utilized only rarely. He finds
> that he can handle the assignments given him
> with very little effort. He finds no chal-
> lenge, low compensation and poor chance for

advancement in police work. Small wonder
that he strays, either from his assigned
duties or to a completely different utilization of his college investment.

Occupational Recruitment and Socialization

Traditionally recruits have been a demographically homogeneous group of individuals. Police work
is a relatively low prestige occupation (Skolnick,
1966; McNamara, 1967; Niederhoffer, 1967; Edwards,
1968; Bayley and Mendelsohn, 1969) attracting personnel to whom income, security and prestige are greater
than what they might otherwise achieve. Most studies
of urban police officers note their blue collar
origins and suggest that they come mainly from the
working class, upper-lower class and lower-middle
class (Skolnick, 1966; Niederhoffer, 1967; McNamara,
1967; Wilson, 1968; Bayley and Mendelsohn, 1969;
Watson and Sterling, 1969; Westley, 1970). To many
in the working class, the police occupation
represents a step up on the social and economic
scales. Study after study of incoming recruits to
police work has shown that the reason for seeking a
police job is related in some fashion to perceptions
of job security or a better job (Niederhoffer, 1967;
Alex, 1969; Bayley and Mendelsohn, 1969; Westley,
1970; Harris, 1973). In addition to their blue
collar origins and attraction to policing because of
its job security, police recruits are similar in
other ways. Typically they have been found to be
young, white males with little college training
(Skolnick, 1966; McNamara, 1967; Niederhoffer, 1967;
Bayley and Mendelsohn, 1969; Van Maanen, 1975).
Lundman (1980) attributes much of this homogeneity in
race and gender to discriminatory selection practices, that is, biased civil service written exams
eliminate blacks and harsh physical agility tests
screen out females. He attributes homogeneity in
educational achievement to the traditional lack of
relevant college programs in criminal justice and
police science. Both Lundman (1980) and Goldstein
(1977) note that the emergence of college programs
and recent court actions prohibiting discriminatory
practices are resulting in demographic diversity in
urban police recruit classes: now recruits are
female as well as male, black as well as white, and
college educated as well as high school educated.
While the portrait of the typical policeman has begun

to change in recent years, the fact remains that most of the persons patrolling our streets today are still white males with little college training.

Like other organizations, police departments are concerned with problems of providing an identity for their members, assuring their loyalty, controlling their actions and in general socializing them into a police occupational culture. Socialization is the process whereby new officers learn the values, attitudes and actions characteristic of their work group. While all writers agree that the occupational socialization of policemen is not confined to the early "breaking in" period but is a continuous process that occurs to some degree throughout the police career, recruit socialization can be divided essentially into two general stages--academy training and on-the-job training.

Formal socialization is the province of the police academy, and one of its main purposes is to try to standardize behavior. It is at the academy that the recruit is exposed to the ideal expectations and practices of his occupation. Manning and Van Maanen (1978), for example, note that at the academy the emphasis is far more on attitudes than acts in that formal processes stress the "proper" or "correct" way of behaving in lieu of the "practical" or "smart way." In his study of police academy training, Harris (1973) lends validity to this point of view by demonstrating the heavy focus on creating norms of defensiveness, professionalism and deperson-alization in new recruits. Specifically, the formal content of the classroom instruction is dispropor-tionately weighted toward the law and physical training (Harris, 1973; Lundman, 1980). Recruits spend a great deal of time learning the law and the proper way to enforce it, fully and without bias. Additionally, they spend a lot of time learning the physical skills (e.g., weapons use, high-speed driving and self-defense) thought to be fundamental to policing. These facts have led critics to charge that academy training gives recruits a distorted image of police work by suggesting that the applica-tion of the law is not discretionary and that most of the officer's time is devoted to law enforcement and arrest. Stated differently, critics charge that formal academy training fails to recognize the reality of everyday police work, that is, that most time is spent in non-law enforcement activity and

14

that the application of law is, in practice, discretionary. While most scholars would not argue that academy training is totally irrelevant to on-the-job needs, a number of them have noted, on the basis of their recruit studies, the striking disparity between class lectures (the ideal) and conditions of patrol (the real). They conclude that academy training is, on the whole, a failure and may, in and of itself, contribute to disenchantment with the occupation (McNamara, 1967; Niederhoffer, 1967; Harris, 1973; Van Maanen, 1973, 1975).

It is also at the academy that the recruit's first real contact with the occupational environment occurs and where s/he is first exposed to the often arbitrary discipline of the organization. Van Maanen (1975:221) notes:

> A man soon learned that to be one minute
> late to class, to utter a careless word in
> formation, to relax in his seat or to be
> caught walking when one should be running
> may result in a "gig" or demerit costing him
> an extra day of work or the time it may take
> to write a long essay on, say, "the
> importance of keeping a neat appearance."

Relations between recruits and instructors are formally pedagogic and punitively oriented. A number of scholars have noted the quasi-military nature of the academy with its emphasis on inflexible rules, following orders, looking sharp, discipline and harsh sanctions (Harris, 1973; Van Maanen, 1973, 1975; Lundman, 1980). Perhaps the most significant unanticipated consequence of the academy and its nature is the development of a strong sense of in-group solidarity among recruits which they carry with them into their later work. Because all recruits share the same lot (a degrading role) they learn not only to identify with their fellow patrolmen and to rely on them for rewards, but also that the best way to "stay low and avoid trouble" (Van Maanen, 1975) is through internalization of and adherence to the informal "no rat" rule which protects fellow recruits and themselves from departmental discipline. Most scholars agree that the development of solidarity is a latent function of academy training (McNamara, 1967; Niederhoffer, 1967; Harris, 1973; Van Maanen, 1973, 1975).

Formal academy training is followed by a period of closely supervised, informal on-the-job training in which the recruit learns the more practical "ropes" of his occupation usually through assignment to an experienced field training officer. It is in this latter phase that the "proper" information is separated by the recruit from the "smart," and the recruit begins to gain full recognition of the police role and to build an identity along lines that are thought to be occupationally appropriate (Manning and Van Maanen, 1978). Moreover, it is during this period of apprenticeship that the recruit is introduced to the complexities of the "street" and the reality shock encompassing full recognition of being a police officer is likely to occur (Van Maanen, 1973). Recruits are usually instructed to forget academy training and are informally indoctrinated into the norms of group life and the attitudes and behaviors which are appropriate and expected of a patrolman within the social setting. They are provided informal rules for how to get the job done and learn by watching and doing what "real" policing is. In short, during the period of on-the-job training recruits learn what Davis (1979) terms the "working role" of police through informal coaching relationships. Most scholars agree that this traditional feature of police work--patrolmen training patrolmen--ensures continuity from class to class of police officers, regardless of the content of academy instruction. It helps to account for the stability of the pattern of police behavior from one generation to another (McNamara, 1967; Niederhoffer, 1967; Harris, 1973; Van Maanen, 1975).

Occupational Role and Function

The policeman's role, unlike many other occupational roles, is ambiguous and his mandate is unclear. From a historical point of view there has been a vast expansion of police function (see, for example, Richardson, 1974) resulting in the fact that at present a great variety of tasks are performed by police. Many of these present-day duties of police have been assumed by default. Petersen (1968:104), for example, notes:

> Society has increasingly transferred many
> responsibilities other than law enforcement
> to police. For example, regulation and

16

control of traffic has become a general duty
of the police. Yet the police have acquired
many duties by default because they are on
duty 24 hours a day. In particular, problems that arise on weekends or late at night
are perhaps of necessity referred to police
because no other agency is available to
respond.

In an earlier work, Cumming et al. (1965) provided
some support for Petersen's argument by noting that
there has been a sort of "division of labor through
time" resulting from the fact that police have been
forced to take over many emergency health and welfare
services, especially on nights and weekends, because
other agents are not available. Regardless of how
duties have come to be relegated to the province of
police the fact is that today there is much more to
policing than enforcing the law, apprehending
criminals and preserving the public peace. Today,
the police render service and assistance in many
matters once not remotely thought to be police
business. Today police do many things where there is
no formal legal mandate.

Although the principal mission of the police is
popularly portrayed as reflecting a narrow emphasis
upon controlling crime, a prominent theme in the literature dealing with the work behavior of police
stresses that the role of the uniformed officer is
not a strict legalistic one (see, for example,
Banton, 1964; Cumming et al., 1965; Skolnick, 1966;
Bittner, 1967b; Petersen, 1968; Wilson, 1968;
Webster, 1973). A number of studies suggest that
policemen usually engage in numerous activities that
are only tangentially related to their responsibilities in law enforcement and that only a limited percentage of police work involves law enforcement.
Research analyzing police calls and time spent on
assignment suggest a duality of roles--law enforcement and order maintenance (peace keeping).[9] In an
analysis of incoming calls to an urban police
complaint desk over an 82-hour period, Cumming et al.
(1965) found that more than half of the calls
required help or some form of support for personal or
interpersonal problems. They conclude that the
policeman on the beat spends more than half his or
her time as an amateur social worker, playing a
supportive rather than a law enforcement role.[10]
Bercal (1970), in an analysis of calls received by

police in several large urban departments, found that the largest proportion of requests from citizens for police assistance involved services rather than a violation of law. He concludes that, to a certain extent, the public perceives non-law enforcement duties as a salient and significant function of police departments.11 In a classic time-motion study of police, Webster (1970, 1973) found that patrolmen spend about two-thirds of their time in administrative or social service tasks rather than law enforcement. Webster (1973:104) concludes that the popular image as a crime fighter bears little resemblance to the reality of a policeman's role. In general, a growing literature indicates that patrolmen spend at best only 10 to 15 percent of their time in law enforcement activities (Epstein, 1962; Bittner, 1967b; Misner, 1967; Wilson, 1968). In other words, police work is more peace keeping than law enforcement, and the role of the typical patrolman is much less that of an agent capturing law violators than that of an agent who mediates personal and community problems (Banton, 1964; Skolnick, 1966; Petersen, 1968; Wilson, 1968; Bayley and Mendelsohn, 1969; Reiss, 1971).

Despite the fact that some research has found police to accept a conception of their role that includes extra-legal activities as a routine part of their job (see, for example, Petersen, 1974), most writers in this area argue that police continue to define their role in terms of law enforcement and that rewards internally and externally concentrate on law enforcement, not service work. Cummins (1971), in an observational study of service calls, found police to view service work as "knit-shit stuff" and relegate it to low status in the department because it goes beyond their perception of what a policeman should do--namely, enforce the law. Police continue to measure their efficiency in relation to controlling crime. Given that the majority of all police work has little relationship to law enforcement it is somewhat ironic, and more so problematic, that policemen are evaluated by the public and themselves against functions such as arrest and crime control which they rarely perform (see, for example, Misner, 1967; Manning and Van Maanen, 1978).

Nature of Work and Routine Policing

Police work is typically depicted in the literature as unpleasant, dirty, difficult, dangerous, requiring long and undesirable hours, and highly discretionary (Banton, 1964; Skolnick, 1966; Niederhoffer, 1967; Wilson, 1968; Whittemore, 1969; Westley, 1970; Rubinstein, 1973; Davis, 1979). In addition, police are usually portrayed as operating in a fishbowl and, even more importantly, functioning in a highly varied social world. The police deal with a wide variety of problems and they come in contact with people from all social strata who hold varying expectations and attitudes toward them. Not only do police enter highly variable social situations but the nature of their encounters with citizens and the outcomes of those encounters are highly variable. Police contacts with the public, for example, can range from incidents in which the policeman plays a friendly, sympathetic and helpful role through those in which there is a strained but highly antagonistic relationship to cases in which the most violent of emotions and behavior occur. In short, interpersonal contacts are unpredictable[12] and, hence, police work itself is unpredictable. Generally it is espoused in the literature that this aspect of police work has a strong bearing on routine policing.

To date, considerable systematic attention has been directed at police citizen encounters (Piliavin and Briar, 1964; La Fave, 1965; Bittner, 1967a and 1967b; Black, 1970; Black and Reiss, 1970; Reiss, 1971; Petersen, 1972; Lundman, 1974). Examination of this literature reveals several major features of routine policing. First, as previously noted, most routine patrol activities do not involve criminal incidents; rather, the vast majority of the patrol-man's time is spent on maintaining order and providing assistance (Cumming et al., 1965; Reiss, 1971; Webster, 1973).

A second feature of routine policing is that it is largely reactive; that is, most police-citizen encounters are citizen invoked (Wilson, 1968; Black and Reiss, 1970; Westley, 1973; Sanders, 1977; Manning and Van Maanen, 1978; Lundman, 1980). For example, Webster (1973) found nearly three-fourths of patrol activities were citizen invoked and Westley (1970) found about four-fifths of patrol assignments

19

were not patrolman initiated assignments. In a classic study of methods of police mobilization, Black and Reiss (1967:17) conclude that "initially police are mobilized more by the actions of private citizens and police headquarters than patrol initiative."

Third, in contrast to popular conception and media portrayals, the majority of police-citizen contacts are primarily polite, civil and nonviolent in nature (Piliavin and Briar, 1964; Black, 1970; Black and Reiss, 1970; Lundman, 1974). For example, in a study of the relation between demeanor of an adult victim and police writing of an incident report Black (1970) observed 96 percent of the victims to be polite in conversations with police. In studies focusing on police-juvenile encounters, Piliavin and Briar (1964) found two-thirds of juvenile suspects were cooperative and polite in their interactions with police and Black and Reiss (1970) found over 80 percent of juvenile suspects were civil or very deferential with police.

Fourth, routine police work involves the use of "typifications" to enhance efficiency13 (Skolnick, 1966; Sacks, 1972; Rubinstein, 1973; Van Maanen, 1978b, 1978c; Lundman, 1980). Because encounters are highly unpredictable in the sense that police deal with a wide variety of problems and types of citizens and are required to make numerous decisions, on the basis of experience, police develop and apply typifications in their encounters with citizens. Accompanying these typifications are guidelines for behavior. For example, Skolnick (1966:45) coined the term "symbolic assailant" to describe the policeman's psychological response to the continual threat of violence.

> The policeman, because his work requires him to be occupied continually with potential violence, develops a perceptual shorthand to identify certain kinds of people as symbolic assailants, that is, as persons who use gesture, language, and attire that the police-man has come to recognize as a prelude to violence.

Skolnick goes on to argue that based on this typification and the identification of a person as a symbolic assailant, police will act accordingly to protect themselves. Other examples of the use of typification processes in routine police work include: (1) the development of notions about what is the "normal" character of behavior and appearances in different sectors of a beat at different times which an officer uses to recognize incongruities (i.e., the out of ordinary) and to decide how to handle cases (Sacks, 1972; Rubinstein, 1973); (2) a division of problems police routinely deal with into "real police work" and a large residual category of "bullshit" (Van Maanen, 1978b); and (3) a division of citizens in reference to their attitudes--good or bad (Van Maanen, 1978c).

Fifth, research has demonstrated that routine police work is highly discretionary (Goldstein, 1963; La Fave, 1965; Bittner, 1967a, 1967b; Black and Reiss, 1967; Buckner, 1967; Wilson, 1968; Black and Reiss, 1970; Petersen, 1972). One author, Reiss (1971), argues that the core feature of police-citizen encounters is discretionary decisions on both the part of the police and the citizen. To date, numerous studies have been conducted of police decision making and discretion. Generally these studies of police discretion show that: (1) there is a normal tendency among patrolmen to underenforce the law (Banton, 1964; La Fave, 1965; Wilson, 1968); (2) citizen attitudes and demeanor are key elements in shaping police reactions (Piliavin and Briar, 1964; Buckner, 1967; Black, 1970; Black and Reiss, 1970; Westley, 1970; Reiss, 1971; Petersen, 1972; Lundman, 1980); and (3) a number of factors other than demeanor also influence police decisions and discretionary behavior. Among these other factors are the following: police bureaucracy and policy (Black and Reiss, 1967; Petersen, 1968; Wilson, 1968; Gardiner, 1969), locational setting (Black and Reiss, 1967; Petersen, 1968, 1972; Rubinstein, 1973; Lundman, 1974), policeman's desire to appear efficient and competent (Skolnick, 1966), officer's knowledge of the law (Buckner, 1967; Petersen, 1968), work group norms (Petersen, 1971), visibility of offender behavior (Petersen, 1968; Black and Reiss, 1970; Lundman, 1974), demographic nature of the offender (Petersen, 1968), legal seriousness of the offense (Black and Reiss, 1967 and 1970; Buckner, 1967), situational demands such as the desire to avoid time consuming arrests when a shift is almost over (Buckner, 1967; Petersen, 1972), predispositions such as the mood of the officer or the manner in which he

21

approaches the situation (Piliavin and Briar, 1964; Black and Reiss, 1967; Petersen, 1972), type of mobilization (Black and Reiss, 1967; Wilson, 1968; Black, 1978), and presence or absence of a complainant (Black, 1970; Black and Reiss, 1970; Lundman, 1974).

The final major feature of routine policing is solidarity. Numerous scholars have addressed this issue and have noted the unusually high degree of occupational solidarity among policemen (Banton, 1964; Skolnick, 1966; Petersen, 1968; Wilson, 1968; Westley, 1970; Rubinstein, 1973). We now turn to a general discussion of this literature.

Solidarity

Solidarity is a subjective feeling of belongingness to a group and implication in each other's lives among members of a group; it is a sense of unity, loyalty, common identification and inclusiveness. As noted earlier, the development of solidarity among policemen is a latent function of training in that the norms of defensiveness, professionalism and depersonalization taught in the academy and reinforced in early street experiences are carried with officers into the field. On a broader level, there are two factors which appear to influence police solidarity--the need for support in situations of danger and the isolation of police officers from the rest of society.

The threat of danger is always present while police officers are on duty. They need to be alert continually to the possibility of being assaulted by some citizen and to recognize that danger may become a reality even in commonplace situations. Officers are trained to recognize and expect danger. Moreover, due to the nature of their occupational responsibility, policemen are not only expected but required to become involved in dangerous situations which ordinary citizens would generally avoid (e.g., a fight between two men, a high-speed chase of a fleeing felon, an arrest of a law violator, and so on). Not only is there always the possibility of danger in police work, but there are real situations of danger for officers in their work. As most officers are deployed in solo patrol, they must believe they can depend upon their fellow officers for support in times of need. Stated differently, the need for support in situations of danger leads to the occupational necessity of having workers who have a strong sense of solidarity. Most scholars agree that solidarity among policemen is a result of the objective dangers policemen face and hence the need for trust, dependability and support between colleagues (Banton, 1964; Skolnick, 1966; Buckner, 1967; Petersen, 1968; Alex, 1969; Harris, 1973; Rubinstein, 1973).

Another major influence upon police solidarity is occupational isolation. A number of writers have noted that police as an occupational group share a position of isolation within the larger society (see, for example, Banton, 1964; Clark, 1965; Skolnick, 1966; Bayley and Mendelsohn, 1969; Westley, 1970).[14] The police play an outsider role in the community. The forces contributing to their isolation from the mainstream of society are numerous. Clark (1965) notes that policemen are isolated community members because of: (1) a desire for privacy by people and a resentment of intrusion into their private affairs; (2) a history of incompetence and occasional brutality by police; (3) the occasional dirty nature of police work and the general social avoidance of seamy elements in society; and (4) the occupational, professional and official policies of policing groups themselves (e.g., the tendency among police groups as a matter of policy to isolate themselves from the public to avoid charges of favoritism). Rubinstein (1973) argues that police are isolated from most other people because of the nature of their obligations.[15] While they work an eight hour shift, policemen are generally sworn to duty 24 hours a day. Often they are required to enforce rules and regulations that the public does not observe or does not want to observe. Hence, by isolating the police, the public reduces its risk of social sanction. Perhaps the best arguments in support of police isolation relate to the antagonistic and indifferent manner in which police are treated by the public. Police work is a low status occupation (Skolnick, 1966; McNamara, 1967; Niederhoffer, 1967; Edwards, 1968) and police perceive they are held in low esteem by the public (Bayley and Mendelsohn, 1969; Westley, 1970; Johnson and Gregory, 1971). Not only do police lack respect from the public but frequently they are in an adversary relation with the public. Often police are subjected to abuse from the public (Banton, 1964; Bayley

23

and Mendelsohn, 1969) and their encounters with the public are unpleasant (Westley, 1970). Because their attitudes are molded by encounters with citizens, police typically perceive the public to be hostile to them (Skolnick, 1966; Wilson, 1968; Westley, 1970). Moreover, they feel the mass media is unfair to them (Banton, 1964; Bayley and Mendelsohn, 1969; Johnson and Gregory, 1971). Given the nature of police work and the perceived manner in which they are treated by the public, several scholars have argued that police tend to think of themselves as a minority group in society (Skolnick, 1966; Bayley and Mendelsohn, 1969; Watson and Sterling, 1969). The analogy to a minority group derives from the fact that police display many of the characteristics and self concepts associated with minority groups--police are frequently thought of in terms of a stereotype, they lack respect and their status in the community is not congruent with their own self image, they are persistently portrayed in the mass media in a simplistic and detracting fashion, they are regularly treated to verbal and physical abuse and perceive the community as the enemy, they are highly sensitive to criticism, they tend to socialize within their own group, and so forth. Generally the most far reaching ramification of police minority group status is isolation within the community.

Not only are policemen isolated from the mainstream of society relative to other occupations, but they also feel socially isolated (Clark, 1965; Skolnick, 1966; Bayley and Mendelsohn, 1969; Westley, 1970). In general, this perception of isolation is seen in the literature as further strengthening occupational solidarity and cohesion existent in policing. In search of support, understanding and a feeling of common identity policemen turn to their own colleagues. As in other occupations, common work experiences become the basis of colleagial groups. Policemen find it more comfortable to socialize with other officers, who know and understand their feelings, and over time they begin to spend most of their off-duty time with other police workers, relying on them for support and identity. In other words, over time police officers withdraw into a relatively closed world peopled chiefly by other police.

Not only do the policeman's need for support in situations of danger and his or her sense of isolation enhance solidarity, but they result in the development of a distinctive subculture or code among officers by which they can live. This provides a basis for self-respect and support independent, to some degree, of civilian attitudes. Alex (1969) notes, for example, that objective dangers, requirements of work, and the police occupational role operate to create an occupational character that transcends personal differences, racial antagonisms and political ideologies. When an officer puts on a uniform s/he enters a distinct subculture governed by norms and values designed to manage the strain created by his or her outsider role in the community.

One of the chief elements of the police subculture is a norm of secrecy--a rule of silence which requires officers to never inform on or criticize a fellow officer. Generally, an officer becomes accepted within the police group to the extent s/he acquires a reputation for silence. Interestingly, Westley (1970) found that 77 percent of the officers he studied would rather perjure themselves than testify against another policeman. While numerous scholars have noted a code of secrecy among policemen (see, for example, Buckner, 1967; Stoddard, 1968; Wilson, 1968; Bittner, 1970; Rubinstein, 1973), the notion is perhaps most developed by Westley (1970). He argues that secrecy is one of the ways by which policemen defend themselves against the presumed hostility of civilians; as the perception of public hostility by police grows, so does police utilization of and informal legitimation of violence and secrecy. According to Westley, secrecy is a form of loyalty for it represents sticking with the group and its maintenance carries with it a profound sense of participation; it is also a form of solidarity because it represents a common front against the outside world.

To date, much emphasis has been placed on the police code as reflecting one aspect of police subculture (see, for example, Skolnick, 1966; Niederhoffer, 1967; Westley, 1970; Manning, 1977). Central to the subcultural perspective is the notion that actual police practice is mediated by an informal code, indoctrination into which is conducted for recruits by experienced officers. References to the code are commonly used to explain police deviancy and corruption. Stoddard (1968), for example, examines "blue coat crime" and the informal code whereby it is perpetuated. He argues that officers are socialized into unlawful practices, preservation of secrecy and group acceptance for practitioners. He concludes that the illegal practices of the police are socially prescribed and patterned through the informal code rather than being a function of individual aberration or personal inadequacies of the policeman himself. In other words, police deviance and corruption are group phenomena reflecting solidarity rather than an individual phenomenon, and they may be fruitfully analyzed from a subcultural perspective.

In recent years there has been some indirect criticism of the theme of police subcultural solidarity.16 Rubinstein (1973), for example, emphasizes the solitude of the patroman's job in contrast to the more frequent emphasis upon solidarity and cohesion. He notes that while there is a high degree of loyalty and solidarity among policemen, this solidarity is not harmonious and trusting—cliques and coalitions develop for specific purposes and much of what a policeman knows remains secretive. Rubinstein argues (1973:438-439):

> The solidarity policemen feel for each other is said by some observers to be a central feature of their personalities. But the relationships among colleagues in a squad are anything but harmonious and trusting. No squad is a cohesive unit whose members openly discuss their work experiences. While most men willingly acknowledge and frequently stress their dependence on each other, no patrolman tries to disguise the secretive nature of much of what he knows. A policeman's information is his private stock, which nobody may presume to make claims on, unless invited to share.

Rubinstein's position is supported by Van Maanen (1978b) who argues that while unavoidable task demands and organizational features of work promote strong mutual concern among patrolmen, the police brotherhood is far from a harmonious and trusting one. Another critique of the solidarity theme is provided by Manning (1974) who implies that police solidarity may be undermined by relatively common-place everyday lying between patrolmen themselves as well as between patrolmen and their supervisory officers. In short, while scholars such as

Rubinstein, Manning and Van Maanen are not denying that solidarity exists among policemen, they are suggesting that the themes of solidarity and cohesion may be overrated.

The Effect of Occupation

To date, sociological research on the police has emphasized the study of the police as an occupational group (Banton, 1964; Skolnick, 1966; McNamara, 1967; Niederhoffer, 1967; Bayley and Mendelsohn, 1969; Westley, 1970). Underlying much of this work are two assumptions. First, in modern society work groups are an important part of a man's social identity and participation in such groups structures the attitudes and self conceptions of members. In other words, the attitude and action orientation of police are in part determined by their particular occupational position. The effect of occupational role may be strengthened in the case of the police due to the adversary nature of their relationship to the rest of society and, hence, their relative social isolation and forced reliance on occupational role as a source of identification (Banton, 1964; Skolnick, 1966; Alex, 1969; Westley, 1970). Second, it follows from the first assumption that certain attitudinal and behavioral complexes of the police originate not from peculiar personal qualities of officers but rather from occupational demands, formal responsibilities, informal expectations and everyday experiences of police. Illustrative of these two assumptions is a body of literature that delineates the "working personality" of the policeman.

Policemen are often thought to display a distinctive set of values and behavior which are generally subsumed under the heading of an occupational or "working personality." The attributes commonly said to be part of the patrol officer's working personality include authoritarianism, suspicion, racism, hostility, insecurity, conservatism and cynicism. While there is some controversy over whether there is, in fact, a police personality (see Balch, 1972), sociologists tend to argue that the world in which policemen work tends to produce certain common characteristics among them. Skolnick, (1966:42), for example, argues:

The police, as a result of combined features
of their social situation, tend to develop
ways of looking at the world distinctive to
themselves, cognitive lenses through which
to see situations and events. The strength
of the lenses may be weaker or stronger depending on certain conditions, but they are
ground on a similar axis.

Skolnick goes on to argue that police develop a characteristic "working personality" which, though modified to some extent by the nature of the officer's
specific assignment, is nevertheless similar in broad
concept to that of other officers. Niederhoffer
(1967) argues that authoritarian elements of the
police personality develop after appointment as a
result of socialization and experience in police
work. Thus, it would appear that assuming it is
possible to locate a working personality of police,
sociological studies emphasize the occupational
sources of it rather than personal background
sources; that is, there is something in the police
system itself that generates a particular world view,
rather than the particular world view of police
having its origins in the fact that certain personality types are inadvertently recruited for police
work.

Arguments with respect to two aspects of the
police personality--suspiciousness and cynicism--are
illustrative of the point of view that policing does
not attract a distinctive type of personality but
rather creates one (Skolnick, 1966; McNamara, 1967;
Niederhoffer, 1967; Lundman, 1980). Not only are
police trained to be suspicious but suspiciousness is
an occupational requirement arising out of the danger
policemen face. Skolnick (1966:40-45) extensively
documents the effect of a man's work on his outlook
on the world. He argues that three outstanding
elements in the police milieu--danger, authority and
efficiency--combine to generate distinctive cognitive
and behavioral responses in police or a working personality, which is most highly developed in the role
of the man on the beat. Skolnick notes, for example,
that the perception of danger lurking unpredictably
in every encounter constitutes the most important
fact of daily occupational life for the patrolman.
Because of the potential for danger inherent in
police work, beat patrolmen necessarily become suspicious persons, identifying certain kinds of people

and situations as a threat, or symbolic assailants, and reacting to their surroundings and the public on the basis of these typifications. Skolnick further argues that to reduce the perception of danger in their operational environment, beat policemen will resort to the use of authority in their encounters with citizens.

Cynicism among policemen is generally seen as arising from the police officer's continual exposure to the seamy side of life and from public antipathy toward police as experienced in the abuse patrolmen absorb day after day (Banton, 1964; Westley, 1970), biased reporting and editorial attacks in newspapers (Niederhoffer, 1967; Bayley and Mendelsohn, 1969), and the low prestige of police work in general (Skolnick, 1966; McNamara, 1967). Niederhoffer (1967) demonstrates that cynical, suspicious and authoritarian personality types are not recruited into the police system, but rather people in the police system become cynical, suspicious and authoritarian. Although his theory is not without critics and qualifications (see Regoli et al., 1979), Niederhoffer notes, for example, in his theoretical model of police cynicism a succession of typical stages in the growth of cynicism that runs parallel to occupational career: cynicism is directly related to length of time on the force.[17] According to Niederhoffer, cynicism is learned as part of the socialization process,[18] is absorbed through contact with an established police subculture, and is a product of occupational anomie created by the transformation of the police occupation into a profession. In conclusion, Niederhoffer argues that it is the police system itself, not the personality of the candidate, that is the more powerful determinant of behavior and ideology.

The Study of Campus Policing: What's Needed?

We have noted that although there has been a considerable amount of research conducted on police procedures and practices in municipal settings, little attention has been paid to campus police organizations. Of the few studies that have been conducted in this area, all have tended to concentrate on the structural characteristics of campus police departments rather than campus police officers. Moreover, they have tended to place emphasis primarily on the official aspects of campus police work rather than the everyday reality of that work.

The present research addresses this gap in substantive knowledge. The research effort is aimed primarily at understanding various aspects of organization and everyday activity of policing in an urban university environment. It seeks to detail the world as a university policeman might see it and to delineate the consequences of that world view. Specifically, as a study in occupational sociology, this research offers a detailed descriptive account of the organization of a university police force and the world view of workers--it describes what officers do, how they are organized, their attitudes and values, and the nature of their work.

A second focus of the study is an examination of the extent to which urban university police are similar to or different from other urban police forces in terms of several broad dimensions of work organization and activity. In addition to describing the world of the campus policeman, this research seeks to explain how differences in police practice are related to the local context in which police departments operate. Explicit comparisons are made between the work worlds of campus and municipal police based upon the existing model of urban policing and the analysis of data on campus policing is organized around these key features of current knowledge concerning policing in an urban context.

Notes

¹To date campus policing has not been well defined in terms of theoretical classification. Some refer to campus law enforcement officers and organizations as "police," others refer to them as "security" and still others see them as a unique form of both. Because of the lack of clarity in theoretical classification, a comprehensive search was made of all available publications which might have some bearing on campus police.

²It is also somewhat surprising that even the more general organizational literature on institu-

tions of higher education, how they operate and the future of the academic community written during the time of student protest movements makes no mention of the role of campus police. See, for example, Barzun (1968), Caffrey (1969) and Nichols (1970).

[3]For a complete review of the literature on police-community relations and projects designed to improve relations (e.g., operation empathy, human relations laboratories, t-group and sensitivity training, speaker programs, and so forth) see Johnson and Gregory (1971).

[4]It is in connection with the inherent conflict between law and order that questions arise of whether police intervention is necessary and how intervention should occur. Skolnick (1966), for example, suggests that such factors as perceived presence of danger in the community, social dissimilarity of police and groups serviced by them, prevailing political conceptions of the locality, and the formal organization of the police department will affect the policeman's perception of the amount of social uniformity necessary and the amount of force necessary to maintain it. Other scholars who have addressed this issue include Chevigny (1969), Bittner (1970), Westley (1970) and Muir (1977). In general this literature suggests that in order to understand police interventions one must understand the conflict in police functions as well as other occupational problems faced by the police (e.g., measure of efficiency based on arrest, nature of work environment, and so forth).

[5]Often police organizations are referred to as "semimilitaristic bureaucracies" in the literature (see, for example, Bittner, 1970). The semimilitaristic analogy is usually drawn on several bases including the notions that police departments: (1) are bottom-heavy organizations with all power flowing from the top of the organizational pyramid and concentrated in the hands of the chief; (2) emphasize protocol and ceremony; (3) have a virtual monopoly on the use of force to defend or achieve an objective; (4) have many rules and regulations bearing on the behavior of members both on and off duty with an emphasis on discipline; and (5) have a style of internal regulation and control based on a command organization in which men are expected to

follow orders regardless of their individual judgment.

In recent years there has been some criticism of the paramilitaristic bureaucratic model of police organization. Specifically, several scholars have made distinctions between the military and the police (Edwards, 1968; Wilson, 1968; Rubinstein, 1973; Clark and Sykes, 1974). For example, Edwards (1968) notes that whereas the military seeks to strike with sufficient force to destroy the enemy, police employ only the minimum force necessary to gain obedience to the law. Wilson (1968) argues that police departments are not military or quasi-military organizations because patrolmen typically work alone rather than as part of a unit and police communications generally cut across rather than work through a chain of command. Clark and Sykes (1974) make essentially the same point as Wilson by noting that the paramilitary facade of police organization is contradicted by the internally decentralized, officer-centered mode of operation in practice.

[6]In recent years there has been some systematic attention to the study of how leaders of police organizations attempt to ensure that individual action in the field is consistent with directives. For example, Kornblum (1976) found that the major strategy used by police administrators to assure compliance from subordinates was functional anxiety (fear). For an analysis of organizational control structure focusing on lower level supervisors (i.e., sergeants) in a large municipal department see Tifft (1970).

[7]From a theoretical point of view the police occupation simply does not meet many of the ideal criteria of a profession including high standards of admission, a special body of knowledge and theory, altruism and dedication to the service ideal, lengthy period of training for candidates, and publically recognized status and prestige (see, Ritzer, 1977). Banton (1964:105-110), for example, argues that police are not a profession because they acquire most knowledge and skill on the job rather than in separate academies, are emphatically subject to the authority of their superiors, have no serious professional society, and do not produce in systematic written form new knowledge about their craft. Niederhoffer (1967) notes two major barriers to the professionalization of the police occupation--a code

of ethics and ideals which are not consistent with reality and refusal of the public to grant high status and prestige to the police occupation. In recent years there has been a general movement among police to try to transform their occupation into a profession. Most scholars agree that this movement has led more to the professionalization of the department (e.g., upgrading of personnel qualifications and training) than of the occupation (Banton, 1964; Bordua and Reiss, 1966; Skolnick, 1966; Niederhoffer, 1967; Wilson, 1968; Reiss, 1971).

[8]It should be noted that while most scholars agree that police organization resembles a profession and a bureaucracy, many argue that in fact police are neither professionals (i.e., capable of exercising free discretion) nor bureaucrats (i.e., completely rule bound) but are rather members of a craft. See, for example, Banton (1964), Skolnick (1966) and Wilson (1968).

[9]While definitions of order maintenance or peace keeping vary in the literature, most scholars include service and assistance in their definitions. Banton (1964), for example, defines peace keeping as all occupational routines not directly related to making arrests. All of the studies cited in this section include service work as part of peace keeping.

[10]In contrast to this portrayal of peace keeping activities as amateur social work, Bittner (1967b) contends that keeping the peace contains certain elements of control and support in a unique combination and that its pursuit has nothing amateurish about it. He views peace keeping as a craft involving skilled performance.

[11]This conclusion finds support in the works of Cumming et al. (1965) and Bayley and Mendelsohn (1969) which suggest that the poor and uneducated appear to use the police in the same way that middle-class people use family doctors and clergymen--they call on police in noncriminal and emergency situations.

[12]Because encounters are unpredictable and police are required to move into highly unpredictable situations on a minute's notice where they stand to make few gains and the possibility of loss is great (e.g., be assaulted or killed), police develop strategies

for gaining and retaining control of situations. One of the most common means of gaining control of inter-personal relations is through the use of force and violence (Banton, 1964; Buckner, 1967; Bittner, 1970; Westley, 1970; Rubinstein, 1973; Muir, 1977). With respect to force and violence it is generally assumed by scholars that: (1) police are not able to rely on the authority of their uniform in the field and, hence, are compelled to establish their personal authority which may in turn lead to violence (Banton, 1964; Black and Reiss, 1967; Westley, 1970; Reiss, 1971); (2) police assume force and violence as tools of their trade and accept them as a solution to their problems--a culture of violence grows in police work (Buckner, 1967; Westley, 1970; Rubinstein, 1973); and (3) the use of force and violence is largely a defen-sive reaction on the part of police (Skolnick, 1966; Muir, 1977).

[13]Typifications are general classifications of problems and citizens. One of the earliest uses of the idea of typifications was made by Sudnow (1965) in his study of public defenders. In essence Sudnow argues that typifications of problems or people permit efficient processing of cases because they are not based on the unique characteristics of individual cases.

[14]Despite the prominence of the theme of occupa-tional isolation, there has been some evidence to suggest that American police may not be as isolated from the public as generally assumed. Banton (1964) contends that American police, unlike their British counterparts, are able to segregate police work from the rest of their lives. He argues that American police are not as isolated as many have claimed. Banton concludes that because U.S. social structure is looser and less dense than British social struc-ture, American police are less set apart from society and more socially integrated than their British counterparts. Banton's conclusion is supported by Clark (1965). Whereas Banton found that 67 percent of his Scottish respondents said their job affected their private lives, Clark found that only 40 percent of the officers he studied in three Illinois cities said their job affected their private lives. Additionally, Bayley and Mendelsohn (1969) found little evidence of social isolation among Denver police. Only 12 percent of their sample said they had difficulty making friends with non-police

families and less than 25 percent complained of
difficulties in their relationships because of their
job. Findings such as these raise questions about
the degree of isolation of American police, not the
fact of isolation. In other words, while there is
disagreement over the degree of isolation of American
police, most authorities agree that the policeman is
relatively isolated compared with members of other
occupations by virtue of the nature of his or her
occupation (Clark, 1965; Skolnick, 1966; Bayley and
Mendelsohn, 1969; Watson and Sterling, 1969; Westley,
1970). Even Banton agrees that relative to other
American occupations policemen in this country can be
considered socially isolated.

   [15]The nature of the policeman's obligations may
have an isolating effect upon him or her personally
as well as upon his or her occupational group.
Watson and Sterling (1969) note, for example, that
the policeman's occupational status and the 24-hour
nature of his or her occupational responsibility tend
to color off-the-job relationships with neighbors and
friends. They argue that the identification of the
policeman with official coercion may inhibit his or
her full acceptance as just another neighbor or
friend. In general, it is postulated that the nature
of police work (e.g., danger, dirty work, shift work,
and so on) may have a deleterious effect on social
relationships by virtue of cutting off social ties
with friends and placing a strain on marital and
family relationships (see, for example, Reiss, 1971;
Rubinstein, 1973). Banton (1964) notes, for example,
that policemen may suffer in their private lives
because of their occupation. Rubinstein (1973) goes
further by arguing that the policeman's work imposes
a burden on his or her family by virtue of the fact
that the policeman cannot tell them some things, and
this creates a barrier between the officer and his or
her family. Stated differently, the nature of the
policeman's job disrupts his or her life.

   [16]While much has been made in the literature of
the factors necessarily leading to solidarity among
police (e.g., isolation, danger, shift work, and so
forth), little attention has been directed at the
specific factors and processes which may undermine
that solidarity.

   [17]McNamara   (1967)   provides   support   for
Niederhoffer's conclusion in that he found evidence

of increasing authoritarianism over time, that is, the most experienced officers in his sample had the highest authoritarianism scores. Like other sociologists, McNamara concludes that the police experience itself intensifies authoritarianism.

18Given the importance of socialization for the working personality several scholars have recently begun to argue that contemporary changes in training practices toward less emphasis on discipline and more emphasis on human relations and counseling are resulting in diversity in the working personality (Muir, 1977; Lundman, 1980). Muir (1977), for example, found not one but rather four working personalities (i.e., enforcers, avoiders, reciprocators and professionals) among officers. He concludes that changes in police socialization practices may lead to diversity rather than homogeneity in police personality.

CHAPTER II

SOCIAL ORGANIZATION OF POLICING

In this chapter the social and organizational arrangements university policemen utilize within their work world are described. A discussion of the nature of campus police bureaucracy is provided in which attention is focused on internal structure, the organization of line operations, relations among role incumbents, and evaluative and disciplinary processes. In addition, the jurisdiction and authority of campus police are discussed, and the nature of university police community relations are explored.

Campus Police Bureaucracy

Internal Police Organization

There are essentially two features of general police organization at the Downtown University Police Department (DTU)[1] worthy of note. First, the DTU Police Department is located within the university administrative structure under a vice-president rather than under the physical plant department or the dean of students' office.[2] The major advantage of this placement is that it permits the campus police department to operate autonomously relative to other departments within the University and, thus, to maintain a separate identity and function. Second, at DTU the Police Department is the major division of the more encompassing Public Safety and Security Division. Under the public safety concept those functions of the university which are directed at the elimination of campus environmental hazards (safety functions such as fire and accident control) and related to the protection and preservation of life, property and order (police/security functions) in the academic community are incorporated in one professionally staffed service organization under one director. In most municipalities organized under a public safety concept, while each division (e.g., fire, police) is located under the same department (i.e., public safety) under one director, each division typically has its own chief and performs separate though complementary services relative to other divisions. In contrast, division of services and organization is not as distinct at the University. Consequently, police officers who are formally labeled "public safety officers" at DTU are expected on a daily basis to perform a range of tasks, including safety and security as well as general law enforcement. The organizational structure of the DTU Police Department is graphically depicted in Figure 1.

Like its municipal counterpart, the DTU police organization is bureaucratically structured. The Department is highly centralized with bureaucratic authority vested in formalized positions which are hierarchically organized with officers at each level reporting to persons at a higher level. All ultimately report to the Chief. Like nearly all police departments, the DTU Department displays a relatively fixed division of labor with clearly defined duties and responsibilities. Organizationally, division of tasks is by function--administrative, staff and line.

The administrative staff is charged with maintaining and increasing organizational efficiency, which is accomplished by coordinating and integrating member activities. At DTU there are essentially two major administrators of the Police Department--the Director of Safety and Security and the Chief of Police/Security. The Director is vested with and responsible for the administration and operation of the Department of Safety and Security; he is responsible for all aspects of personal safety and well-being of those in the campus community, the police/security force, and the fire and safety program. In addition he is responsible for the direct management of noncommissioned safety personnel (usually student aides) who supplement the police function by manning fixed security posts in the library and parking areas.3 In addition to his overall administrative duties, the Director acts as sort of a "commissioner of police" and also serves as Chief of Safety. The Chief of Police/Security assumes the responsibilities of the Director in his absence but is directly responsible for the overall administration and coordination of the divisions and personnel within the Police Department on a daily basis. For example, the Chief is responsible for establishing operational procedures with regard to

FIGURE 1

DTU POLICE DEPARTMENT ORGANIZATIONAL STRUCTURE

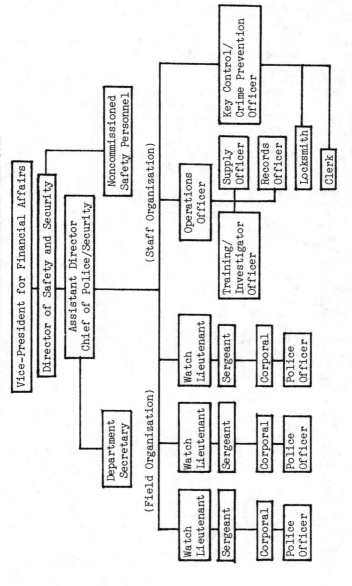

39

the responsibilities of the Department, recruitment, personnel management and discipline, handling press relations, maintaining a liaison with other law enforcement agencies, and so forth.

Other than upper-level administrators, line and staff personnel constitute the two basic types of personnel found within the DTU Police Department. The staff is composed of those forces (five officers and two civilian employees) organized to service the line and assist them in their primary function. Staff operations include personnel administration, forms and records control, equipment supply and maintenance, personnel orientation and training, investigations, key control and crime prevention. With 55 officers,[4] the uniformed line division is by far the largest subdivision within the Department in terms of number of personnel. It is composed of those forces organized to provide delivery of police services (e.g., patrol, traffic, investigation and other services). Line operations are police field activities.

Line operations are organized into three watches or shifts. Each watch is composed of supervisory personnel--one lieutenant, one sergeant, two corporals--and varying numbers of patrol personnel. The lieutenant on each watch is the shift commander and has ultimate responsibility for the coordination and operation of all activities on his or her assigned shift. Specifically, the lieutenant is responsible for general supervision of beat activities and manpower, maintenance of daily personnel records, monitoring of personnel performance, developing and implementing strategies of patrol, carrying out special orders of the Chief, recommending disciplinary actions, scheduling of personnel, and so forth. In short, the lieutenant sees to it that his or her shift operates properly. The sergeant is responsible for the shift in the lieutenant's absence and may conduct all the functions normally assigned to the lieutenant. On days when the lieutenant is present, the sergeant is more or less "the right arm and eyes of the lieutenant, spotting areas that need attention." The sergeant usually spends most of his or her time in motor patrol, responding to nonroutine problems and exercising supervision of patrolmen. Corporals are the lowest level supervisors on each watch. While they will assume the responsibilities of upper-level supervisors in their absence, their normal duties include working as communications dispatcher, substituting for the sergeant on mobile patrol, and engaging in flexible foot patrol responding to routine and mundane problems and exercising close supervision of foot patrolmen. In addition, corporals act as a liaison between supervisors and patrolmen and are instrumental in on-the-job training, indoctrinating new men or women in the policies, practices and procedures of the Department. If the shift is shorthanded the corporals will act as patrolmen.5 The following comment of one supervisor summarizes the role and function of corporals:

> A corporal is sort of half supervisor and half patrolman. He runs the shift in the absence of upper level supervisors or he fills in as a patrolman and is assigned to a duty post if the shift is short of officers. A corporal is really a glorified officer. He has few powers and solves only mundane problems. He is the eyes and ears of the watch and acts as a middleman between officers and supervisors, counseling patrolmen and reporting observances to other supervisors.

Most of the police personnel are patrolmen or public safety officers. Patrolmen are the backbone of the department for it is their duties which comprise the basic function of the campus police service. In contrast to municipal police departments in which the basic line organization falls naturally into the uniformed officer on the beat and the nonuniformed detective force on the basis of task specialization (Banton, 1964; Skolnick, 1966; Niederhoffer, 1967; Watson and Sterling, 1969; Westley, 1970; Sanders, 1977), there is no such functional specialization at the university.6 Each university officer is a "jack of all trades" who performs all functions. Patrolmen are responsible for: patrolling all campus buildings and grounds; enforcing laws and arresting offenders; conducting investigations of all criminal, traffic and other incidents; controlling and directing traffic; inspecting campus buildings and grounds for safety hazards; and providing general public services to those on campus (e.g., giving information, assisting those in distress, and so forth). The lack of specialists at DTU may be attributed to two facts: (1) there is little call for specialization on campus, and (2) the relatively

41

small size of the Department tends to render specialization a waste of manpower.

In short, the DTU Police Department closely
resembles municipal departments in structure; it is,
in fact, modeled after municipal law enforcement
agencies. It should be noted, however, that while
the DTU Department is highly structured, exhibiting a
hierarchical arrangement and fixed division of labor,
it is not elaborately structured. The lack of functional specialization at the line level and the fact
that the Chief assumes direct responsibility for both
field and staff organization with the heads of both
types of operations reporting directly to him[7]
suggest a somewhat simpler structure than that found
in large municipal departments.

Status arrangements

Similar to many municipal police organizations,
the DTU police use military ranks to enhance internal
efficiency by making status distinctions clear and
reminding everyone of his or her position in the
unit. Other than the relative power of position, as
reflected in these ranks, there is little basis for
status distinctions among DTU officers. This is particularly true among patrolmen, who hold the lowest
status position in the organization. Furthermore,
there is no dramatic way that a patrolman can gain
status vis-a-vis his coworkers within the Department.
For example, there is no status differentiation on
the basis of assignments since all line patrolmen
perform all tasks.[8] Moreover, there are no assignments that officers define as most desirable. Each
uniformed patrolman was asked the following question:
"What duty assignment on the force would you choose
if you had free choice?" Thirty-two percent (31.6%)
of the officers reported they could not choose one
because they would prefer to perform a variety of
assignments on a daily basis. An additional 22 percent (21.6%) indicated they would choose general foot
patrol, 14 percent (14.3%) said vehicle patrol, 14
percent (13.5%) said traffic, 11 percent (10.8%)
indicated radio dispatcher, and the remainder were
unable to make a choice. When probed as to the
reasons for their choice, patrolmen mentioned such
things as "it is more interesting," "it affords more
autonomy and freedom from supervisors," or "I just
like it," but never mentioned the prestige or status

associated with any particular assignment. These data suggest a lack of prestige assignments among officers. In contrast to their municipal counterparts who can gain status with their coworkers on the basis of assignment, particularly detective and vice assignments (Skolnick, 1966; Niederhoffer, 1967; Westley, 1970; Rubinstein, 1973; Sanders, 1977), officers at DTU have no prestigious assignments which can be used as a means of advancement. Moreover, unlike their municipal counterparts, who advance within the department and are considered "good officers" on the basis of their law enforcement activity (e.g., number of arrests, or good arrests), university officers have no comparable measure. In university policing, the "good officer" is merely someone who does his or her job and is not a trouble maker. When questioned about the criteria they use to distinguish a good university policeman from a bad one, 57 percent of the officers mentioned someone who does his or her job, 47 percent mentioned someone who displays a positive attitude (e.g., does not complain, is interested in his or her job, and so forth), 30 percent mentioned neat appearance, 27 percent listed humanistic approach (i.e., cares about and is sensitive to people), and 25 percent indicated reliability and attendance.[9] While university officers progress within the department on the basis of these criteria, they are not the basis of status differentiation among officers.

Organization of Everyday Line Operations: Watches

The University Police Department operates 24 hours a day, 7 days a week, 365 days a year. Patrol service is provided around the clock and is divided into three watches or shifts: day watch (7 A.M. to 3 P.M.), evening watch (3 P.M. to 11 P.M.) and morning watch (11 P.M. to 7 A.M.). As stated previously, each watch is organized similarly being composed of a consistent rank structure[10] and varying numbers of patrol officers. The number of patrolmen employed on each shift varies with the nature of demands. Maximum manpower is made available when the greatest demand for service is needed. Most classes at DTU start around 8 A.M. and end around 10 P.M.; thus, more police and security services are required during these hours. At the time of the data collection, 35 percent (N=19) of the line personnel were assigned

43

to the day watch, 38 percent (N=21) to the evening watch and 27 percent (N=15) to the morning watch. Thus, in contrast to urban police departments whose busiest hours are from about 6 P.M. to about 4 A.M. and only a skeleton crew is employed during the day (see, for example, Cumming et al., 1965; Buckner, 1967; Petersen, 1968; Rubinstein, 1973), the greatest concentration of university officers is found on the day and evening shifts.

Common features

There are several features common to all watches which have a bearing on the line patrolman's everyday work. These features include preparation for patrol and the organization of operations.

Preparation for patrol

All officers are required to report for duty no later than twenty minutes before the hour that their shift begins. The first thing that each officer does upon arriving at work is to check in with an outgoing watch supervisor at the operations room to ensure that his attendance for the day is recorded. Officers usually begin gathering in the briefing room about half an hour before their watch begins. They use the time before formal briefing to accomplish a number of tasks, including checking out a radio and radio case, buffing their shoes, checking the bulletin board for all posted orders and communications, engaging in informal conversations with their fellow officers, and so forth.

Formal roll call or briefing begins at twenty minutes before the hour and is conducted by one or more watch supervisors from the incoming shift. It is at this point that patrolmen receive the information they need to perform their routine duty: they receive their assignments for the day, special instructions such as schedule changes and particular things to pay attention to, and knowledge of the events occurring since their last tour of duty as recorded in the incident reports. In addition to the dispensement of information needed for patrol, time during formal roll call is also used to distribute keys, conduct inspections, and record identifying numbers of each officer's radio, radio case and keys.

Upon completion of these activities, which usually takes five or ten minutes, officers are immediately dispatched to the field, and the previous watch is officially relieved.[11]

In reality, the tone of roll call is more informal than formal in nature. For example, inspections are rarely conducted unless it is close to evaluation time. When one is conducted, the officers do not stand at attention, nor are all sides of their persons checked. Another example of the informal nature of briefings is the way in which information about incidents is dispensed. Usually briefings on previous incidents are conducted "tongue in cheek" and oftentimes informal editorial comment is added. The following examples, taken from field observation, are illustrative:

> Well, I see we have another theft by opportunity...so what else is new.

> Here's a good one. A woman reported on the last shift that she saw a man in the hallway outside a classroom masturbating. You'll never believe when the incident actually happened...two days ago. God!

The informal tone of roll call, especially in relation to incident reports, may be viewed as part of the continuing socialization of the university officer. It serves to inculcate in the officer certain attitudes and ways of looking at things. (Socialization of the university officer is discussed more fully in Chapter 3.)

Organization of Operations

The operations room, which is referred to as Operations, is the "nerve center" of the University Police Department. It is here that all watch records are kept and all communications equipment (e.g., centralized radio, telephones, and so on) and other electronic equipment (e.g., communications tape machine, crime information center machine, closed circuit TV monitors, elevator alarm panels, and so on) are located. Operations is usually staffed by a two person supervisory team with one supervisor working the desk and the other working the communications equipment. On the days s/he is present the

45

lieutenant of each watch mans the desk[12] and is responsible, among other things, for keeping a permanent daily log of all incidents, criminal and non-criminal,[13] maintaining department records and files, answering the telephone or radio if the dispatcher is busy, maintaining a daily attendance record of all duty personnel, handling walk-in complaints and giving information. Usually the radio is manned by a corporal who acts as dispatcher. The dispatcher's major duties include receiving, routing and dispatching messages which come through the communications center, maintaining an accurate status record of various field units and directing their activity, making a periodic radio test every hour on the half hour,[14] and observing the closed circuit television monitors.[15] On those days when supervisory personnel are at a minimum, especially on weekends, an experienced, non-ranked senior patrol officer is brought into Operations to act as dispatcher. The rationale behind permitting only experienced officers to act as dispatcher was perhaps best summed up by one officer who said: "You have to know what is on the outside before you can work the inside."

Communications. Each officer is equipped with a portable two-way walkie talkie that ties directly to the central radio located in Operations. S/He is identified on duty by a code composed of his or her watch number followed by the radio number s/he is using that day. For example, if s/he is working the evening watch, departmentally designated as watch "3", and is using radio number 10 the officer is identified as "3-10." The officer uses this designation in all radio communications for his or her tour of duty.

According to FCC regulations, all routine radio communication must be kept to a minimum and unnecessary traffic avoided. Hence, like all police, university police make extensive use of standard radio codes to shorten transmission time (e.g., a signal "13" specifies that an officer is in trouble, "10-11" means to return to Operations). In addition, these codes provide a certain amount of secrecy in handling police communications. Furthermore, lengthy messages of a non-emergency or confidential nature are not broadcast on the radio but are transmitted over the telephone. Oftentimes during the course of routine patrol an officer is instructed by radio to call Operations on the phone. Usually the officer proceeds to the nearest pay phone, informs Operations of its number by radio and Operations returns the call according to the number given.16 Moreover, in the course of his or her routine duty an officer will often initiate telephone calls to Operations on his or her own to apprise supervisors of a situation and/or receive instructions for action. The following example taken from field observation is illustrative:

> One day an officer was dispatched to the
> game room (located in the DTU student
> center) to check on an incident involving
> the use of equipment in this area by
> unauthorized personnel. Upon arrival at the
> scene the officer assessed the situation and
> phoned Operations to find out how to
> proceed. He was instructed to escort the
> unauthorized person off campus, which he
> did.

It would appear that the telephone serves an important consultive function for university officers.

From a sociological point of view, one of the most significant features of radio communication is its potential use as a supervisory tool. All officers are required to inform Operations at the beginning and end of each assignment of their whereabouts. This information, along with the time of the transmission, is formally logged in Operations on a piece of paper termed a "round sheet." Not only does this log enable Operations to know where everyone is in case of emergency but it can be used to analyze officer performance because it reflects units of work accomplished by an officer in relation to time spent in the field. For example, there are certain informal understandings regarding the amounts of time it takes to patrol each building. If an officer violates these informal time norms it appears to supervisors that s/he is not doing his or her job properly. In reality there is some problem with using round logs to analyze officer performance. On many occasions when the dispatcher was away from his or her desk other Operations' personnel were observed receiving transmissions from field officers and neglecting to record that information on the round sheet. While the dispatcher was usually informed of the communication upon his or her return the information relayed was usually inaccurate with regard to

47

time. Thus the potential use of the round sheet to analyze officer performance is reduced. Nevertheless, there is no doubt that the use of radios, which allow constant communication with field units, increases control over patrolmen's movements and, thus, enhances supervision.

Unique features

Though all watches are organized the same way and use many of the same operational procedures, they operate independently and differently. Major differences between watches can be found in the duties that officers perform at different times of the day, foot patrol patterns, and the atmosphere in which officers work.

Duties

University policemen perform a wide variety of duties. However, the tasks which officers may be called on to perform vary with shifts. For example, day and evening officers "pull" traffic duty and may be assigned to the flag detail but morning watch personnel are never responsible for these duties; the day watch opens doors, the evening watch closes them, and the morning watch has only minimal responsibility for openings and closings; all watches have certain locations which require officers to maintain stationary surveillance, with the evening watch having the most (usually five) and the morning watch the least (only one); the evening watch and morning watch must pull an officer off patrol to cover the Primate Center located off campus but the day watch has no responsibility in this area; officers on the evening and morning watches are more likely than those on the day watch to have to provide escort to cars; officers on the day watch are more likely to provide "money escorts" for university personnel on official banking business; officers on the day and evening watches are more likely to be confronted with criminal incidents, and so forth.

In short, the evening watch is probably the most active in terms of compulsory obligations and varied activities, with the day watch running a close second and the morning watch coming in last in terms of degree of activity. In other words, in the perform-

48

ance of their everyday duty, day and evening watch
officers are likely to perform a myriad of other
duties which remove them from patrol, while morning
watch officers engage almost exclusively in patrol
activities. Furthermore, the security emphasis
varies with shifts. Officers perceive variations in
shift emphasis also. Most officers think of the day
and evening watches as requiring a mixture of police
and security duties and the morning watch as requiring primarily security work. The following comment
is typical:

> The day watch is about 50-50 police and
> security work. The evening watch is about
> 80 percent police work and 20 percent secur-
> ity work. The morning watch is 90 percent
> security work. On the morning watch all you
> do is engage in constant patrol to make sure
> everything is secure and to check for smoke
> odors. You rarely get to use your policing
> skills.

Patrol patterns

On all watches when officers are not otherwise
engaged (e.g., investigating an accident, assigned to
a stationary post, on break, and so forth) they are
expected to be on interior or exterior patrol of
buildings. Since there are different things to look
for and do during different hours of the day, foot
patrol patterns vary according to shift. On the day
watch patrolmen usually conduct four rounds of all
campus buildings at two hour intervals. The first
round is a "shake down" round in which "every door
knob is rattled" on a thorough patrol of each building. The second round is a "quick shakedown" in
which officers attempt to catch anything which they
might have missed on the first round by covering all
floors but not shaking all knobs. The third and
fourth rounds are largely "walk through" fire and
safety rounds in which officers are attuned to the
"out of ordinary" and make themselves visible to the
public. In short, the day watch begins with a
thorough shakedown style of patrol and ends with a
walk through style. In contrast, a typical day for
an evening watch patrolman begins with a walk through
the buildings in his or her zone. His or her second
and third rounds are more thorough because there are
now knobs on locked offices to be checked. The last

49

round on the evening watch is by far the most
thorough and involves a complete shakedown and securing of buildings. On the morning watch the first and
last rounds are the most thorough, with the rounds in
between being mostly walk through fire checks.

Morning rounds are the most patterned because
officers are rarely removed from patrol to perform
other assignments. Day and evening rounds are less
patterned. One line officer summed up the differences in patrol patterns across watches in the following manner:

> Patrol rounds on the day watch are somewhat
> patterned, but officers are pulled off
> patrol to perform other duties. Rounds on
> the evening watch are the least patterned.
> Those officers just sort of check buildings
> between other assignments. Rounds on the
> morning watch are the most patterned.
> Officers on that watch are pretty much con-
> stantly on patrol.

Atmosphere

The atmosphere of each watch varies with the type
and amount of community members present during
different hours of the day. The day watch is known
as the "PR Watch" (public relations watch) because it
is during this time of day that the university
community is most heterogeneous, being composed of a
wide variety of faculty, staff, students, and departmental and university administrators. Because of the
type of people that are around, as well as the fact
that so many people are around, most officers feel
that the day watch is the most tense watch in the
sense that it makes the greatest demands upon
officers to be tolerant, to use their discretion, and
to remain professional at all times. Comments such
as the following were typical among officers:

> The day watch is primarily a public rela-
> tions shift because the big university
> bosses are around and there are more
> faculty, staff and students on a wider scale
> than on other watches. On the day watch you
> deal with people more and have to display a
> sincere interest in helping them. To most
> people the day watch is the police depart-

ment and therefore it is important to always
look good, act good and smell good.

On the day watch you deal with a non-
working, younger set of students that are
likely to do things like throw people in the
fountain. There are a lot of kids right out
of high school who pull a number of pranks.
You really have to be tolerant. You also
have to keep on your toes because the big
wigs are here during the day.

The evening watch is also characterized by involvement with the public, thus requiring that
officers stay alert at all times. However, the
nature of that public is significantly different from
that found on the day watch. Evening watch personnel
deal with a more mature, working and career oriented
student and are not subjected to the scrutiny of high
level departmental and university administrators
throughout their entire tour of duty. Consequently,
the tension which characterizes the day watch is
somewhat relieved on the evening watch. The following officer comments were typical:

On the evening watch you deal with more
business and professional people. You get
only about two hours of what the day shift
has and then you get an older, more mature
generation and you get into the working
group. You don't have to worry about
childish pranks anymore but you do get more
problems at the decks (parking decks).
People coming into the decks between 5 and
6 P.M. having had a hard day at work are
frustrated and lose their cool easily. It
can get pretty tense but after the parking
problems are solved the tension wears away
fast and you can pretty much relax for the
rest of the shift. Older people just don't
try your patience as much as the younger
ones although they can be trying at times.

After the big brass heads home for the
evening around 5:30 or 6:00 you can let your
hair down a little. You still have to stay
on your toes because a lot of people are
around and they will report you if they
think you are goofing off. But you don't
have to stay on your tippy toes like when
the big brass is around.

51

The atmosphere of the morning watch is by far the most relaxed of the three watches. This is the case because there are few people around campus during the morning hours and there are a minimum number of duties, other than patrol, which officers are required to perform. The following comments are representative:

This watch is characterized by non-involvement with other people. There is no one around but custodians and workers in the computer center. Occasionally custodians will complain if they see an officer sitting around but not very often. In contrast to other watches there is far less community on the morning watch to keep their eyes on you and get you in trouble. It's a more relaxed atmosphere.

There is not much public to deal with on the morning watch and there is a lot less happening. You have a lot of slack time and nobody bothers you if you stop to take a cup of coffee several times throughout the night. You just don't have every Tom, Dick and Harry breathing down your neck like you do on the other watches where people are constantly around. Things are a lot less tense and more relaxed on the morning watch.

In short, the nature of the community present during a particular watch has a strong bearing on the atmosphere of that watch. The most tense watch on weekdays is the day watch and the most relaxed is the morning watch. On weekends and during vacations when fewer community members are present during normal working hours, the day and evening watches most closely approximate the morning watch; they are substantially more relaxed and their major function is patrol.

Watch preference

Like all police work, university police work is shift work. When officers initially enter the Department they request a particular watch assignment. These requests are taken into consideration by Department administrators but in the final analysis assignments to watches are based upon manpower needs.

Nevertheless, most officers seem to be satisfied with their watch assignments. Each uniformed line officer was asked the following question: "Do you prefer this watch to others?" Seventy-four percent of the officers indicated that they actually prefer their current watch to others. Of those officers, 84 percent suggested they prefer their current watch because the hours are convenient to their life style. Of the 26 percent who would prefer to work another watch, 77 percent indicated that they would prefer the day and 23 percent said they would prefer evening. Again, the major reason offered for wanting a particular watch was related to convenience more in line with life patterns.

In general, watch preference seems to be related to some extent to the degree to which life patterns and activities are disrupted. Most officers prefer the day watch because it does not disrupt daily activities as much as the other watches. The following officer comment is illustrative:

> You have to get up early but you get off at 3 P.M. You can lead pretty much of a normal life just like the rest of the world. Your home life is not really disrupted.

The evening watch is seen by most officers as the most life-disrupting shift. The following comments were typical:

> This watch is pretty isolating. You come to work about two hours before the rest of the world is getting off and you don't get home until around 11:30 P.M. when the rest of the world has gone to bed. Believe me this can put a lot of strain on your relationships with other people who work more normal hours.

> I'm a single parent. When I was assigned to the evening watch I had to send my kid to live with my parents out of town because I could no longer look after him. I mean I'm just not home when he is home. If that's not disruptive of my life I don't know what is. If I was on the day watch I could have him live with me.

The morning watch is seen by officers as more disruptive of one's life than the day watch but less disruptive than the evening watch. While it involves "non-normal" working hours, the morning watch does not totally preclude participation in "normal" activities and relationships. The following officer comment was representative:

> When you work the morning watch you are working while normal people are sleeping and you are sleeping when they are awake, but you still have some overlap time with them. You can use this overlap time to engage in normal activites.

In reality there are a myriad of factors other than convenience of one's working hours that can influence individual watch preference (e.g., degree and nature of demands placed upon officers, like or dislike of shift co-workers, atmosphere of the shift, and so forth). However, one factor which seems to be an overriding consideration in a general lack of preference for the morning watch among university officers is the negative stereotype associated with working this shift. Oftentimes officers are assigned to the morning watch by department administrators for disciplinary reasons. Consequently, over time the watch has become known informally among officers as the "fuck-up watch" and any officer assigned to this watch must contend with the "fuck-up" image other members of the force hold of him or her whether or not s/he in fact fits this image. At the time of data collection twelve patrolmen were assigned to the morning watch. The following comments about this watch were typical among officers:

> Because of a lack of manpower and high turn-over the Department can't afford to suspend people. So all disciplinary problems are eventually sent to the morning watch. It is sort of the on-your-way-out shift. Once you get assigned there you are pretty much through as a campus policeman.

> The morning watch is well known among officers as a dumping ground for goof-offs and fuck-ups. Once you get transferred there other officers start to think of you as a problem and after awhile they sort of look down on you. It's degrading. After awhile you just don't give a damn and your

work begins to reflect it. You might as
well quit and look for another job.

In short, among other things, the negative stereotype
associated with working the morning watch has a
strong bearing on patrolman's lack of preference for
that watch.

Relations Among Role Incumbents

Each university officer was asked his or her
opinion on the following statement: "The university
police department is a very efficient, smoothly
operating organization." Only 22 percent of the
officers agreed. Random probe of responses to this
statement suggested that while most university
officers believe the Department is efficient in
getting the job done, it is not smoothly operating.
Lack of smoothness in operation is generally seen as
deriving from the nature of relations between role
incumbents, especially those between supervisors and
subordinates.

In a bureaucracy the primary relation is between
superior and subordinate. Within the DTU Police
Department these relations are neither formal impersonal nor friendly informal (personal). Despite the
fact that the Department utilizes military rankings
to make status distinctions between role incumbents
clear, the absence of military formality in relations
is demonstrated in several ways. First, communications often cut across rather than go through a rigid
chain of command. Perhaps this is a result of the
fact that the DTU force is a rather small and concentrated force with all subordinate personnel having
daily contact with a variety of ranked personnel.
Stated differently, on a daily basis high ranking
personnel are not socially and physically isolated
from nonranked personnel: this increases the possibility of direct communication. Second, there is
little emphasis placed on protocol and ceremony within the Department, and there is little attention paid
informally to rank. While patrolmen are always aware
that their superiors have authority over them, there
is little outward formality in interaction between
various ranks. For example, officers display little
deference towards their superiors as illustrated by
the facts that they never salute ranked personnel or
stand at attention in their presence. In both of

these respects--the cutting across of communications and absence of attention informally to rank--university police are no different from their municipal counterparts (see, for example, Edwards, 1968; Wilson, 1968; Rubinstein, 1973).

In contrast, however, to the intensely personal relations scholars have reported existing between patrolmen themselves and to some extent between officers and their immediate supervisors (see, for example, Banton, 1964; Skolnick, 1966; Wilson, 1968; Westley, 1970; Rubinstein, 1973), relations between line supervisors and patrolmen at DTU are generally unfriendly and unsatisfactory. Both supervisors and patrolmen reported that relations between them are characterized by poor communication, friction, hostility, and a lack of respect and understanding. As a consequence of the nature of these relations there is a definite rift between the two groups and a feeling of "officers versus supervisors" existing on all shifts. The comment of one uniformed patrolman is illustrative:

> There is not good interaction between officers and supervisors here. Supervisors stick together and officers stick together. There is more of a "them" rather than "us" feeling around here.

The basic reason offered by both groups for the friction between them varies with position in the organization. Supervisors claim officers lack respect for authority and do not understand that they too have a job to do, that is, to supervise. Officers, on the other hand, see low quality relations with supervisors stemming not so much from differentials in authority inherent in position but rather from the approach supervisors take in exercising their authority on a daily basis. To most officers this approach is nonsupportive, negative, demeaning, critical, nonconstructive, harrassing and authoritative.[17] In the course of this research, numerous interactions between officers and supervisors were observed. More often than not, negativism characterized these interactions. Only once was a supervisor observed giving an officer constructive advice in a positive, noncritical and nondemeaning manner. Moreover, oftentimes officers were chastized and berated in front of anyone who happened to be standing within ear shot (e.g., other officers, the researchers, the general public, and so forth). The "openness" of these communications can only serve to increase feelings of their demeaning nature among officers. The following comments are representative of officer's attitudes regarding their relations with supervisors:

> Supervisors are not loyal to officers. They are more interested in covering their own ass than backing you. They work against you instead of with you. Anything an officer does he has to stand on his own because he never receives backing and support from his superiors.

> Officers are constantly being talked down to...they are treated like a child rather than an adult. Supervisors dwell on negative things...they cut you down instead of help you. They criticize too harshly. Most of the verbal abuse in this job comes from supervisors not the public. Even if supervisor criticism is meant to be constructive they leave a negative impression because of the way they do it. How do you expect the public to treat us like police officers when supervisors don't even treat us like security guards.

> Some supervisors are power crazed. They say, "things are this way because I say they are." Supervisors want officers to be their clones. They have an attitude of do as I do, think as I think, and say as I say. If an officer follows this rule he is unlikely to be harrassed by a supervisor, but if he doesn't he is going to be given a hard time.

Despite their feelings about supervisors, most officers are aware that in the long run it does not pay to oppose a supervisor. Evaluations, discipline, assignments, raises, and so forth within the Department are based upon the opinions of supervisors. By virtue of their authority and position within the organization supervisors "hold all the cards." The system operates in their favor rather than the officers'. To counteract this system bias and avoid getting into trouble, officers employ essentially two techniques. First, they may attempt to avoid getting in trouble by "getting something on a supervisor."

The fear of mutual disclosure reduces the power supervisors have over officers. The following comment is illustrative:

> Supervisors will slack off on riding you if you can get something on them. One supervisor was really giving me a hard time until her boyfriend came down here on a weekend and I walked up on them smooching on duty. After that the supervisor slacked off on me.

Second, and more commonly, officers may attempt to avoid getting into trouble by keeping a low profile. The following comments were typical among officers:

> The best way to stay out of trouble at work is to hang low from supervisors. That means keeping your mouth shut and staying out of the supervisors' way.

> Supervisors have all the power. The less contact you have with them the better off you are. You have to stay low if you want to survive. I try to keep as much distance between myself and supervisors as possible. I also don't make waves and try to avoid controversial situations. Keeping your mouth shut and not making waves will get you anything you want around here. You're better off keeping a low profile and not giving a supervisor any static because they will come down on you if you do.

Evaluations

The performance of each university officer is formally evaluated monthly for the first six months of employment while s/he is on probation and then every six months thereafter for the remainder of his or her term of employment. Usually patrolmen evaluations are completed by the watch lieutenant after consultation with other supervisory personnel and, hence, officer evaluations are done as a group. Using a standardized departmental form each officer is evaluated in terms of attendance, appearance and care of equipment, demeanor, attitude, report writing skills, and compliance with rules and regulations.18 Thus, in contrast to their municipal counterparts,

58

whose performance is appraised in terms of law enforcement activity (e.g., number of arrests, convictions) and involvement in the visible and dramatic
aspects of policing, performance appraisal of university officers rests largely on more general personal
characteristics and not on law enforcement activity.

Given that numerous scholars of policing have
pointed out the fallacy of evaluating municipal
policemen in terms of law enforcement tasks they
rarely perform (see, for example, Cumming et al.,
1965; Niederhoffer, 1967; Rubinstein, 1973; Webster,
1973; Lundman, 1980), it would appear at first glance
that university officers receive a more realistic
appraisal than their municipal counterparts. However, the evaluative process used to appraise DTU
officers is not without its problems. The evaluative
criteria themselves are based largely on superficial
personal characteristics rather than assessment of
actual work. The measurement of such things as
attendance, appearance, compliance with rules, and so
forth, says nothing about proficiency on the job.
Moreover, despite attempts to objectify evaluations,
in the final analysis they are based on the subjective opinions of others. Hence, they remain arbitrary and reflect, to a large extent, the degree to
which an officer manages to stay out of trouble.
This again does not measure proficiency. In short,
because evaluations do not really measure actual job
performance, they provide little incentive in and of
themselves among officers to maintain superior performance.

Discipline

As a bureaucratic organization, university police
have many rules and regulations bearing on the
behavior of members, including a myriad of stipula-
tions concerning dress, conduct and job performance
both on and off duty.[19] These rules and regulations
designed to guide and control the actions of officers
are formally stated by the Department in the DTU
Police Manual. Thus, the police manual defines what
is expected of officers, and officers are encouraged
to "stick to the book" to avoid getting into trouble.
All officers are aware that any violation of the
book, that is, the rules and regulations of the
Department, may result in disciplinary action.

It is inevitable in any organization that personnel will engage in some form of misconduct which requires review and disposition. All violations of standards of conduct are handled internally within the Department. When an officer is caught in an infraction of a rule, one of three possible outcomes can occur. First, the infraction may be overlooked and no action taken against the officer. Second, the officer may be informally "written up" with no immediate action taken against him or her. Informal write-ups simply involve a supervisor making a written notation "in his little black book" of the infraction and later using this information to document a poor evaluation of the officer. Since evaluations affect salary raises, informal write-ups could eventually result in disciplinary action, that is, reduction or cancellation of merit raise. Finally, if an officer commits an infraction of a rule s/he may be formally written-up by a supervisor with a typed copy of a letter describing the circumstances of the infraction being forwarded to the Chief for his review and disposition. Usually formal write-ups bring some form of immediate formal action from the Chief who has a wide gamut of disciplinary measures at his disposal including reprimand, raise cancellation, transfer to a less desirable watch, probation, suspension, dismissal, and so forth.[20]

Official write-ups, whether informal or formal, seem to be the most common result when there is a known rule infraction by a patrolman. Rarely are even minor violations ignored. On numerous occasions supervisors were observed making a written notation of misconduct to be used to refresh their memories when evaluation time arrived. Moreover, the researcher had knowledge of approximately 10 percent of the sample (five officers) who were formally written-up and against whom formal disciplinary action was taken during the period of data collection--three officers were suspended, one was fired, and one was forced to resign.[21] These observations suggest that disciplinary actions are common in university police work. This conclusion is supported by officer's perceptions. Each uniformed officer was asked his or her opinion on the following statement: "Disciplinary actions are frequently taken against members of the force." The majority of officers (53%) agreed. Thus, it appears that the use of negative sanctions and the threat or fear of their use does pervade day-to-day operation.

While infractions do occur and disciplinary action either of a formal or informal nature is frequently taken, many officers suggested that formal discipline is probably not as severe as it could be. The comments of several officers were typical:

> There is not really enough discipline here. Things have to progress to a point where they get really bad before anything is done. The Chief bends over backwards to give people a chance...in other words, not to fire them.

> There is a lack of harsh discipline here. It is very lax. People commit offenses that they would be fired for elsewhere. Once two supervisors were caught having sex on duty and they are still here. Not only is this unprofessional, but it does not set a good example for others to follow.

Despite the perception among officers that the severity of disciplinary action is not as great as it could be, there is a strong feeling among DTU officers that the disciplinary process itself is unjust. Several factors contribute to this feeling of unjustness. The first factor pertains to the right of appeal. Ideally the campus police disciplinary process is based upon the principle that every officer is entitled to due process. Each officer who has been employed longer than six months and is thus not on probation is given the right of appeal to higher authority if s/he disagrees with any disciplinary action taken against him or her. Most officers feel that this right of appeal is more lip service than reality. The following comment was representative of this attitude:

> We don't really have any appeal here. All we have is paper appeal. If you go before the Chief he always takes the supervisor's side. If you appeal to the Director he always backs up the Chief. So it doesn't really do any good to appeal although it looks good on paper for the Department to say you can. If you do appeal all you succeed in doing is getting a reputation as a trouble maker. You can't win when you appeal so you don't really have the right to appeal.

61

Second, while the Department has policies covering what will happen if one does not adhere to rules of conduct the actual disciplinary actions that will result are not made explicit in a formally written policy. Hence, when an officer is caught in a rule infraction s/he knows s/he is in trouble but s/he is unsure what action will be taken against him or her, if any. As a consequence, no matter what action is taken it is viewed by officers as arbitrary and unpredictable. This lack of predictability increases feelings of unjustness among officers. The following comment of one uniformed patrolman is illustrative:

> You never can tell what the Chief will do in a disciplinary situation. He likes to mull things over. Sometimes he lets an officer go and other times he fires them. One officer will get fired for insubordination and another one won't.

Finally, officers feel that the disciplinary process is unjust because it is based on inconsistent policy--the rules of conduct do not apply equally to all employees. To most officers a double standard between patrolmen and supervisors exists at DTU in terms of the application of rules and regulations--supervisors commit offenses without being punished for which officers are disciplined. This double standard is one source of friction between officers and supervisors. The following officer comments were typical:

> Supervisors don't obey their own rules. The rules aren't for them. They are just for officers. This creates a lot of problems. They don't set an example and we get blamed for doing the same things they do all the time.

> Supervisors are at liberty to do anything we get written up for...like eating on duty, walking with their hats off, reading on duty. They don't set an example. Yet they throw the rules and regulations in your face and use them to punish you. Nothing is consistent around here. They should have a police manual that reads "Supervisors Only."

Officer's perceptions of a double standard in disci-

pline were supported by observation. Supervisors
were often seen engaging in such behavior as reading
newspapers and popular magazines, working crossword
puzzles, and listening to commercial radio stations
while on duty. Though this was observed by other
supervisors, nothing was ever said. In contrast, on
several occasions patrolmen were observed being rep-
rimanded by a supervisor for engaging in similar
acts, particularly reading while sitting at a stationary post.

As in all police organizations, discipline at DTU
is problematic because police command is precarious.
Like all police operations, campus police operations
are highly decentralized involving the deployment of
patrolmen alone (or occasionally in teams of two)
where control over their routine duties is problematic. Since supervisors are not with officers on
patrol, they are not in a position to know with any
degree of certainty what an officer is actually doing
or whether s/he is following the regulations.
Patrolmen spend much of their day-to-day work-time
without direct supervision.

In its attempts to control subordinate behavior
the Department generally assumes a supervisory style
which Tifft (1970) termed "the inspector," that is,
supervisors spend time in the surveillance of patrolmen to see if they are doing the job and to detect
infractions of rules. At DTU oftentimes supervisors
will "stroll around campus keeping their eyes open
for officers." If they see an officer in a violation
or where he or she is not supposed to be, the officer
is in trouble and is written-up. Occasionally a
supervisor will stand on a particular floor of a
building and wait to see if an officer passes by. If
the officer does not pass by, the supervisor knows
the patrolman is not making his or her round of the
building. In addition to surveillance, another major
technique of subordinate control is through radio
communication. If officers are in contact, they are
controllable to a greater extent than if they are not
in contact. The importance of radio communication to
supervision at DTU has been previously noted; supervisors use the information logged on the round sheet
to satisfy themselves that at least part of an
officer's assigned district is patrolled during the
time s/he is not under direct supervision. Despite
these techniques of control, police command still
remains precarious.

While police command is precarious at DTU, it is probably less precarious than in most municipal police organizations in which patrol operations are conducted under weak or nonexistent supervision. At the university they are conducted under far greater supervision. The greater supervision to be found in campus policing at DTU is probably a result of two factors. First, DTU police operate in a geographically limited and confined area. Since most officers are deployed on foot, they are less mobile and remain highly visible to all supervisors as well as all campus community members present. The more confined and visible subordinates are, the easier they are to supervise and control. Second, the ratio of campus police supervisors to police patrolmen is extremely high. Of the 55 DTU uniformed line personnel, 11 or 20 percent were supervisors. This results in a ratio of one supervisor for every four officers. It is noteworthy that the same ratio holds across all watches. The higher the ratio is of supervisors to subordinates the greater the likelihood of increased control. The degree of control in campus policing is reflected in officers' perception of supervision. Each uniformed patrolman was questioned as to his or her opinion of the following statement: "My on the job activities are strictly supervised." Fifty-two percent (52.4%) of the university patrolmen indicated that they agreed with the statement, 21 percent (21.4%) remained neutral, and only 26 percent (26.2%) disagreed. The fact that police command is less precarious at DTU suggests that campus police operations may in fact be more bureaucratic than municipal operations.

Jurisdiction and Authority

The DTU security force officially became a police force in 1974 with officers deriving their authority from state legislation.22 According to statute, each university policeman is a fully empowered peace officer with the authority to exercise his or her powers within five hundred yards of any property under the jurisdiction of the state university system. Realistically, each officer's authority is limited to five hundred yards beyond any property under the control of the specific institution to which s/he is assigned. Like all other police, university police have authority to perform police functions only within their jurisdiction except when they

64

have a warrant or are in "hot pursuit" of a felon; beyond their jurisdictional boundaries their powers revert to those of an ordinary citizen. Thus, university police are at no greater disadvantage than municipal police because of jurisdictional boundaries. Beyond the five hundred yard geographical limitation, there are no other statutory restrictions placed on university policemen in the exercise of their authority. For example, university police are not restricted by law to dealing only with university-affiliated persons, but may deal with anyone within their jurisdiction who violates the law.

There is, however, a formal departmental policy restriction on campus police jurisdiction which in effect limits the exercise of the university policeman's authority to the campus proper and streets and sidewalks adjacent to campus.²³ In reality the term "adjacent to campus" is interpreted in relationship to whether or not a university member is involved in an "adjacent" incident. For example, if an incident occurs in a park located across the street from a main campus building and a student is involved, the campus police handle the incident; if no campus community member is involved, the incident is referred to the city police. The following comment of one line officer is illustrative of university officer understanding of "off campus but adjacent:"

> We enforce the law off campus proper when-
> ever it has an effect on DTU. There is sort
> of an understood policy agreement with the
> city of whoever gets there first. However,
> if we get there first and it has nothing to
> do with DTU, we turn it over to the city.
> Vice versa, if they get there first and it
> has something to do with DTU, they turn it
> over to us. This policy avoids a lot of
> problems of dual jurisdiction and double
> statistics. Community member involvement is
> the key to whether we handle an incident
> adjacent to campus.

The formal policy with respect to jurisdictional boundaries is understood by both university and city police. University police do not actively pursue incidents outside their area and city police do not actively pursue incidents on campus. Thus, the line of demarcation between what constitutes the responsibility of the DTU police and the city police is clearly delineated by policy.

In short, University police are granted wide jurisdiction by state statute but their jurisdiction is formally restricted by policy. The major effect of this formal policy is to limit the university officer's routine work and the exercise of his or her authority to the immediate campus area rather than the large area granted him or her by state statute.

Community Relations

When questioned about the necessity of public support for police operations, 96 percent of the university officers agreed that "public support is imperative if police are to be effective." In other words, police operations cannot hope to be successful unless the police themselves gain the respect and confidence of the community they serve. Gaining this respect and confidence is no easy matter for any police organization, but it is particularly problematic in the university environment for several reasons. First, as is the case with municipal police, the public often holds contradictory opinions about campus police. They welcome official protection but resent official interference. They want to know that campus police are doing their job but they do not want campus police to interfere with them. A proper mixture of freedom and restraint is needed on campus. On the individual officer level this means that each officer needs to project a picture of helpfulness (service) rather than suppression while at the same time being firm and businesslike in his or her dealings with the public. If officers are too lenient or too repressive, the result is a loss of respect, support and cooperation within the community.

A second factor rendering community respect and confidence in campus police problematic is the stereotyped image many community members have of the campus cop. In contrast to the public image of municipal police, which is centered on the dramatic nature of a small portion of all police work (i.e., crime fighting), the campus police image is centered on security work. In fact, most university officers think the majority of the university community thinks of them as security guards rather than as police. The following comment was typical among officers:

66

Nine-tenths of the community thinks of us as
security. They think we don't do anything
and they look down on us and show us no
respect. They think we are inadequate just
because they think of us as security and not
police.

The fact that university officers are perceived as
security guards rather than policemen within the university community creates many situations in which
the university officer's authority is likely to be
questioned. The following comment is illustrative:

Sometimes we deserve a lack of respect
because we are inadequate, but most of the
time it is not our fault. One day a city
police officer was standing down at the
parking decks with me. He told a car to
move on that was blocking traffic while
waiting to get into the parking lot and the
driver blurted back that he was going to
tell the Dean. The city officer replied, "I
don't work for the damn Dean, so move it."
The point is that simply because he was
standing there the student assumed he was
DTU security and gave him static.

Overcoming the stereotype as security guards and thus
enhancing the campus police image within the community is no easy task because the composition of the
university community changes with each quarter--
masses of new students arrive and old ones leave. As
one officer noted:

We have to establish who we are four times a
year and that's hard. A lot of people mis-
understand who we are and what we are here
for. They think of us as security servants.
Every three months a new batch of people
come in here and we have to teach that new
batch what we are all about. City police
don't have this problem. In the city the
community already knows who you are and what
you can do--they grow up knowing what your
function is and what your powers are.

In short, university officers are in essence under
pressure to sell their profession to the community
with each new quarter.

The selling of the university police profession to the university community is made difficult at DTU because the police department lacks an active, determined and well organized community relations program. Given the lack of a formal community relations program at the university, the responsibility for engendering support from those who are to be served falls informally to the individual officer. Every officer is a community relations officer; everything s/he does affects community relations. Given his or her key position with respect to daily interactions with the public, each officer becomes an "image maker" or public relations officer. From the time they are first employed officers are instructed that their appearance, demeanor, approach, courtesy, contacts with the public and day-to-day performance of their duties will determine the Department's image on campus and thus affect community relations.

The university police department places a strong emphasis on good public relations. This emphasis on public relations is not only the result of the need for good relations but also the desire to upgrade the image of campus police. In fact the "image factor" is of such concern to campus police administrators that a number of the rules to which officers are subjected are designed to prohibit officers from doing anything that might reflect negatively upon the Department. For example, officers are prohibited from securing a second job without the written permission of the Chief, and any such job which might by nature bring embarrassment to the Department or university is automatically denied. Illustrative is the officer who held a second job as a bouncer in a topless bar and was instructed to resign from that job by the Chief for fear that any type of scandal would reflect negatively on the Department.

In general, university police attempt to control their image on campus through the management of appearances. For example, they try to convince the public that they are professional by focusing on superficial criteria such as demeanor and physical appearance that are closely aligned with the professional image. Outward conformity to the professional image is seen by most officers as the crux of obtaining community support and respect. The following officer comments were representative:

Being police depends on how you carry your-

self. If you look like a duck, walk like a
duck and act like a duck, you are a duck.
If you look like police, walk like police
and act like police you appear to others
that you are police and they respect you.

We need to protect ourselves image-wise.
Here there is a lot of emphasis placed on
the appearance an officer makes. They don't
want you to lean against buildings, have a
ciggy (cigarette) hanging out the side of
your mouth or to blow smoke in someone's
face. Your appearance is an indicator of
your personal standards as well as the
standards of the department you represent.
If you look good, people think good of you.
Image is what is important.

Relations Within the Campus Community

Effective policing ultimately depends upon the
cooperation and good will of the policed and, hence,
their attitudes toward the police are important.
While the present research did not obtain scientific
information on the publics' opinion of campus police,
it did obtain data on the policeman's definition of
the public and him or herself with respect to the
public. One can assume that this is largely a
product of his or her interaction with the public and
the conclusions s/he draws from this interaction.

Officer perception of image held by others

Sixty-three percent of the officers indicated in
interviews that overall they think the university
police have a favorable image within the academic
community. However, this image is seen as varying
among different campus groups. Officers' perception
of the image held of them by different groups within
the community is summarized in Table 1. The data in
this table suggest two conclusions. First, university police perceive they have a more favorable
image with some groups than with others--favorability
of image is highest for staff, followed by faculty
and students, respectively. Interestingly, the staff
group, which is overwhelmingly perceived as thinking
well of the DTU police, is composed of service
workers, who are roughly equivalent to university

police with respect to pay and status level within the university community. Hence, they are the kind of community members campus police are likely to get to know as people. In fact many officers suggested that the better community members get to know campus police, the more likely those members are to think well of the campus police. The following comments were typical among officers:

> Most of the community thinks of us as
> security and they tend to look down on us
> unless they have had contact with us. When
> they have contact they think better of us.

> We are here to help people with their
> problems. When groups get to know us they
> think well of us. Secretaries, for example,
> are always calling on us for this and that.
> We always respond and help them. They are
> always appreciative and courteous. I'd say
> they think pretty well of us.

Second, as noted above, DTU officers generally perceive other campus community members as thinking well of them. While students as a group were perceived as about equally split between thinking well of university officers and looking down on them, a majority of faculty and staff were perceived as thinking well of the campus police. Overall, DTU officers believe they are thought well of within the campus community.

TABLE 1

OFFICER PERCEPTION OF HOW VARIOUS
CAMPUS GROUPS FEEL ABOUT THEM (PERCENTAGES)

	Look Down On	Ignore	Think Well of	Varies
Students	41	18	39	2
Faculty	31	10	55	4
Staff	4	4	90	2

Officer attitudes toward
community components

Most officers believe that the community group from whom they are most likely to receive abusive treatment is students. Thus, students are seen by officers as the group most trying of their patience. On the whole, most students are perceived by officers as "okay" but the small minority of students that "give officers a hard time" are intensely disliked. Such students were described by officers as "rude," "inconsiderate," and as presenting "a real hassle." The following officer comments are illustrative of these attitudes:

> Ninety-five percent of the people go here to school to learn and are adults. It is the other five percent who don't know why they are here that give us a hard time. Our contacts with the public are only unpleasant with this five percent fringe. You can't help but hate someone who continuously gives you a hard time.

> Some students are real wise jerk-offs and others are not. Some will abuse you on this job. A few students will test you out... they will call you names, cuss you out and give you the finger. You just have to bite your teeth and put up with it. It is just part of the job to put up with the minority of students who are this way but you sure can't help but disliking them for it.

Officer's attitudes toward faculty members are largely ambivalent. As with officer's attitudes toward students, negative attitudes toward faculty are not generalizable to all faculty members. To university officers most faculty members are "okay." However, there is a small minority of faculty that officers resent. This resentment stems from two sources. First, faculty members constitute the group within the university community that is most likely to complain to departmental administrators and thus get officers in trouble. Second, and perhaps most important, faculty members are perceived by officers as having higher status within the community and thus oftentimes treating officers like servants. The resentful nature of officer attitudes toward faculty is readily apparent in the following officer comments:

> Faculty members think they have all kinds of
> privileges and priorities. Once they say
> they are faculty they think we are supposed
> to bow down and kiss their feet. They look
> down on us and expect us to cater to them.
> Well, I don't like their attitude. I don't
> care who they think they are.

> Some faculty members think they are God's
> gift to the University and we're scared of
> them because they have enough clout to make
> waves. So we're expected to cater to them
> and be their servants. I resent being
> expected to open doors for them because they
> are too lazy to remember their keys.

> We're supposed to ask faculty members for an
> ID if they want in a secured area. If they
> don't have an ID and we don't let them in
> they get pissed off and try to pull rank on
> us even though we are just doing our job.
> We are merely a convenience at their whim.

In short, it would appear that officer attitudes
toward various community groups reflect their perception of different groups' attitudes toward them.
This contention is further supported by the fact that
no officer expressed any negative opinion about staff
members. It should be recalled that staff members
are perceived by officers as espousing the most
favorable image of campus police as reflected in
their appreciative and courteous manner.

Press relations

The Department's press release policy is rather
stringent. Only the Chief and Director of Safety are
authorized to issue information to representatives of
the news media on investigations, arrests or any
other activities of police officers in the discharge
of their duties. If a member of the department has
reason to believe that s/he is being questioned for a
news release s/he is obligated to refer the
questioner to the proper authority. The purpose of
this policy is to reduce and control public criticism
to the greatest extent possible. The Department has
no real strategy for using the media to create a

positive image and negate public criticism. Its policy is geared more toward avoiding criticism than creating a good image.

Each of the officers were asked to agree or disagree with the following statement: "The university police force does not get a fair deal from the university newspaper." A majority of university officers (54%) agreed. While some officers suggested that the press image they get varies with the incident, many officers felt that the Department gets "burned" by reporters from the school paper. As one officer stated: "The university newspaper rarely gives us any credit...it is mostly all criticism. We get very negative press here." Examination of the university newspaper during the three months of data collection revealed that the school media does, in fact, generally portray the Department in a negative light. In most articles in which the DTU police were mentioned (a total of nine articles), an unfavorable image or impression was left. Articles tend to play up police inefficiency rather than sing police praises. Never was the Department patted on the back for a job well done. Moreover, occasionally the campus police were blamed for things that are not under their control (e.g., not providing the community with a short term parking lane).

As with all police departments, the negative press the university police have received has had an influence upon police operations. For example, the DTU police received rather harsh criticism from the school press over an incident involving the theft of a human skull from an anthropology display case because they failed to take fingerprints. Once the story broke, an internal memo was sent to all watch lieutenants instructing that fingerprints should be taken in all cases and that a supervisor should accompany officers on all important calls. The purpose of this shift in operational procedure was to avoid further public criticism.[24] The press does influence police operations.

Relations with Local Police

Despite the fact that DTU police are now the legal equivalent of their municipal counterparts, they continue to perceive themselves to be second-class citizens in the community of law enforcement.

73

Most university officers think that other police look
down on them and do not recognize their legitimacy as
"real" police. The following comment was typical
among officers:

Members of other police think of us as high
class security guards. They look down on us
and refer to us as Keystone Kops. Since
they are ignorant of our status, they don't
recognize us as a legitimate police force.

Even with this perception of "illegitimacy" attributed to other police perceptions of them, most university officers feel that other police respect them
for what they do. The following comments were
typical among officers:

Other police respect us in the area we are
in but not as police. They think we do a
good job for what we do but they still look
down on us as police.

Our image with other police has improved in
recent years as we got training. As we got
training and they became more familiar with
us we have gradually earned their respect.
If they didn't respect us they wouldn't
constantly be trying to recruit our
officers.

University and other local police operate autonomously. For example, they never conduct joint investigations. While the DTU Chief has regular confer-
ences with heads of other agencies, the average
officer has little contact with other police except
at the academy. What relations do exist are friendly
and courteous. For example, university officers on
exterior patrol or working traffic wave, smile and
nod to passing city officers in marked cars and the
amenity is returned. On the whole, however, there is
little association between departments on a daily
basis. This lack of association results in a feeling
among university officers that they are professionally isolated. The following comment is representative:

We have little association with other law enforcement officers and are not well versed in
what is going on around us. For example, with
respect to the recent string of murders

74

plaguing the city, we might be able to see something if we knew what to look for. But we're not given any information and therefore we are isolated.

Although the departments operate autonomously and there is little association between municipal and campus officers, the relations that do exist between DTU police and other local police are cooperative and good. Both agencies assist the other. Local police provide assistance to university police by supplying emergency manpower if needed,[25] training campus police in their academies, detaining suspects in the county jail, and informing campus police of incidents in their jurisdiction. DTU police have occasionally assisted local police with arrests and have provided them information regarding incidents within city jurisdiction on numerous occasions.

Notes

[1]Downtown University or DTU is a pseudonym for the actual location of the study used to protect the anonymity of the University and its police department.

[2]Historically many campus police departments were located under the physical plant department or the dean of students office. On many campuses today this is still true. The campus police literature is replete with calls for placement under an executive vice-president of the university noting many disadvantages of placement elsewhere (e.g., loss of identity, lack of automomy, less respect within the community, and so forth). Arguments for placement of campus police departments under vice-presidents are emotionally charged and comparisons with municipal police are often made in the literature. For example, Nielsen (1971:14)notes that locating a campus police department under a dean is like placing municipal police under the supervision of the city judiciary. Further Powell (1981:50) argues that the head of a campus security department answering to the physical plant director might be compared to the chief of police in a municipality answering to the head of the public works department. Today both situational

75

placements are viewed as unacceptable by most campus police administrators.

[3]These noncommissioned safety/security personnel, for example, patrol parking areas at night helping people who are having trouble with their cars and keeping their eyes open for safety hazards. They are equipped with the necessary means of reporting incidents that require police action but they do not make arrests or conduct investigations because they are vested with no power beyond that of an ordinary citizen.

[4]Although there were 55 uniformed line officers at the time of the study, two refused to be formally interviewed by the researchers. Consequently, all computations derived from interviews in this work are based on a sample size of 53 officers.

[5]This is also true of sergeants and lieutenants when there are severe manpower shortages.

[6]The basic line organization of the DTU police falls naturally into supervisors and patrolmen. This division derives more from the bureaucratic features of the organization than the nature of policing like the differentiation between patrol and detective divisions found in the line organization of municipal police. Thus, while there is general task differentiation between officer and supervisor there is no specific task differentiation among patrolmen at DTU.

[7]In large municipal departments a watch commander, for example, may have several persons intervening between him and the chief.

[8]There are only two permanent assignments among patrolmen--scooter driver and motor vehicle driver. These assignments are not the most desirable.

[9]This was a multiple response item (up to four responses coded) so percentages do not total to 100 percent.

[10]On any given day the rank structure will vary on each watch. Since the days off of various supervisors are scatterd throughout the week there are in reality only two days a week when all four supervisors are present. Usually there are only two or three supervisors present on any given day.

[11]Upon relief each officer is required to turn in the radio, radio case and keys s/he used during his or her tour that day. It is the responsibility of out going watch supervisors to account for these items before they leave work for the day.

[12]On the lieutenant's off days the sergeant of the watch will man the Operations desk and is, in turn, replaced on motor patrol by one of the corporals.

[13]This log is usually less than one page because on an average shift on an average day few incidents occur.

[14]To comply with FCC regulations and to serve as a periodic radio test the dispatcher will broadcast the time every hour on the half hour. Additional radio checks are made by officers before they go in the field at the beginning of their shift and then every hour on the hour during their tour of duty.

[15]The cameras accompanying these monitors are directed at strategic locations on campus including, for example, the student accounts area, the hallway outside of the DTU president's office, and several major access entrances to campus buildings. Observation of the monitors results in more rapid deployment of patrolmen to these areas should an incident occur.

[16]Officers normally use pay telephones because there is a departmental regulation against entering locked offices to use telephones. Occasionally if there is an open office and the officer is not near a pay telephone s/he will request permission of the office personnel to use their phone. If granted s/he will avail himself or herself of the opportunity.

[17]Most officers view the low quality relations between themselves and supervisors as providing a catylyst for high attrition within the Department. Many officers suggested that the rift between supervisors and patrolmen could be alleviated and turnover among patrolmen significantly reduced if supervisors were given some training in management techniques.

[18]It should be recalled, as previously mentioned, that DTU officers tend to evaluate informally their coworkers largely on the basis of these same

criteria.

[19]Examples of official prescriptions aimed at controlling officers off duty include prohibitions against taking a second job without the Chief's permission and requirements that officers remain financially solvent.

[20]Common infractions resulting in formal disciplinary action include lateness in reporting to work, neglect of duty (e.g., claiming to be on a round of a building when you are not), insubordination (e.g., refusal to obey an order or accept an assignment) and abuse of sick leave.

[21]It is noteworthy that the officer actions which precipitated formal negative sanction included insubordination and neglect of duty. Hence, it would appear that officers were disciplined for good reason.

[22]Gelber (1972) indicates that almost every state has legislated in varying degrees to provide some peace officer status to campus security personnel. Moreover, he found that many states grant full peace officer status to them.

[23]The policy limitation on university police jurisdiction is in the interest of both the university and city in which the university is located. The 1974 legislation granting university police jurisdiction to 500 yards beyond any property owned by the university created several major problems. First, it expanded the geographic area of responsibility of the university police beyond the point which they desired and had sufficient manpower to cover adequately. Second, the legislation created some friction and ill will with city police by technically usurping a large geographic area which normally fell under the jurisdiction of the city. Furthermore, each time the university purchased a new piece of property the university police jurisdiction technically increased and city jurisdiction decreased. Finally, much confusion and numerous problems related to dual jurisdiction were created. The formal policy agreement between the city and university police effectively eliminated these problems created by the 1974 legislation.

[24]The senior researcher personally observed

several occasions in which fingerprints were taken following the skull incident. On each occasion the taking of prints was prejudged by officers as futile because the prints were smeared. Nevertheless prints were taken to avoid potential criticism.

25The DTU police have never had to seek assistance in this area and given the nature of the community they are not likely to have to seek emergency assistance. However, local police do provide a potential for emergency assistance if needed.

CHAPTER III

OCCUPATIONAL ENTRY AND SOCIALIZATION

For any organization to survive it must have a pool of potential members from which to draw, procedures and processes to weed out qualified from unqualified applicants, and processes for training those selected to become effective, participating members of the organization. In this chapter the recruitment, selection and socialization processes utilized in campus policing are discussed. Basic to the entire presentation is the notion that persons <u>become</u> university policemen; they are processed, managed, manipulated and trained to become policemen and they, in turn, adopt, learn and internalize the accepted expectations of their vocation.

Recruitment

Recruitment Procedures

Like all organizations, the university police department must, in some way, attract qualified personnel to meet manpower needs. In order to ensure a sufficient number of applicants from which the department can selectively choose the most qualified, aggressive methods of making positions known to prospective applicants are implemented. These procedures to recruit actively are of two basic types-- formal (including university newspaper, radio, bulletin board, and employment service advertisements) and informal (including dissemination of information about position availability by word of mouth and personal contacts). Since 67 percent of the line officers indicated that they had heard about their job from a friend, coworker or other university employee, it would appear that informal methods of making positions known to prospective applicants are by far the more effective. In general, the fact that recruitment procedures are effective in making position availability known is illustrated by the fact that there are always many more applicants than the number of positions open. As one high ranking official indicated, "On an average we get a minimum

81

of ten applicants for every one position." While
this does not imply that those persons applying for
university police work are necessarily qualified, it
does imply that there are sufficient numbers of
applicants from which the department can select the
most qualified for employment. Stated differently,
the university police department is not forced into
accepting "whoever comes through the door" to meet
its manpower needs.

Occupational Choice, Career and Commitment

The available literature suggests that the occupation of policeman is viewed by those who enter as
simply one job among many and considered roughly
along the same dimensions as other jobs including,
for example, security, salary, interesting work, and
so forth (McNamara, 1967; Niederhoffer, 1967; President's Commission on Law Enforcement & the Administration of Justice, 1967; Sterling, 1972). The
major reasons for seeking employment in university
police work are essentially the same, that is,
related to economic and experiential considerations.
Each uniformed line officer was asked the following
questions: "Why did you join the university police
force?"[1] Thirty-eight percent of the officers
mentioned among their reasons the fact that they were
unemployed and needed a job, 20 percent indicated
that the job pays well and 18 percent reported they
joined because the job offered good fringe benefits
and job security. The following comment was representative among officers who joined the Department
for economic reasons:

> When you really need a job, most any one
> will do. This job is just as good as any
> other and it pays better than most. I
> joined the Department because I needed a job
> and the money was good.

Among their other reasons for joining the department, 10 percent of the sample mentioned they wanted
their job originally just for the experience of doing
it and an additional 26 percent of the officers
specifically indicated the opportunity the job
afforded to gain low level experience in law enforcement. The following comment of one officer is illustrative:

82

I just wanted to see what the work was like.
You grow by your experiences. How are you
going to know if you like something, if you
don't try it?...This job is a good introduction to police work if that's your game.
It is a good way to get your feet wet in law
enforcement and see if you like this kind of
work without laying your life on the line.

Many university officers noted that some of their
colleagues joined the university force because university police work provides the opportunity for
experience in law enforcement. Not only does the job
offer one the opportunity to discover if they would
be interested in making police work their career, but
it also provides the opportunity for those who have
chosen police work as their career to gain experience
and training before moving on. In other words,
campus law enforcement is often thought of among
officers as a stop gap to other law enforcement jobs,
that is, as a training ground for officers who might
want to or actually aspire to move on to "real
police" agencies. The following officer comment is
supportive of this belief:

A lot of officers who come here use this job
as a stepping stone to other police jobs.
Once they get hired they get a taste of
police work and they can move on if they
want. We lose a lot of our officers to
municipal departments. The qualifications
you need for this job are the same as you
need elsewhere. We are sort of a training
school. Officers stay here until they get
certified and then they move out. It is a
lot easier to get a job if you are already
certified. No one can accomplish what they
want in law enforcement here but they can
gain the experience and qualification they
need to do it elsewhere.

These findings with respect to the "experiential
value" of university police work suggest that a
number of officers may actively choose university
police work over regular police work rather than just
fall into it because they cannot get a job with a
regular police department. In fact, only one officer
indicated that she joined the university department
because other police were not hiring at the time she
needed work.

83

Whatever their reasons for joining the force, the fact remains that most officers who enter university police work do not view it as their lifetime occupation. It is only a temporary stop gap or fill-in job while they are finishing their degree or searching for something else. Comments such as "I don't intend to stay here forever" or "this isn't my life's work" were typical among officers. The data suggest that many who enter university police work do so not thinking of it as a career but rather as "just a job." This attitude is perhaps best summed up in the following comment of one officer:

> This job is not a career job but more or less a transient job. It is just something to sustain a person...it is not a career.

Moreover, most officers have concrete career plans that do not include university police work. Each officer was questioned about his or her future plans utilizing the following question: "What do you expect to be doing five years from now?" Seventeen percent of the officers stated they plan to remain in law enforcement at the university, 19 percent plan to remain in law enforcement elsewhere and 64 percent indicated they plan to do something else.[2] Of the 64 percent who plan to do something else, only 32 percent have career plans loosely related to law enforcement (e.g., lawyer, probation officer, security, juvenile case worker, and so forth) and the remainder plan to do something totally unrelated (e.g., computer programmer, engineer, architect, accountant, salesman, and so forth). In short, most university officers contemplate leaving policing and doing something else.

The perception of university police work as a job and not as a career is strongly influenced by two factors. First, like all police work university police work is a low status occupation. Since the type of work one does reflects upon others' perception of the worker, university officers are constantly open to other job possibilities which may afford greater status and opportunity. In this respect university officers are no different from workers in other low status occupations. In terms of their relative prestige with respect to related occupations most officers believe that their job falls between police work and security work. When questioned about their perception of how members of other occupational groups perceive university police, 89 percent of the uniformed line officers indicated that members of other police forces look down on the university police occupation and 94 percent indicated that private security guards look up to their occupation. University officers perceive they have less prestige than regular police, and numerous scholars have argued that regular policing is itself a low status occupation (Skolnick, 1966; McNamara, 1967; Niederhoffer, 1967; Edwards, 1968; Bayley and Mendelsohn, 1969).

The second factor influencing the perception of university police work as a job rather than a career is the general lack of job mobility found within the police organization. The traditional type of mobility in police work is almost exclusively vertical--there is little lateral entry and promotions come from within the department for which the officer works. However, in reality vertical mobility is uncommon because few positions are open. Like all bottom-heavy organizations there is little chance for advancement because there are only a limited number of ranked positions. The lack of career opportunities provides little incentive for officers to remain in university police work and to think of it as a career. The following comment was typical among officers:

> This is a dead end job. Once you get in, there is no place to go within the organization. Chances for advancement are severely limited...there are no career opportunities. Part of the reason for high turnover is due to this lack of opportunity for advancement.

Those persons who enter any job thinking of it as just a job or who are just putting in time are more likely to lack commitment to their work. Such is the case with many university officers. In addition to the fact that few officers plan to stay in university policing, lack of occupational commitment may be illustrated in several other ways. First, during the course of numerous conversations with officers, few expressed real interest in their work or loyalty to the department. Second, each officer was asked the following question: "Would you recommend your job to someone you really cared about?" While 55 percent of the officers responded in the affirmative, 15 percent said no, and 30 percent said yes with qualification, that is, only if the person needed a temporary job or was seeking experience in law enforcement. Third, only 20 percent of the officers agreed with the statement: "I always wanted to be a police officer." Finally, 94 percent of all officers indicated that they belong to no professional organizations or associations related to their work. These data suggest a lack of strong commitment to university police work among officers. In general, in any occupation the less occupational commitment there is the greater the likelihood that an individual will leave that work. As one officer phrased it:

> Many officers enter this job saying it is just a job and thinking they can always get another temporary one. That's like entering a marriage and saying at the wedding ceremony that I can always get a divorce. Lack of commitment to marriage is why divorce rates are high and lack of commitment to work is why turnover rates are high.

In general, older officers with seniority who lack education and have no place else to go are more likely to express commitment to their job and perceive it as a career than younger officers who are better educated, lack seniority, have not obtained their career goals and are still striving for career advancement. While 43 percent of the supervisors said that they planned to still be in police work at the university in five years, only approximately 13 percent (12.5%) of the patrolmen plan to remain. In other words, younger, better educated officers who are more competitive on the job market and have little invested in their university job are more likely to leave their job than older coworkers. The following officer comments are illustrative:

> Many officers stay on a temporary basis because the job market is tight or they are trying to finish school so they can get a better job. Most young patrolmen that remain two or three years haven't finished school yet. As soon as they get their degree they become more mobile and leave. Officers with only a high school education are not hot stuff on the job market so they stay.

By the time you have been here awhile you
have too much seniority and familiarity with
everything to pull up stakes. The longer
you remain here the less serious you consider the possibility of leaving. You have
just too much invested to start all over.
Older officers stay because they're working
a second retirement and nobody else wants
them.

Officer Profile

Essentially, university and urban police draw
from the same labor pool. Research on municipal
police generally shows the typical patrolman to be a
young, white male from a lower or lower-middle class
background who is likely to have attended college but
does not hold a degree (Skolnick, 1966; McNamara,
1967; Niederhoffer, 1967; Wilson, 1968; Bayley and
Mendelsohn, 1969; Van Maanen, 1975). University
policemen essentially meet this profile. Analysis of
the demographic characteristics of non-supervisory
personnel found the typical university patrolman to
be a black male about 29 years of age (mean age of
28.8) with one to three years of college and from a
lower class background. Thus, with the exception of
race (i.e., university police are more likely to be
black than their municipal counterparts), DTU
officers are the demographic equivalent of municipal
officers in terms of sex, age, education and class.

With respect to university policemen, only one
major qualification needs to be made in the model of
police career choice offered in the urban police literature. While 88 percent of the university patrolmen come from distinctly lower class and lower-middle
class backgrounds, the choice of a university police
career does not generally result in upward mobility.
Comparison of father's social class rank to respondent's social class rank using Hollingshead and
Redlich's (1958) two-factor index of social position
revealed that 36 percent (35.7%) of the sample had a
lower social class ranking than their father, 48 percent (47.6%) had the same ranking, and only 17 percent (16.7%) had a higher ranking than their father.[3]
Among those with a higher ranking than their father,
the essential difference appears to lie in the
greater amount of education of the respondent rather
than the greater prestige of his or her choice of

work. While these data are not conclusive, they do suggest that the choice of university policing may be seen as a distinctly lower and working class phenomenon. At the same time the data suggest that the upward mobility assumption concerning the choice of police careers generally found in the urban police literature (McNamara, 1967; Niederhoffer, 1967; Alex, 1969; Bayley and Mendelsohn, 1969; Westley, 1970; Harris, 1973) does not necessarily hold for university policemen or is at least overrated.

Selection

Selection Requirements

According to state statute all applicants for any commissioned police position in the state must meet certain minimum requirements. Since university policemen are commissioned peace officers, their requirements for employment are in line with those of all other police departments in the state. To be considered for employment an applicant must be a citizen of the United States, at least 18 years of age, have a high school diploma or its recognized equivalent,[4] and not have a felony record nor have been convicted of sufficient misdemeanors to establish a pattern of disrespect for the law.

Selection Process

In the final analysis any program can only be as good as the quality of its personnel. Hence, the selection process is important in the long run for the effectiveness of the program. The police officer selection process at DTU is similar to that of most municipal departments in the country. The applicant must pass progressively through a fingerprint record check designed to disclose any criminal record, a background character investigation, a general medical examination conducted by a licensed physician to ensure the applicant is in good health, and an oral interview with the hiring authority to determine the applicant's appearance, demeanor, background and ability to communicate.[5] In addition, the university department requires that each applicant successfully pass a polygraph test designed to determine whether s/he has ever been involved in any serious undetected crime or has any serious drug involvement, including

the use or sale of illicit drugs. If the applicant
is successful in all these areas, s/he is hired into
the department on the basis of authorized openings.

In actual practice the importance of the initial
application for employment to the university
screening process cannot be overlooked. As with
other organizations this application is used by the
department as a "weeding out" device. There are two
items on the application of significance in the
weeding out process. First, the application provides
a complete record of the applicant's prior work experience. While prior experience in related fields
is not necessary for employment, it is desirable. As
one high ranking official stated:

> We are biased toward selecting people with
> related kinds of work. We like people with
> prior experience in security, police work
> and the military. These people seem to
> adapt best to university police work because
> they are already used to the routine and
> discipline required of the university
> officer.

Analysis of the sample data yielded that in fact
there is a slight bias toward the selection of
persons with prior experience in related fields.
When asked their major job (i.e., the job they held
the longest) before entering university police work,
25 percent of the officers stated security, 21 percent indicated other police work and seven percent
said they were in the military. In short, 53 percent
of the officers had prior experience in a related
field as broadly defined by the department.6 The
second reason why the initial application is
important to the screening process relates to the
fact that it affords the opportunity to assess the
applicant's writing ability. In contrast to many
municipal departments which require some form of
written examination (Niederhoffer, 1967; Harris,
1973), the university requires none. However, on his
or her initial application each applicant is required
to provide a written statement expressing the reasons
why s/he would like to become a university police
officer. One high ranking official summed up the
purpose and importance of this written "test" in the
following manner:

> One of the most important things an officer

89

may have to do in his routine duties is write reports. Yet report writing is notoriously one of the major weaknesses of many law enforcement officers. If an officer can't write an accurate and coherent report he just isn't of much value. Given that we only require a high school education it is doubly important that we screen the applicant for writing ability. We do this by requiring him to express himself in writing on the application form. If he can't express himself, we weed him out right then and there.

While the selection procedures outlined above appear useful in weeding out unqualified personnel, they do not guarantee the selection of quality personnel. In actual practice the department's screening process can be viewed as problematic in several major ways. First, and perhaps most importantly, there is an almost total reliance upon the oral interview to assess the psychological fitness and emotional stability of the applicant. In contrast to many municipal departments which require a psychiatric exam (see Niederhoffer, 1967; Harris, 1973; Lundman, 1980), the university police department requires none. The absence of preemployment testing for psychological fitness, attitudes and emotional stability is particularly surprising given the attitude of departmental administrators and the fact that resources for such testing are readily available on campus. One high ranking official described the situation as follows:

When you're thinking about hiring people who are going to be given guns and power over other people you have to be careful. They need a personality which allows them to relate to the campus community but most of all they need to be psychologically and emotionally stable. We rely on the interview to check out communication skills and look for negative personality traits. While we have thought about instituting some kind of psychological testing through the university counseling center, we haven't because our turnover is so high that it would be a waste of time and resources.

Despite this official's claim that psychological

testing would be a waste of time and resources due to high personnel turnover, it might, in fact, be time and resources well spent. By aiding in the selection of types of individuals who are prone to find satisfaction in university police work and be successful in it, psychological testing might enhance the selection process and, thus, might in the long run reduce personnel turnover.

A second aspect of the department's screening process which might be viewed as problematic is also related to the oral interview. In contrast to many municipal departments in which a screening board is utilized (Cohen and Chaiken, 1973; Harris, 1973; Gray, 1975; Van Maanen, 1975), at DTU the interview is conducted by one individual who is given the sole responsibility for hiring decisions. While the department used to employ a screening board it has not for several years. Among their recommendations for improving the department several officers suggested a return to the screening board as a possible means of improving officer selection, performance, and the length of time s/he stays at the university. One officer stated: "Most of the officers who have stayed around here a long time came in under a screening board and are the better officers." Another officer noted the difficulty involved in one man being able to assess another man adequately. "It is a lot harder to fool five people than one. You are bound to get better people when they have to pass the five test."

Third, in contrast to many municipal departments where physical strength and agility tests are required prior to employment (Niederhoffer, 1967; Harris, 1973), at DTU little attention is paid to physical fitness in the selection process. While applicants are required to be in good physical health, their medical exams do not include physical agility or stress tests. Perhaps the lack of attention paid to physical strength and agility in the selection process is a function of the nature of university police work. In the exercise of his or her routine duties the university policeman is rarely confronted with a situation requiring physical stamina and agility. For example, s/he is not likely to be called upon to give chase to a fleeing suspect nor is s/he likely to have to use physical strength in his or her encounters with the public.[7] Being in shape and staying in shape seem to be more a matter

91

of individual concern than departmental concern. Yet
an increasing number of departments are now beginning
to stress the importance of physical fitness in the
selection process (Cohen and Chaiken, 1973; Harris,
1973; Lundman, 1980). As one officer noted:

> If you are physically fit you are less
> likely to have to use physical force or
> shoot someone. Suppose, for example, you
> are on foot chasing a dude down the street
> who you just saw stab a pretty coed. Cause
> you're too fat and out of shape, for every
> step you take he gets further away. Well,
> what are you gonna do...let him get away?
> No, you're gonna pull your gun and shoot.
> But the whole shooting could have been
> avoided if you were in shape in the first
> place.

Given the departmental policy against the use of
force and firearms except in the most dire circumstances combined with the fact that DTU police work
requires officers to be on their feet for hours at a
time, it would seem that more attention might be paid
to physical fitness in the selection process.

The final aspect of the department's screening
process relates to the time frame encompassing selection and hiring. In contrast to most municipal
departments where there is a long, arduous selection
procedure often taking up to a year or more
(McNamara, 1967; Niederhoffer, 1967; Harris, 1973;
Van Maanen, 1975), it may be only a matter of a few
weeks between the time an application is filed and
hiring as a university officer takes place. The
absence of a protracted screening has several important implications. First, while in theory all selection procedures are completed prior to hiring
actually taking place, in practice they are not. The
record-checking process and background investigation
can often take a long time; many officers are hired
before their completion. Since the entire screening
process is not completed before hiring, it might be
possible for an "undesirable" to sneak through and
embody the authority of a peace officer for some time
before discovery. The potential for serious consequences of this situation is obvious. Second, the
absence of a protracted screening factor to some
extent precludes the assurance that those who join
the occupation will have strong positive attitudes

concerning their new job. Van Maanen (1975), for example, argues that an arduous selection procedure over a long period of time represents the organizational or structural side of what Merton (1957) calls anticipatory socialization. He suggests that the very length and nature of the selection process serves to increase the recruit's motivation and commitment toward his or her new job. If Van Maanen is correct, we can conclude that university policemen may not enter their occupation with the same degree of commitment and motivation as their municipal counterparts, given the relatively short duration of the selection-hiring sequence within the university department.

Occupational Socialization

Occupational socialization is the process by which individuals acquire knowledge, skills and dispositions that enable them to participate as more or less effective members of an occupation (see for example, Ritzer, 1977). It involves the learning of social roles and specific role expectations, patterns of thought and action, skills and procedures. It may be either formal or informal in nature; oftentimes it is both. While occupational socialization occurs throughout all career stages, the concentration here is upon the recruit's entry into the occupation. The focus is upon the training phase of the process of preparing a person to perform a job.

There are essentially two phases in the recruit's training within the first year of employment in university policing at DTU: (1) entry level in-service including orientation training and on-the-job training, and (2) academy training. The nature of training for the first six months of the university policeman's occupational life is of two general types, classroom and on-the-job. It is during the second six months of his or her career that s/he receives further classroom instruction at one of the local police academies.[8] At all times the recruit's first assignment upon joining the university department is to the training officer for a formal two week training program provided by the department.

93

Orientation Training

The first two weeks of each recruit's employment are spent in a formal in-house orientation training program. The overall objectives of this course are to introduce the new employee to his or her job and to departmental policies and procedures, and to familiarize him or her with the campus, campus community and its problems. From the onset recruits are informed that the basic intent of the training is to introduce and familiarize them with the minimum amount of knowledge they will need to function in their role. As the training officer stated:

> Here what you get is an overview. You are not going to be an accomplished officer when you finish, but you will have just enough information so you can go out on the street and function.

While instruction takes place in both the classroom and field, most of the knowledge transmitted to the trainees is theoretical rather than practical. Ideally the orientation training is tailored toward the specialized knowledge and skills needed to police in a university environment, but in reality it is more like a condensed version of the academy. In fact many of the substantive areas covered in lecture follow the lesson plans of the state-mandated basic course at the academy. The essential difference between the in-house orientation training and academy training is the fact that due to limitations of time the former program provides an overview rather than indepth coverage. On the last day of orientation training each recruit is given a written exam which s/he must satisfactorily complete with a minimum score of 70 in order that employment not be terminated.[9]

The atmosphere of the entry program is at the same time both formal and informal. While there is a specified formal curriculum through which trainees are led, combined with a strict adherence to rules, regulations and standards, at the same time there is an air of flexibility and informality that pervades the training process. Rather than being punitively oriented as are most municipal programs (see McNamara, 1967; Harris, 1973; Van Maanen, 1975; Lundman, 1980), the DTU training officer assumed a more informal. guidance-oriented role. For example,

94

upon several occasions some of the trainees were a minute or two late reporting to class. Rather than taking any disciplinary action against the recruits, the training officer merely expressed his displeasure and pointed out the trouble they would bring upon themselves if they were even one minute late reporting for duty in the field. In this way the trainees began to learn the need to obey departmental rules in order to avoid trouble. While a certain amount of formal social distance was always maintained between the training officer and the recruits, there was a relatively strong rapport between them. Recruits felt free to raise questions and discuss their concerns openly. Furthermore, the training officer occasionally stopped in the middle of his formal lectures to offer the trainees informal tips on how to be a "smart officer." For example, during the course of a lecture on search and seizure, the training officer stated:

> Search and seizure is very technical.
> Sometimes you have to be sneaky and guily.
> Suppose you are making a search incidental
> to a lawful arrest. According to the Chimel
> rule you are only allowed to search the
> suspect's person and the area under his
> immediate control. You go into Smith's
> office to arrest him and you find him
> sitting at his desk. Well, legally you can
> only search him and the open areas of his
> desk. But you think there might be some
> important evidence in a closed closet
> several feet away. As you are taking him
> out of the office all you have to do is ask
> him if he wants his coat. As soon as he
> makes one step toward the closet, you tell
> him to hold it right there and then proceed
> to make a legal search of the closet.

While training in being a "smart officer" was employed on a very limited basis, it was instrumental in the maintenance of a sense of rapport between the instructor and recruits. The mixture of informality with formality, the lack of a punitive orientation, and the guidance-oriented role assumed by the training officer during orientation training served to defuse the development of strong recruit solidarity and feelings of degradation in the recruit role that research has shown to be so characteristic of academy training (Niederhoffer, 1967; Harris, 1973;

95

Van Maanen, 1975).

A summary of the orientation program in terms of major content areas and the amount of time devoted to each is provided in Table 2. Essentially, recruits receive two types of instruction--classroom lecture and field practice. Noticeably, for only about 58 percent (58.1%) of the 80 hours of training was the recruit engaged in actual formal instruction (either classroom or field) related to his or her job. The remainder of his or her time (about 42%) was spent in lunch and study breaks or administrative processing including such activities as getting signed up with the department and university, selecting insurance plans, obtaining equipment supplies and uniforms, driving to and from the firing range, and taking and reviewing substantive exams.

Formal classroom instruction covers a wide range of subjects in an overview fashion: departmental rules, regulations and policies; firearms safety and techniques; police community relations; criminal police procedures; watch procedures; note taking and report writing; police ethics and professionalism, and so forth. The data in Table 2 reveal that the training curriculum places strong emphasis on criminal procedures, note taking and reports, the use of force and firearms, and police liability, respectively. One major theme was apparent in all content areas--the temperance of authority. Recruits are taught that they are policemen with all the policeman's authority yet they need to temper that authority in the university environment; that is, a "gung ho" attitude has no place on campus.

There are three basic means through which the training officer tries to instill an attitude of temperance in the trainees. First, recruits are instructed in the need to be sensitive to the campus community. For example, they are informed of problems in dealing with foreign students. As a representative of the Dean of Foreign Students instructed recruits:

> Foreign students think of you as police and
> most of them have a fragile relationship
> with authority. In many of their countries
> when they are asked to go with a policeman,
> they never come back. They have a fear of
> police. You need to be sensitive to their

96

TABLE 2

ORIENTATION TRAINING SUMMARY: CONTENT AREAS & TIME

Area	Major Areas Raw Time Hrs.	Mins.	Major Area % Total Time	Area Topics Raw Time Hrs.	Mins.
Classroom	30	30	38.1		
Introduction to Org./Prof. administrative info*	4	30	5.6		
addresses				1	45
authority/jurisdiction				1	15
ethics/professionalism				1	30
Basic Law	9	25	11.8		
criminal procedures				6	25
police liability				3	
Community Relations	2	5	2.6		
Police Procedures	14	30	18.1		
patrol				1	50
traffic direction					50
notetaking/reports/forms				5	20
use of force/firearms				5	
watch procedures					45
use of specialized equipment					45

TABLE 2--Continued

Area	Major Areas Raw Time Hrs.	Mins.	Major Area % Total Time	Area Topics Raw Time Hrs.	Mins.
Field Practice in Police Skills	16		20.0		
Vehicle	1	10	1.5		
Traffic Direction		40	0.8		
Firearms	3	25	4.3		
Zone Patrol	10	45	13.4		
Miscellaneous	33	30	41.9		
Administrative Processing	13	5	16.4		
Breaks/Study Halls	20	25	25.5		
TOTALS	80		100.0		

Note: While relatively accurate time records were kept, the raw times on each topic are not absolute. For example, while discussing criminal procedures a brief question pertaining to police liability may have arisen, but the time spent on the question and answer were logged under criminal procedures rather than liability. Raw times are therefore approximate and, consequently, so are percentage times. Nevertheless, percentage times do reflect the emphasis of content instruction in terms of gross categories and how time was spent during training.

* This category included discussion of fringe benefits and departmental policy with respect to such items as overtime, outside employment, holidays, leave, and so forth.

feelings or things might get out of hand and
that would certainly mean trouble for everyone...including you.

Second, emphasis in instruction was placed upon
learning and obeying departmental rules, regulations
and policy. Recruits were told that a breach in any
of these areas would only serve to get them in
trouble. The instruction by the training officer in
firearms policy is illustrative:

> Your gun is a defensive weapon which is to
> be used only under the most extreme circum-
> stances. The front office takes a dim view
> of the use of your weapon unless you are
> positive that the situation warrants it.
> Most officers that have been dismissed
> around here have gone because of violations
> of the firearm policy. Your gun is a defen-
> sive weapon only. The mere fact that you
> take it out of your holster means that you
> are threatening deadly force. The depart-
> ment frowns upon threats. You just can't go
> around making them here. So if you take
> your gun out of your holster you better use
> it...and you better damn well be sure you're
> justified when you do.

The final means used to instill temperance in the
trainee was through the heavy emphasis in instruction
placed on liability. Recruits were instructed in the
civil and criminal liability of a peace officer under
state and federal statutes. The importance and purpose of liability instruction to the university
officer were summed up by the training officer in the
following comment:

> Suits against officers have increased in
> recent years because the media has made
> individuals aware of their rights.
> Liability is one of the most important parts
> of your instruction. You may face both
> criminal and civil charges on the same
> incident and that is not double jeopardy.
> There is a tendency for recruits after
> training to be action oriented but your
> actions must be within legal limits. Many
> situations you face will be ambiguous and
> open to varying interpretations. You are
> responsible for your actions both on and off

duty. Your badge is not a guarantee against prosecution or civil suit. This liability may extend to your supervisor and department. You better be careful.

Common to all three means of instilling an attitude of temperance in the recruit was an element of fear: fear that lack of sensitivity to the community, breaches of department rules and policies, and violations of individual rights will only serve to get an officer in trouble. Upon completion of orientation training one recruit expressed the sentiments of all recruits in the following way:

> This may not be a dangerous job, but it sure is a hazardous profession in terms of liability. There are so many ways to get in trouble. I guess you are better off doing nothing than risking prosecution or the department coming down on you. I'll tell you this...I sure don't plan on throwing my weight around.

It would appear from this comment that the trainees did learn through formal classroom instruction that a "gung ho" perspective may only serve to get them in trouble. Being action oriented may lead to violation of some rule, regulation or policy and, hence, lead to punishment not reward. In short, in conjunction with learning an attitude of temperance each recruit also learned that the best way to stay out of trouble is to minimize the set of activities s/he pursues. In other words, s/he learned s/he should do what is required and little more.

Approximately 20 percent of the recruit's time during orientation training is devoted to gaining brief practical experience in the operation of vehicles, firearms, traffic direction and zone patrol (see Table 2). This instruction is geared toward familiarizing the recruit with each task rather than toward complete mastery of the skills needed to perform the task. For example, each recruit is given about six minutes of practical experience in directing traffic on a one-way street. As one experienced officer commented:

> You can't learn to direct traffic in five or ten minutes. During training they put you out there and give you a chance to blow your

whistle and wave your arms around. You get
a taste of what it is like to make a car
stop or have the weight of pedestrian safety
on your shoulders. But you don't have any
confidence after five or ten minutes. It
takes a couple of hours to develop your
ability and you have to wait until you pull
traffic duty on your watch before you get
that much practice.

Firearms range training provides another example
of the emphasis on familiarization rather than
proficiency in the orientation training program.
Recruits spent only two hours and fifteen minutes at
the shooting range with the training officer.10
During this time each recruit fires 150 rounds in
various positions at varying distances from a
stationary target.11 Obviously someone who has never
handled a gun before cannot expect to become proficient with a weapon with this minimal amount of
training and, in fact, s/he is not expected to. As
the training officer noted:

Your whole purpose for being here today is
to learn how to use your weapon...how it
works and how it feels. Accuracy is not our
major consideration today.

Beyond this initial training in firearms, officers
receive no other formally instructed training with
weapons. They are expected to practice on their own
and become proficient by themselves. Each officer is
required to qualify with his or her weapon a minimum
of two times per year and during his or her qualification if s/he is having difficulty s/he may receive
some informal individualized instruction from the
training officer. Nevertheless, formal firearms
training is minimal and while proficiency is expected
it is largely self taught.

The bulk of practical field training (about
67 percent) is devoted to familiarization with the
patrol zone divisions, buildings and techniques of
patrolling campus. Sixty percent of the practical
zone patrol is instructed with the training officer
pointing out particular problem areas and the unique
difficulties of patrolling various buildings, rapid
access passages between buildings, locks and appropriate keys, and the location of boiler rooms, emergency equipment, elevator switches, power valves,

fire panels and indicators, alarms, sprinkler systems, and so forth at every campus building. This instruction was decidedly oriented more to security and safety than to law enforcement. It is during this phase of training that recruits get their first real glimpse of what their everyday activity on the job is likely to be. It is here that they begin to gain an appreciation of the scope of their responsibilities on patrol in terms of security, protection and safety, and the extent of walking (physical stamina) and planning which are required to make sure that everything is covered that is supposed to be covered. It is also at this point that the recruit begins to experience his or her first difficulties with the job. As one trainee suggested:

> I feel like a lost needle in a hay stack.
> This place is a lot bigger than it looks.
> There are so many nooks and crannies and
> things to learn.

Another recruit remarked:

> Damn, we have all this equipment to help us
> in our job and it's either inaccessible or
> doesn't function. That is just going to
> make our job that much harder.

Given the need for familiarization with the campus each recruit spent the remaining 40 percent of practical patrol training walking the zones on his or her own, testing his or her keys and testing himself or herself on his or her knowledge of the campus.

On-the-job Training

Following the two week orientation training each recruit is assigned to a watch where s/he is introduced to his or her daily work by a watch supervisor rather than an experienced patrolman as in most municipal departments. One supervisor expressed the rationale behind assigning a recruit to a supervisor rather than another officer in the following manner:

> An officer can develop bad habits and the
> wrong attitude from the start if an "old
> timer" trains him. Older officers still
> make mistakes and if they don't show the
> trainee right, that would be just too bad.

It would still be the trainee's fault if he screwed up. We (supervisors) don't want to hear any excuses. Each officer is responsible for his own actions. If a supervisor trains him, you know he has been trained right.

Essentially the supervisor's responsibilities in on-the-job training are two-fold: (1) walk the trainee through his or her duties instructing him or her in his or her responsibilities (e.g., techniques of patrol, lockups/openings, proper keys, and so on), and (2) review with the trainee the rules, regulations and policies of the department coupled with a discussion of what is expected of him or her.

In contrast to the situation in most municipal departments, where an officer's on-the-job training covers an extended period of time (McNamara, 1967; Niederhoffer, 1967; Van Maanen, 1973, 1975), the university officer's supervisory training is usually concluded within three or four days after assignment to the watch. Upon completion, each university officer is sent out on solo patrol rather than assigned to a permanent partner. Much of what s/he learns from this point on, s/he learns on his or her own. The fact that the trainee is essentially "on his own" within several days after joining the watch to a great extent formally precludes the opportunity to learn informal norms and practices from his or her fellow officers and to develop ties of loyalty with other members of the force which are so characteristic of municipal on-the-job training (McNamara, 1967; Niederhoffer, 1967; Harris, 1973; Van Maanen, 1973; Manning and Van Maanen, 1978).

While informal socialization does continue on the job after an officer is assigned to solo patrol, it is largely self-initiated and achieved in a haphazard fashion. Opportunities for learning informal norms from fellow officers present themselves on a daily basis in the form of lunch breaks, waiting for shift changes, roll calls, exchange of stationary posts, and observation of fellow officers in the performance of their duties. Since encounters with fellow officers during work are usually of very brief duration and usually occur on a hit-and-miss basis, informal learning by the new officer occurs in a piecemeal fashion. It is left largely to the new officer to synthesize on his or her own whatever cues

s/he receives from his or her coworkers on the job.
In short, after completion of the several-day supervisory training, much of the university officer's
training may be thought of as self-socialization
rather than as socialization by others. Officer perceptions reinforce these observations.

Each uniformed patrolman was asked his or her
opinion on the following statement: "My best
training for this job has been on-the-job training."
While 80 percent of the officers indicated that they
agreed with the statement, many added that they
essentially trained themselves on the job. Comments
such as the following were typical among officers:

> They don't really train you here. They just
> sort of walk you around and leave you to
> your own devices. You learn this job on
> your own. You have to teach yourself and
> sometimes it can be frustrating.

The frustration that officers feel in being left to
their "own devices" for most on-the-job learning is
demonstrated in the comments of two patrolmen:

> The supervisors expect you to know things
> too fast. There is a lot to know around
> here. When you come to a watch a supervisor
> shows you around and then you spend a couple
> of days going over the rules and regula-
> tions. But you can't really learn something
> until you do it and it may be over a month
> since they told you something before you
> actually do it. Well, officers are human.
> With so much to know they are bound to
> forget and fuck up. When they do, they are
> in trouble.

> In training they don't teach you what you
> need to know. They halfheartedly show you
> the ropes but leave some things out. But
> when you do wrong cause they didn't show you
> it's your ass that is on the line and you
> get a black mark. You pretty much have to
> teach yourself everything just to protect
> your own butt. Learning this job is doubly
> hard since you are mostly on your own and
> there is nobody around to help you.

In short, officers are given several days of walk-

through training on the job. At the end of that time
they are expected to be able to function on their own
and are left to their own resources. What they do
not learn in the two week training, they must pick up
on their own or suffer the consequences. The fact
that they are held responsible for things they have
not been taught creates a sense of frustration in new
officers.

Adequacy of Entry Training

The two week orientation training and the supervisory on-the-job training in essence constitute the
bulk of training that a university officer receives
for at least the first six months of his or her
employment. By the time the officer finishes both
programs and several weeks in the field learning on
his or her own, s/he is pretty much able to handle
routine duties but lacks confidence in his or her
ability to function properly in emergency and law
enforcement situations. Many officers recalled their
feelings of unpreparedness and inadequacy when put on
the street after their entry training. Comments such
as the following were typical among patrolmen:

> As a new officer I feel a lot of things
> still have not been made clear. I'm just
> not sure what to do.

> Entry level training is helpful but in-
> adequate. When I finished I felt lost and
> had no confidence. They just gave me a gun
> and told me to get out there. They throw
> you in the mainstream right away before you
> really have enough knowledge and are really
> capable of handling certain situations.

Officer's feelings of being inadequately prepared
to be put on the street on their own derive from
several topical omissions in entry training. First,
while a great deal of attention was paid in the
classroom to the legal rules governing police practices and procedures as they relate to arrest,
search, seizure, warrants, and so forth, there was a
noticeable lack of instruction in the law (penal
code) per se. In other words, officers were not
taught what constitutes an arrestable offense. Lack
of knowledge of the penal code may potentially lead
to errors in action. On the one hand, if an officer

105

sees a crime happen s/he may not perform his or her duty because s/he is unaware that s/he should be performing his or her duty. On the other hand, if s/he sees something happen that s/he thinks is against the law s/he may act only later to discover that the individual did not break any law. In short, lack of knowledge of the penal code may lead to underaction or overaction on the part of the untrained officer. Either way the interests of the community and department are not served. Furthermore, in view of the emphasis in training on liability and temperance of authority, it is important to note that trainees receive no formal instruction in the penal code. The following example provided by an officer who had been in the field for only a few weeks illustrates the problems that lack of knowledge of the penal code can create for the officer in the street:

> I had been on patrol about a week when one day I came across a guy who seemed somewhat suspicious. I asked him for his ID (identification card). He refused to show it to me. Well, I didn't know what to do so I decided to bring him in. As I was getting ready to take him to operations it dawned on me that if I did I would technically have him under arrest and may be laying myself open to trouble if I didn't have a good reason for arresting him. Well, I knew refusal to show an ID was not against the law, but I thought maybe he could be charged with criminal trespass. After all he was in a place he shouldn't be at a time he shouldn't be there and did not seem to have any good reason to be where he was. Then I thought to myself that I didn't really know what the law had to say about criminal trespass. Anyway to make a long story short, I just let the guy go. I was too unsure of myself to do anything else.

Lack of knowledge of the penal code does influence officer performance by virtue of rendering him or her unsure of what s/he can do, in particular, and unsure of himself or herself, in general. Feelings of adequacy among new officers on the street could probably be enhanced if formal entry instruction made the law relevant to the officer, especially the small number of codes which are most likely to be needed by the university officer working in the field.[12]

The second major topic omitted in entry training
which results in the questioning by officers of their
ability to function on the street pertains to a lack
of instruction in the actual mechanics of "how to do"
the job, that is, how to make an arrest, cuff a
suspect, approach a suspicious person, handle a
drunk, and so on. While much of recruit training was
task relevant it was rarely situation relevant.
Practical problems and situations were employed in
training only on a limited basis. Often when they
were, examples were drawn from situations more likely
to occur in a municipal environment than a campus
one. One officer who had been on the job approximately three months commented:

> I don't have any confidence when I am on the
> street, because we are not taught how to
> handle situations before we are expected to
> do so. More attention in training needs to
> be given to types of situations we are
> likely to encounter and how to deal with
> them. It would be particularly helpful if
> they concentrated on university examples...
> like how to approach a drunk on the street
> or a pervert in the library.

Most of what the officers learn in entry training is
theoretical with only a limited amount of practical
knowledge. It is this practical knowledge that all
recruits felt they needed before being put in the
field on their own.

The collective solution offered by officers to
feelings of inadequacy due to omissions in entry
training was to send officers to the academy before
putting them on patrol. The basic feeling among most
officers was that if they had academy training prior
to field assignment like their municipal counterparts, they would be equipped with the knowledge and
skills necessary to perform their basic functions as
a university police officer. In other words, they
would know the "how to do" of their job as policemen
if the situation demanded it. Comments offered by
several patrolmen are illustrative of this point of
view:

> Our entry level training is inadequate.
> They only give you a couple of weeks to know
> everything. If there is a man on the street
> with a gun, they tell you to go take care of

it. But you don't get what you need to do
that until you go to the academy. But what
are you supposed to do until then?

There is too much time gap before you go to
the academy. From the time of employment
until you go to the academy you're in a bad
situation. They tell you to handle something and you really haven't been trained to
know what to do or how to do it. All you
know is how to lock and unlock doors and
which ones to lock and unlock when. But you
certainly don't know how to handle a disturbance or deal with a criminal act in
progress. You just don't get that until you
go to the academy.

At the time of data collection 60 percent of the
line patrolmen had completed academy instruction.
These officers expressed confidence in their ability
to function on the street but recalled their initial
feelings of inadequacy on the street before attending
the academy. It was the 40 percent of the line
officers who had not been to the academy who
expressed the greatest concern over their ability to
handle a situation should it arise. These fears
seemed to subside with each passing day though they
were never completely overcome. As each officer
gained increasing familiarity with the job s/he began
to realize that it did not require specialized knowledge in law enforcement on a routine, everyday
basis. The frequency with which s/he might be called
on to handle a situation requiring knowledge of the
law and the "how to do" of law enforcement was
minimal. (See chapter 6 for a more detailed discussion of the nature of crime and law enforcement on
campus.) Consequently, each officer began to realize
that s/he was able to function adequately on a daily
basis without the benefit of more indepth academy
training. Feelings of inadequacy decreased with the
passage of time but were never totally eliminated
until the completion of academy training, because the
potential of a situation arising that required more
specialized training was everpresent.

Academy Training

In contrast to most municipal departments in
which officers are sent through academy training

108

prior to field assignment, university officers do not enter the academy until they have at least six months of field experience. The state requires that mandatory basic training for all entering police officers be satisfactorily completed within twelve months of initial employment. University officers are subject to the same standards imposed upon all other peace officers in the state. Since the university does not have an academy of its own, it sends its officers to those of neighboring departments, usually at the rate of three officers per class or on the basis of position availability. The state-mandated training curriculum includes 240 hours of classroom and practical training. The general content areas in classroom instruction are the same as those offered university officers in their orientation training, but coverage at the academy is in greater depth. Officers must qualify in three areas--first aid, firearms and academics--with at least a minimum exit score of 70 in order to meet successfully state certification requirements and, thus, remain employed.

The academy training is useful to the university officers because it increases their confidence in their ability to meet job expectations at times when such training might be needed. Each line patrolman who had completed the academy was asked his or her opinion on the following statement: "The academy training I received helps me do a good job in my work at the university." Over three-fourths (78%) of the officers agreed. Comments such as the following were typical among officers who had completed the academy:

> The academy teaches you how to do things you
> might be asked to do. For example, you
> learn how to investigate a traffic accident,
> how to respond to calls in progress, how to
> recognize mentally ill or suspicuous per-
> sons, how to go about cuffing a suspect, and
> how to give first aid. When you finish you
> just plain feel more prepared to handle
> things.

Despite the fact that university officers feel more prepared to handle their job upon completion of the academy, over 66 percent of the officers who had completed the academy indicated that their actual work differs significantly from what was taught at the academy. This finding is in line with the urban police literature (see, for example, McNamara, 1967;

Niederhoffer, 1967; Harris, 1973; Van Maanen, 1975). For the university officer the feeling of difference results not so much from a difference in the way they were taught to do things (theory) and the way they actually do them (practice), but rather from the fact that at the academy they are exposed to a good deal of training they cannot use in their routine duties (e.g., discussions of devices used to measure traffic speed, vehicle pullovers, handling of death cases, defensive driving, and so on) or are rarely called upon to use (e.g., handling of riots and mobs, fundamentals of indepth investigation, techniques of crime scene search, fundamentals of courtroom testimony, and so forth). In short, at the academy university officers receive training in many subjects that are irrelevant in the performance of their everyday duties on the campus.[13]

Perhaps the greatest drawback of academy training for university officers is that it may neutralize their previous instruction--it does not encourage them to temper their authority and be sensitive to the campus community. Officers who go through the academy are indoctrinated in a hard-line police approach that may not be acceptable within the university community. The heavy emphasis placed on arrest, use of weapons, defensive tactics and police procedures at the academy inculcates in the individual that s/he should be judging his or her performance in terms of actual law enforcement (e.g., number of arrests) rather than in terms of crime prevention or provision of services. Training in traditional police responses is not a detriment in itself, because training in law enforcement skills is important to the university officer or at least they believe it to be important. However, such training does not recognize that the university officer works in a special environment and is, therefore, a special kind of policeman.

Notes

[1]This was a multiple response item (i.e., up to two responses coded) so percentages do not total to one hundred percent.

[2]It is noteworthy that of the 64 percent of the officers who plan to do something else, two-thirds (66.7%) have been employed as university policemen for two years or less. Thus, many of the officers who plan to do something else are still sufficiently flexible with regard to job mobility that their career plans cannot be considered unrealistic.

[3]It should be noted that there may be a downward bias in the determination of the university patrolman's social class ranking. Each officer received a score of six on the occupational scale which is the same score a security guard would have received. Given the fact that university police work is generally perceived by officers and others as higher in occupational prestige than security work, a score of six is somewhat inaccurate. However, to have given each officer a score of five on the occupational scale would have equated him or her with a municipal policeman in terms of occupational prestige despite the fact that university police work is generally perceived as a "cut below" municipal police work. The net effect of assigning each officer a six instead of a five in occupational ranking was to decrease the probability that s/he would eventually be categorized in a higher overall social class position. Had a five ranking been used, the results with respect to the lack of upward mobility would have been less striking, that is 21 percent (21.4%) of the sample would have had a lower social class ranking than their father, 24 percent (23.8%) would have had the same ranking, and 55 percent (54.8%) would have had a higher ranking than their father. Ultimately the choice of a six ranking instead of a five was based on one major consideration. As will become apparent in Chapter 5 university policemen perform many more security-type functions on a daily basis than they do police-type functions. Thus, intuitively university officers seem to fit more in an occupational category with security guards than in one with city policemen.

[4]There seems to be an increasing interest among colleges and universities in requiring a college education for campus officers (Kassinger, 1971; McDaniel, 1971; Nielsen, 1971; Webb, 1975; Powell, 1971b and 1981). There are two basic arguments in favor of educated officers on campus. First, since educated people can more effectively deal with other educated people, it does not make much sense to have

uneducated persons functioning in an important role in an educational environment. Second, if an officer has functioned as a college student s/he will be more sensitive to the community, and can better understand student problems and the campus environment. It is interesting to note that when the DTU Police Department was first formed in 1974, all applicants were required to have completed two years of college. While this may be viewed in light of the more general attempt to professionalize, the requirement was soon dropped because no other police department in the state required more than a high school education.

[5]It should be noted that these four selection procedures are mandated by state statute and required of all police agencies in the state. That they are mandated accounts for much of the similarity between the university's selection procedures and those of municipal departments.

[6]When asked if they had _ever_ had any prior police experience before joining the university force, 38 percent of the sample responded in the affirmative. Interestingly, 50 percent of these officers received their experience in either municipal or metropolitan area county policing. This finding suggests that university police work may be attractive to those who for whatever reason have left urban departments, but still wish to remain in law enforcement. An additional 45 percent received their policing experience in the military and the remaining five percent gained it at another university. Moreover, of the 38 percent of the officers who stated they at some time had had prior police experience, 32 percent (31.7%) reported they had less than one year of experience, 37 percent (36.6%) said they had one to two years of experience, and 32 percent (31.7%) indicated four or more years of experience with one officer reporting 29 years.

[7]It is also rare for municipal policemen to be confronted with these situations but relatively speaking such situations are even rarer in university police work.

[8]Upon hiring, each recruit is given temporary certification as a peace officer for up to one year, within which time s/he must successfully complete academy instruction and thus become permanently certified. It is the policy of the DTU department that

no recruit will be sent to the academy until they have completed at least six months in the field.

[9]In actual practice the formal two week orientation training program does not appear to serve an additional screening function. Although recruits are told they must achieve a minimum standard of competence, the exam is so easy that virtually all are retained. As one high ranking official noted, "I don't know of anyone who has been terminated because he couldn't pass the entry exam."

[10]The other hour and ten minutes of firearm field training was spent in the care and cleaning of the weapon upon return from the range.

[11]It might be noted that officers do not receive any experience with moving targets during their training program. Even if one became proficient with a stationary target it does not guarantee s/he could hit a moving target. Moreover, firearms training does not necessarily transfer under stress. The following incident related by one university officer is illustrative:

> One time a guy was coming at an officer with a knife...the officer emptied his gun and missed all six shots. By this time the guy was right on the officer so the officer bopped him over the head with his gun...an arrest was eventually made.

[12]According to the cannons of police ethics as stated in the department's training manual, it is the duty of all officers to have a working knowledge of the law. If they do not receive this working knowledge in formal training, then it should be the officer's responsibility to learn it on his or her own. One supervisor expressed this point of view as follows:

> We have a lot of officers who don't know the criminal code. This is a result of weakness in our training but it also points to a lack of initiative on the part of the officer himself. After all, anyone can read.

[13]It is noteworthy that municipal policemen feel the same way, that is, they receive intense instruction in many subjects at the academy which are irrele-

vant to their everyday job needs (McNamara, 1967; Niederhoffer, 1967; Harris, 1973; Van Maanen, 1973, 1975).

CHAPTER IV

ROLE AND FUNCTION

Law enforcement agencies of all types share the broad and vague mandate to enforce the law and keep the peace. Therefore, the role of university police in many respects is the same as the role of municipal police--preventor, protector, and law enforcer. Yet the role of campus police remains unclear. Lack of clarity in definition can be attributed to many causes including the varied historical origins of campus police departments, the changing attitudes and actions of students over time, the lack of recognition by college administrators until a few years ago of the need for an efficient police operation on campus, and the fact that the growth of the campus police field in recent years has been so rapid that the role of campus officers is constantly shifting. In this chapter the nature of the campus police role is explored through an analysis of what officers actually do on a daily basis and officers' perception of their role and function.

Routine Field Work

The normal or characteristic actions performed in the course of one's work are a key aspect of role (see, for example, Biddle and Thomas, 1966). Hence, analysis of what officers actually do on an everyday basis provides insight into the police role on campus. There are three traditional police services which the DTU police offer to the campus community on a daily basis--patrol, criminal investigation and traffic control. In addition, campus police routinely provide a host of other more indirect services.

Patrol

Patrol is the most visible service of the campus police agency. It is generally recognized among officers as the most effective method of preventing crimes from occurring. The high visibility and continuing presence of uniformed patrolmen in every

115

nook and cranny of the campus is seen by officers as a deterrent to crime. Patrol is the surveillance of public places for the purposes of preventing crime, apprehending criminals, assuring public safety, and so on. To the university officer everyday patrolling means more than crime prevention, detection, apprehension of criminals and law enforcement--it means security of buildings and grounds.

Patrol is the primary task of all police officers; yet the nature of patrol on campus is quite different from that for municipalities. First, in contrast to municipal departments, which employ hardly any of their patrol force on foot,1 the bulk of university patrol is on foot. The majority of all DTU buildings are located in a four block downtown area. The numerous buildings comprising the university require that a large portion of patrolling be handled by officers walking a beat. In short, the ecology and physical layout of the campus preclude motor patrol to a certain extent and dictate that officers walk a beat to get the job done. Since the campus does not cover a large area and is more self-contained and closely integrated than a city, foot patrol is viewed by officers as an effective means of coverage. The following comment was representative:

> We don't have a large geographic area to cover. A man on foot can go almost anywhere on campus within two or three minutes, especially if he knows all the "secret" passages and short cuts. Our response time on foot is minimal. However, if we relied on mobile units who have to weave in and out of downtown traffic, our response time would be higher. Foot patrol is more feasible here.

A second difference between the nature of municipal and university patrol is found in the meaning of "walking a beat on the street." To the university officer walking a beat on the street refers not only to campus streets and roads but to campus buildings which may require indoor as well as outdoor patrolling. In contrast to the municipal beat officer who may spend some of his or her time making exterior checks of buildings on his or her beat, much of the university officer's beat time is spent on interior patrol performing security and safety functions (e.g., checking classrooms, offices, boiler rooms, locking and unlocking doors, and so forth). Despite the fact that university patrolmen spend most of their time on interior patrol, the majority (58.8%) prefer exterior patrol over interior patrol. The major reasons for exterior preference appear to be related to increased identification with a police image and an avid dislike for performing security type work.

Foot patrol

Officers are deployed in single-man patrol and expected to handle most situations on their own without calling for backup. Prior to taking over his or her patrol beat each officer gathers all equipment to be utilized during his or her tour of duty, makes a radio test and receives his or her assignment for that day. Operationally the campus is divided into four zones and beat officers are routinely rotated between them, being assigned to different zones on different days.[2]

Organizationally, foot patrol is highly structured at the University. Upon assignment to a zone each officer is ideally required to make four rounds of every building, usually at two-hour intervals. Realistically, a given officer only makes about three rounds during his or her tour of duty because s/he is routinely called off patrol to perform other tasks (e.g., lockups/openings, suspicious person searches, escorts, accident investigations, stationary post coverage, direct traffic, and so forth). The time spent on these other tasks reduces the time spent on patrol and precludes full completion of all rounds. Despite the variability this situation implies, most officers feel patrol is too structured. The following comment of one beat officer was typical:

> We are too patterned in our rounds. We
> would be more effective if we were more
> loose on patrol. Sometimes we have a rover
> who is not assigned to a zone and can go
> anywhere. But this is rare because of man-
> power shortages. Usually each officer is
> assigned to a zone and has three or four
> buildings to cover plus other things he
> routinely has to do. When he finishes a
> round of a building it is usually two or
> more hours before he gets back to that

117

building. Anyone can figure out our pattern
after observing us for a couple of days. A
criminal may not be able to predict exactly
where we are at a particular time but he can
get a good idea where we are not and how
long we are not there.

To combat the organizational structure inherent in
patrol many university officers vary their individual
patrol pattern within specific buildings. For
example, instead of always beginning on the top floor
of a building and working their way down, officers
will sometimes begin in the middle of the building
and work their way up and then back down, or they may
double back on a building a few minutes after leaving
it. Limitations on the officer's time and his or her
responsibility for thorough coverage of all buildings
in his or her zone, however, preclude the ability of
the officer to individually alter his or her patrol
pattern on a routine basis.

     The university beat officer's main function on
patrol is observation. Occupationally s/he is
obliged to search out signs of difficulty and danger
in his or her surroundings--to recognize the "out of
ordinary."[3] A primary function of this observation
is directed toward the security of campus buildings.
A patrolman's security responsibilities include
inspecting all buildings for safety and fire hazards,
protecting the building against illegal entry, preventing the intrusion of unauthorized persons, and
opening and closing (securing) buildings. University
officers try to be as proactive as possible with
respect to the prevention aspects (e.g., seeking out
unsafe conditions) of their security role. In the
actual day to day performance of their security role
(e.g., lockups and openings) university officers
fulfill more of a custodial function than a police
function. In other words, in much of their routine
work on patrol university police are performing traditional "guard" duties.

Mobile patrol

     Mobile patrol supplements foot patrol by patrol-
ling the area surrounding campus on the "thin blue
line principle." The essence of this principle is
that a well marked conspicuous patrol on the perimeter of campus is an effective means of preventing

and repressing crime because it discourages potential law breakers from seeking "a soft touch" on campus. Motor patrol covers a wide geographic area and is not limited to the streets adjacent to the campus proper. It is used often to check university property located at varying distances from campus that is not readily accessible to the foot patrolman. In addition to the preventive function, mobile patrol fulfills a safety and service function. Routinely the mobile units patrol the parking areas for safety hazards (e.g., ice) and the protection of personnel. Each car is equipped with emergency equipment (e.g., first aid box, blanket, road flare, flashlight, and so forth) which can be used to be of service to those in need. Furthermore, cars are occasionally used to transport sick and injured persons to hospitals and students to their cars located in distant parking lots late at night. Routinely the mobile units are "flagged" down by those seeking directions and other information.

The university police use two kinds of marked motor vehicles--three-wheeled scooters and tradition- ally equipped police automobiles. These vehicles make continuous loops around the campus 24 hours a day, day in and day out. The scooters are single man vehicles usually driven by designated senior patrol persons (officers with seniority). While drivers are generally unhappy with scooters--claiming them to be unsafe, too cold in the winter and too hot in the summer--they are both practical and economical for use in an urban setting. They are effective in areas where cars cannot be used and cover a wider area than a man or woman walking. The DTU police have two scooters which are both deployed (assuming they are both operational) to patrol parking areas and uni- versity property located within several blocks of campus. Ideally car patrol is a two man patrol composed of a designated senior officer driver and one supervisor (usually the watch sergeant). The rationale behind this department policy is to keep the car moving even if the supervisor is called out to respond to a call. In reality manpower shortages often preclude two man patrol. Thus, the driver ends up making many rounds alone or the supervisor drives himself or herself without benefit of a designated driver.

In contrast to municipal police, in the perform- ance of their everyday duty at the university DTU mobile units almost never get involved in high speed

119

chases or make traffic stops for moving violations. Units merely make a continuing loop around campus. Like their municipal counterparts (see, for example, Stoddard, 1968; Rubinstein, 1973), some mileage is built up in non-official activities (e.g., coffee stops, dinner runs for supervisors, "observing" prostitutes outside of DTU jurisdiction, and so forth). On the whole, however, abuse of official rules appears to be minimal among the university police studied.

Criminal Investigation

The university police department is not organized to investigate criminal offenses and bring persons responsible to justice but rather to patrol campus grounds for safety and security. While the department does not have an investigative unit patterned after municipal detective bureaus, it does have an experienced, trained staff investigator who occasionally, though rarely, conducts a follow-up or actual investigation of an offense if it is sufficiently serious. On the whole, however, few crimes are actively investigated beyond the taking of an initial incident report.[4]

Preliminary investigation is the responsibility of uniformed patrolmen, who have received little extensive training in investigative techniques. Consequently, in the course of their everyday duty officers are limited to recording complaints regarding thefts and other crimes, but almost never do they conduct an actual investigation. Usually a short report is written to the effect that a crime has been committed. It is filed and the incident is forgotten. Hence, the university patrolman, like his municipal counterpart (see, for example, Buckner, 1967; Wilson, 1968; Rubinstein, 1973), is little more than a reactive report taker or record keeper with respect to his or her investigative duties. The fact that university officers are aware of this limitation to their function is illustrated by the following representative comments:

> Our investigations aren't really investigations. They are merely recordings.
> Suppose some guy "shakes his wand" (exposes his sexual organ) in a hallway. The complainant calls us and we take a report. We

120

come back to Operations and write the incident up on the proper form, it's checked by
a supervisor, filed away and forgotten.

Here there is no follow-up of cases or further investigation unless something real
serious comes down, and that is rare. Even
if a large amount of valuable equipment is
stolen from a department, it is basically
the department's responsibility to let us
know of further information as it develops.
In other words, we don't actively pursue the
investigation after taking the initial
report. We don't do follow-up investigations per se. We just take reports and
keep records.

While in reality patrolmen are limited to the
taking down of the who, when and where of crime and
expressing regret that it happened, many officers
indicated dissatisfaction with this state of affairs.
Officers felt that the lack of follow-through on
cases does little to enhance their self-image or
their image within the community. The following
comments were typical among officers:

We need more follow-through investigation.
I get uncomfortable when I see a victim two
weeks later who inquires what has happened.
Well, I know that nothing has been done
since I took the report, but you don't want
the victim to know that. So what do you do?
You lie. You tell the victim that no
progress has been made in the case but that
we're still working on it. Well, that is a
damn lie because you know that nothing is
being done. It doesn't make you think good
of yourself to lie. But what else are you
going to do?

It really is a shame that we don't do any
follow-up investigations here. If we did we
might be able to solve some cases and improve our image within the community. There
are just so many times you can tell a victim
that no progress has been made in a case
before it comes back on you. In the long
run the lack of follow-up on cases rein-
forces our image as glorified watchmen
rather than police.

Occasionally university patrolmen will be assigned to special undercover details for the purposes of surveillance and detection, especially when there have been a rash of crimes on campus. Ideally, these details are composed of new officers whose value lies in the fact that their faces are not known to the public. Most officers see the use of plainclothes personnel as an effective means of solving and reducing crime. The following comment was typical among officers:

> Occasionally we have special details like decoy squads and undercover jobs which we use especially for sex crimes and burglaries. These squads are pretty effective. For example, in the last several months we have reduced buglaries significantly by having a lot of officers work overtime in plainclothes. The very fact that we have a lot of plainclothes working overtime makes uniformed officers more aware that they need to keep their eyes open. This helps a lot too. Sometimes these squads even lead to an arrest.

Despite the fact that special details are perceived by the officers as effective, they are only rarely deployed by the department.

Traffic Control

Traffic is a real problem at DTU because a number of main city streets open to the public for vehicular traffic flow through campus and around its perimeter. In the course of their everyday duties university patrolmen have three basic responsibilities with respect to traffic services: (1) direct and control traffic at congested points to provide for the free and safe movement of vehicles and/or pedestrians, (2) enforce traffic laws and issue citations for moving and non-moving violations throughout campus, and (3) investigate motor vehicle accidents which occur on university property. The latter requires no further elaboration because in the course of his or her accident investigation duty the university officer plays essentially the same reactive report-taker role as s/he does in criminal investigations. However, the first two duties require more attention.

Traffic direction

While all university patrolmen, as part of their normal everyday duties, are responsible for monitoring vehicular traffic and stopping patrol to direct traffic in times of congestion, the bulk of responsibility for traffic control on a daily basis falls to the two or three officers specially assigned to traffic duty for that day. Since assignments are rotated daily, all officers generally have a special traffic assignment at least once a week. There are two major special area assignments which are covered by line officers Monday through Friday from 7 A.M. to approximately 7 P.M.--the student parking decks and a one-way major public thoroughfare through campus.

Parking decks

Parking problems are universal on university and college campuses (Csanyi, 1958; University Facilities Research Center, 1964; Nielsen, 1971; Gelber, 1972; Holloman, 1972; Abramson, 1974). This is especially true of a downtown commuter school such as DTU where automobiles are not a luxury but a necessity for many and the total capacity of parking spaces is less than the number of cars trying to utilize them at any given time. The problems that this situation creates are perhaps best exemplified by the following comment of one officer:

> Parking is at a premium here. The lack of parking spaces creates more problems for us than almost any other thing. Otherwise intelligent people sometimes just plain become dysfunctional when they can't find a parking place. They become frustrated, abusive, aggressive and just plain mean. I remember one day when a guy had been driving around the block for quite awhile. He finally made it into the lot, eyed a parking space and just as he was about to pull in some lady pulled into the space ahead of him. The guy became irrate, jumped out of his car and started banging in the side of the lady's car. Most people don't flip out that much but they sure do get frustrated. And a lot of times the officer is on the receiving end of that frustration.

Parking lots and multi-level parking decks on campus are self-parking facilities in which entrance is controlled by a variety of means including cashiers, permits, and automatic gates. All parking areas are privately leased from the university and officers have no control over who enters what lot, when they enter, how many enter, nor where and how they park once they enter. Stated differently, university police have no responsibility for parking regulation. The basic responsibilities of an officer specially assigned to a parking area are limited to patrolling the area for theft and/or accidents and, most importantly, keeping traffic moving on public streets by eliminating the backup of vehicles whose drivers wish entrance to parking lots. The officers have no responsibility for the placement of vehicles. Many officers suggested that one of the most common areas of misunderstanding between university police and students pertains to parking regulation. They feel that most students are unaware of their limited responsibility in parking and tend to hold them responsible for their inability to get into a lot. The following comment was typical among officers:

> The parking decks have counters and when
> they reach a certain number they close up.
> The operator (cashier) tells us to stop in-
> coming traffic flow. To keep traffic from
> backing up on the street, we wave people on.
> Usually they get mad because they can see
> open spaces and can't understand why they
> can't get in. They take out their
> frustration on us. What they don't realize
> is that there may be a lot of cars parked
> illegally (not in designated or proper
> spaces) and so while there may appear to be
> open spaces the lot is really full. They're
> also unaware that it is not my fault they
> can't get in. I just do what the operator
> tells me. I'm not responsible for who gets
> in. My responsibility is to keep traffic
> from backing up on the public streets. If
> students were made aware at orientation that
> we are not responsible for parking, maybe it
> would relieve some of the negative feelings
> we get from them.

Most officers say that while the task of "keeping traffic moving" is a routine and relatively simple part of their job, it requires more tact, diplomacy

and patience than almost any other of their numerous
tasks. Since the objectives of students and officers
(i.e., students want to stop on the street and wait
for a parking space to open up and officers want to
keep traffic moving) are oftentimes in conflict at
the parking decks, a potential for stress and abuse
is inherent in the situation.   Officers are expected
to remain courteous while being subjected to a barrage of dirty looks, abusive language and abusive
gestures.   On numerous occasions officers were observed taking this abuse in stride and handling it
routinely. For example, one day an officer was observed telling a woman to move as she was blocking
traffic while waiting to get into a full parking
deck.

> Officer:Miss, this is not a parking space.
> This is a street. You will have to move.
> Woman: Can't I wait here? He is going to
> let me into the lot in a few minutes.
> Officer: I'm sorry Miss but you will have
> to move.
> Woman (shooting a bird): You rotton son of
> a bitch.
> Officer (smiling): Thank you.
> The incident ended when the lady moved on.

One-way Street[5]

The other special traffic assignment to which
officers are routinely assigned is to direct one-way
traffic at a well traveled pedestrian crosswalk on a
traffic-congested public thoroughfare which essentially divides the campus in half and is a major
artery between two major buildings on campus.   The
basic responsibility of the officer is to ensure the
safe movement of pedestrians at the crossing and to
allow members of the university community to cross
from building to building.   This is not as simple a
task as it first appears.   Observation of traffic
duty revealed that there are numerous problems with
which the officer has to routinely contend including
cars and pedestrians stopping in the middle of the
street to ask directions, pedestrians stopping in the
middle of the street to "chit chat," drivers stopping
along the curb to drop off passengers, disobedience
by pedestrians who cross against officer commands,
disobedience by vehicle operators who refuse to stop
against officer commands, pedestrians and drivers who

seem oblivious to the world and thus risk injury to themselves and others, verbal abuse from passing motorists and pedestrians, and so forth. Despite these problems and the potential for injury which they imply, many officers feel that traffic control on One-way Street is a waste of time. Comments such as the following were typical among officers:

> Sometimes I feel like we are running a
> nursery here. There is no reason for an
> officer to be on One-way Street directing
> traffic. These people are grown students
> and they don't need their hands held. Since
> they are grown they should know how to cross
> a street by themselves. If they don't they
> have no business being in college.

> One-way Street traffic is ridiculous because
> everyone here is grown. They can certainly
> cross a street on their own. We don't have
> an officer directing traffic on the one-way
> street by the decks and that street is just
> as heavily traveled as One-way Street.

In spite of officers' attitudes toward traffic direction on One-way Street, observations over a six-hour period spread throughout a typical school day indicated that 6,114 pedestrians crossed the street. Given the tremendous volume of pedestrian traffic coupled with the fact that One-way Street is a major vehicular artery through downtown, it is potentially a hazardous area. One might argue, in fact, that the university police would be negligent if they did not try to protect the community and facilitate the orderly flow of traffic at this spot.

Traffic as difficult assignment

Traffic control causes campus police more annoyances and subjects them to pressure from a greater number of sources than any other task they routinely perform. Most officers perceive traffic as a "hard job." There are three reasons for this attitude. First, traffic is seen as difficult because the officer is exposed to the elements. Comments such as the following were typical among officers:

> During the summer it is hot as hell out
> there on the asphalt. During the winter you

126

freeze your buns off. And when it's raining
you're just damn well miserable.

Traffic is an especially bad assignment.
The weather causes you a lot of problems.
Traffic during winter is bad. Any person
who spends five to six hours in the cold is
bound to get sick. If you do get sick and
don't go to work the next day you are
"unreliable."

The second reason officers see traffic as a
difficult assignment pertains to the personal danger
inherent in the situation. Each officer of the uniformed patrol was asked his or her opinion on the
following statement: "The most dangerous duty
assignment at the university is directing traffic."
Two-thirds of the officers agreed. To most officers
the danger associated with traffic resides in the
potential for being hit by a motorist. The following
comment was typical among officers:

Traffic direction is a nerve wracking experience. You're in the street to tell people
when and how to move and it can be
hazardous. Some of those turkeys are
driving by instinct alone. They come up the
street and they see you but they don't see
you. You can get run over. In fact we had
an officer run over once.

Finally, officers view traffic as a hard assignment because of the "hassles" involved in dealing
with people. These hassles are of two kinds. First,
unpleasant contacts with the public are more likely
to occur when officers are directing traffic. On
numerous occasions while performing their traffic
duty, officers were observed being subjected to a
barrage of insults and malicious comments from motorists and pedestrians, including having degrading gestures directed at them and being called such names as
"mother fucker," "son of a bitch," "asshole" and
"faggot." The following remarks of officers are representative of the abuse they feel they receive while
directing traffic:

People smart off at you when you tell them
to move on and don't let them in a parking
lot. Some students think they have a mono-
graphed parking place and when you tell them

127

to move you get choice words hurled at you.

I got one lady who never says anything to me
when I'm on traffic duty. She just shoots
me a bird every time she rides by.

While directing traffic on One-way Street I
told a student to hold up and he did. When
I let him cross he walked behind me and
said, "I could have made it across,
asshole."

The second hassle in dealing with people on traffic
duty is a function of challenges to the policeman's
authority. Each officer was questioned about
challenges to his or her authority utilizing the
following question: "In the course of your work at
the university, have you ever encountered a situation
where your authority as a police officer has been
questioned?" Nearly two-thirds (64.3%) of the uniformed officers reported that they had encountered
such a situation. When questioned about the circumstances involved, 80 percent of these officers specifically indicated they were traffic-related. Most
officers feel that people do not listen to them
and/or take them for granted especially when they are
on traffic duty. Comments such as the following were
typical among officers:

Jay walking is a big problem around here.
We can't really do anything about it. It
wouldn't be so bad if people would only
respect your judgment. Students dart out
into the street saying they can make it.
Several have almost been hit. You can tell
them to observe your signals but they ain't
gonna pay you no mind.

It is really hard working traffic at the
decks. People won't pay you any attention
when you tell them to move. Lots of times
they argue with you. You have to be a
Dr. Jekyll and Mr. Hyde. You have to play
both roles doing an instant switch between
them and it is hard. For example, you huff
and puff at someone until the gate goes up
and then you have to turn around and be nice
to them. It's real tough dealing with
people that pay you no mind.

Enforcement of traffic laws

All officers, whether specially assigned to traffic or not, are charged with enforcing traffic laws and issuing citations for moving and non-moving violations. University police handle traffic enforcement on a low-key basis, not dispensing many tickets. As one officer noted:

> We're not out there to issue tickets. There is no quota here. Our priority is not to write tickets unless we absolutely have to.

With respect to non-moving violations the opportunities so far exceed the obligations that the individual officer has great freedom in deciding whom and when to ticket. However, several factors limit his or her ticketing activity. First, university officers are limited in their authority to issue tickets only on university property. Since all parking areas are privately leased the university police have no authority to take action against parking violations within those areas. Second, the officers' ticketing ability is limited by departmental policy. While curb parking is not permitted on campus or adjacent streets except where there are meters, there is a department policy against enforcing parking regulations on public streets adjacent to campus unless the vehicle is in some way a safety hazard or interfering with the operations of the university.[6] Since this is rarely the case, few tickets are ever issued. Finally, all fees for parking violations are collected by the municipality in which DTU is located. As one officer noted:

> Normally we don't mess with parking violations and overtime parking meters. The meters belong to the city and the fines are paid to the city. We don't get any money out of it. So if you issue a ticket all you've accomplished is to cause yourself some paperwork.

The fact that issuance of parking tickets is not a priority among university policemen is illustrated by the fact that no beat officer was observed carrying his or her parking citation booklet with him or her on routine patrol.[7]

Department policy with regard to the issuance of

moving violation citations is also very lenient.
This policy essentially states that officers are to
try to avoid issuing tickets but they are to use
their own discretion. In general, DTU officers do
not issue a citation unless a motorist in some way
"hassles" them. As a guide to action, over time an
informal norm has developed among uniformed officers
to the effect that "if a motorist fails to obey an
officer, cite him with resisting an officer." During
1981 ten moving violations were recorded at DTU. All
ten involved the issuance of a traffic citation in
which the motorist was charged with "failure to obey
an officer's order." The informal norm is most
likely to be applicable in the context of challenges
to officers' authority in parking areas. The following comments of officers are illustrative:

> One thing about traffic is that people won't
> move. You tell them to move and they don't.
> They question who you think you are to tell
> them what to do. When you give them a
> ticket they know then what kind of authority
> you have.

> You really need to ticket a motorist if he
> fails to comply with an order. Sometimes
> taking out your ticket book and threatening
> him is enough. If he continues to give you
> a hard time, write him up. If you don't,
> you lose your advantage because you haven't
> backed your words up with actions.

The fact that the informal norm is strong among officers is illustrated by the fact that most patrolmen,
whether assigned to traffic or not, routinely carry
their moving citation book with them during the hours
they may be pulled off patrol and have to direct
traffic. Many officers suggested that one factor
mitigating the issuance of a moving violation ticket
for any reason other than failure to obey an order
was the difficulty in actually issuing the ticket.
The following officer comments are illustrative:

> It is really hard to give a ticket even out
> there at the decks. You are out there to
> keep traffic moving. By the time you write
> a ticket traffic has backed up even more.
> Sometimes it just isn't worth it unless the
> guy is a super bastard and leaves you abso-
> lutely no other choice.

You can't really give a moving violation
ticket on One-way Street. Suppose a motorist doesn't stop when you tell him or stops
but goes again before you tell him. Well,
you are really powerless to do anything
about it. After all his wheels rotate
faster than your legs. Besides you're not
supposed to leave your post. I've been here
a long time and I've never known anyone to
call Operations to run a license because of
a routine moving violation on One-way
Street.

In short, university officers' opportunities far
exceed their obligations with respect to the enforcement of traffic laws. Nevertheless, ability to issue
tickets for both moving and non-moving violations is
effectively limited by the scope of their authority,
department policy, lack of direct reward to the department, and difficulties in issuance.

Officer role

In the fulfillment of their everyday traffic control function university officers play more of a service and safety role than a law enforcement role.
They patrol parking areas to ensure traffic flows on
the street but not to enforce parking laws. They
direct traffic on One-way Street to ensure the safety
of pedestrians. They rarely issue tickets. Even the
approach they take in performing their everyday traffic duties suggests more of a service orientation
(helping) than a law enforcement (controlling) orientation. This service orientation is evident in the
following example taken from field observation:

One day a new trainee was observed directing
traffic on One-way Street. In a controlling
tone he constantly said things to pedestrians such as "use the crosswalk next time,
get back on the curb, and don't cross until
I tell you." The officer was later taken
aside and chastised by one of his supervisors who had also been observing him.
"You can't push people around like that
here. You are here to serve. Next time
just say in a pleasant tone something like
you may get hit by a car if you don't use
the crosswalk."

Other Services

In addition to their more traditional direct services, university police also routinely provide the university community with a myriad of more indirect "helping" services. Many of these special services exist on campus as a result of custom and tradition (e.g., maintaining a lost-and-found at police headquarters) and because the university police are the only agency on campus capable of providing service 24 hours a day, 365 days a year (e.g., raise and lower flag daily). It would appear that like their municipal counterparts (Cumming et al., 1965; Buckner, 1967; Petersen, 1968; Cummins, 1971) university police have assumed some of their services by default. All indirect services are services the community desires. Thus, they are services the university police are obliged to continue to provide as long as they have sufficient manpower to do so.

In the course of his or her everyday work the university officer may be called off patrol to perform a number of social services. For example, s/he may be called on to escort a female to her car thus guaranteeing her safe passage through campus, provide an escort for university personnel carrying large amounts of money to banks, answer requests for information and directions, assist motorists, aid the handicapped, deliver emergency messages, and so forth. In addition the officer may be called on to administer immediate and temporary first aid to the sick or injured until the time when professional medical assistance can take over care and treatment. Finally, s/he may be dispatched to perform a number of safety services such as checking on a smoke report, an elevator malfunction or an overflowing commode.

In addition to maintaining records on all reported criminal incidents, the DTU Police Department maintains incident records on several of the indirect "helping" services provided by officers. While these records are compiled for a number of administrative purposes, they also provide the information necessary for an officer to defend himself or herself in case a complaint is lodged against him or her. The following officer comment is illustrative of the "protective" function of indirect service records:

When a woman comes by for an escort, we fill

out a case card on it that tells the time of
leaving, drop off, return and what happened.
That's a CYOA--cover your own ass. These
people complain about everything. Well,
officers are only human and they may try to
make a date. But the woman may call up the
Chief and complain that the officer tried to
rape her. We can look at the case card and
say he was only gone three minutes and
that's damn near impossible...unless he is a
super quickie.

Presented in Table 3 is an annual summary of recorded
service incidents by type and number from 1978
through 1981. In addition it provides the total
crime reported during the same time period. The data
statistically support the fact that university
officers do provide a number of assistance, health
and safety services. Perhaps the most significant
feature of the table, however, is the ratio of
service reports to criminal reports. In each year
the number of service reports far exceeds the number
of criminal reports and for the total time period
covered by the Table the ratio of service reports to
criminal reports is 4,932 to 1,720 or approximately
four to one. If records were kept on all other
indirect services which university police provide
(e.g., answering requests for information and directions) this ratio would be even greater. In short,
the data suggest that university policemen are
largely engaged in service activities just like their
municipal counterparts.

Multi-Function Responsibility

On an average shift campus police may perform
both police and non-police duties. They have a
multi-function responsibility. University officers
enforce those laws enacted and codified by the legis-
lature, which is largely a law enforcement function
involving the detection, prevention and investigation
of crime in addition to the apprehension of violators. They provide protection for personnel, property and operations of the university, which is
largely a security function accomplished via patrol,
lighting, use of electronic alarms, locks and key
control. They maintain peace and order on campus,
which is largely a preventive function involving the
forestalling of disruptive events and traffic

TABLE 3

ANNUAL SERVICE INCIDENTS BY TYPE AND NUMBER

AND TOTAL REPORTED CRIME

Type of Service	Year				Totals
	1978	1979	1980	1981	
Assistance					
1. bank escorts	403	712	542	713	2,370
2. female escorts	279	363	490	376	1,508
3. male escorts	3		10	2	15
4. handicapped		7			7
Sub Total	(685)	(1,082)	(1,042)	(1,091)	(3,900)
Health					
1. illness	59	58	59	48	224
2. injury	42	62	62	47	213
Sub Total	(101)	(120)	(121)	(95)	(437)
Safety					
1. fire alarm	44	23	41	37	145
2. actual fire	9	8	11	8	36
3. smoke reports	22	19	23	26	90
4. elevator malfunction	60	43	43	37	183
5. water leakage or alarm	8	9	12	11	40
6. gas fumes	4	3	1	1	9
7. miscellaneous				92	92
Sub Total	(147)	(105)	(131)	(212)	(595)
TOTAL SERVICE INCIDENTS	933	1,307	1,294	1,398	4,932
TOTAL CRIMINAL INCIDENTS	372	328	504	516	1,720

control. Finally, they provide public assistance,
which is largely a service function. Law enforcement, security, prevention and service are all functional parts of the university officer's role on
campus.8 All of his or her routine field work is
designed to meet these responsibilities.

Officer Perception of Role and Function

A role is more than what one does, it includes
expectations (see, for example, Biddle and Thomas,
1966; Goodman and Marx, 1978). Moreover, it is what
one defines as appropriate for him or herself. Consequently one way to gain understanding of the role
of campus police is through analysis of how line
officers themselves perceive their role and function
on campus. How do line officers define their role?
What is their image of their occupational self? What
is their perception of real university police work?

Security or Police

While DTU officers are hired as police, invested
with full peace officer authority by state statute,
carry police titles (e.g., chief of police, public
safety officer, patrolman, and so forth), project a
strong police image in their uniforms and equipment,
are taught that they are police in training, and are
paid salaries equivalent to municipal police,9 they
face a genuine identity problem on campus--are they
police or security? As noted previously, many
officers feel that members of the campus community
think of them as security not police. Comments such
as the following were typical among line officers:

> Students and faculty just think of us as
> security. It is really disappointing that
> most people don't even think of us as "real
> pigs."
>
> People think of us as high class security or
> counterfeit police. While our image has
> improved since we became a police depart-
> ment, most people don't think of us as real
> police. They look down on us and don't give
> us the same respect or perks.

In contrast, the overwhelming majority of university

officers perceive themselves as police, not security officers. Each uniformed line officer was asked the following question: "Do you feel there is a big difference between a university policeman and a security guard?" More than three-fourths (77.4%) of the officers responded in the affirmative. Upon further questioning, officers suggested several important dimensions to the distinction between policemen and security guards. Of those officers who felt there was a difference, 64 percent mentioned the greater authority of the university policeman granted by law10 and 22 percent mentioned the greater training of the university officer. The following comment was typical:

> Law and training make the difference between police and security. In both respects we are police not security. Security has no authority to make an arrest. They merely hold you if they can until someone (police) gets there to make the arrest. Training makes the difference status-wise between police and security. Police are trained and certified. Security gets only two or three hours of training.

Most university officers want no part of the name "security." To them the term is associated with a low-level, unprofessional approach emphasizing only the protection of property and does not take into account the policeman's training and responsibility for dealing with people. To most campus law enforcement persons "security officer" is a degrading term which does not enhance the self image or role perceptions of the officer. The following officer comment is illustrative:

> Most people think of a security guard as not much more than a vegetable--he sits at a desk, falls asleep and is just a night watchman. When people see you as a vegetable they treat you as a vegetable and expect you to act like and be a vegetable. Well, I'm not a vegetable. I'm a steak. It is really insulting and degrading to be down-rated and called security when you are certified police.

In addition to the degradation associated with being called security, most officers feel that their perception by others as security makes their job more difficult on a daily basis. Generally the lack of a well-defined police identity on campus creates problems in the officer's everyday work by increasing the potential that his authority to perform his function may be questioned by members of the campus community as well as others. The following comments were typical among officers:

> Naturally it is easier to do your job when people are aware you have the power and authority of police. Most people don't recognize the scope of our authority as police. They think of us as security and as such don't pay much attention to what we say. Because they think of us as security they show us no respect and challenge us. For example, you'll tell somebody something and he'll tell you, "Go to hell...you can't tell me what to do...you ain't nothing but a goddamn security guard."

> We are constantly having to demonstrate our authority as police. Most people on campus think of us as security with no power. Even off campus they think of us the same way. I remember one time not too awfully long ago when we arrested someone and took him to court. The judge had to go look it up in the code to see if we had the authority to arrest. Imagine, the judge didn't even know we could arrest. Then there was another time when a guy who worked for the FBI was trying to lift some materials from the library. He didn't know we could arrest him until we read him his rights and cuffed him. Then he believed it.

As previously noted the most common circumstances under which the university officers' authority is likely to be questioned are traffic related. However, virtually any area of interaction with the public may result in a questioning of authority because of the public perception that the university officer lacks legal authority. Challenges to police authority are not unique to university policing. Numerous scholars of municipal police have noted that challenges of authority are a daily fact of life among municipal officers (see, for example, Banton, 1964; Buckner, 1967; Bittner, 1970; Westley, 1970;

Clark and Sykes, 1974). These scholars have also noted that the use of force and violence is an accepted solution to such challenges among municipal officers. What is unique about campus policing is that university officers do not have a comparable solution. Because of the nature of the environment in which they work and the emphasis upon temperance of authority within the department, many officers feel they are not in a position to "use any means necessary" to gain control over everyday situations in which their authority is challenged. As a consequence officers will often back down when challenged beyond a certain point; virtually never do they resort to violence. Several field observations are illustrative:

> One evening during lockup a woman approached an officer requesting admittance to a building. The officer informed her he would need to see her ID. The woman refused and quickly brushed by the officer and entered the building. The officer did not pursue her. Later the officer remarked, "I didn't know what to do so I decided it would be better to forget about it."

> One afternoon while working the parking decks a motorist who was blocking traffic on a public street refused to move on upon an officer's request. After several minutes of telling the driver to move the officer decided to issue the motorist a ticket. Hence, the officer requested the motorist's license. The motorist refused to produce it and continued to block traffic. The officer walked away from the car. Several minutes later he commented as he observed the motorist pulling into a parking lot, "I didn't really know what to do...there wasn't really anything I could do. We're not supposed to throw our authority around here. It makes me mad that the driver won. It makes me feel inadequate. But when you get right down to it we are powerless in most normal situations."

In short, university officers seem to identify more with police than with security because of the negative stereotype associated with the security guard concept and the enhancement of self-image and reduced challenges to authority in public interaction that such an identification imply. The image factor appears to be instrumental in university officers' identification with and desire to be identified with police rather than security. As one officer noted:

> Using the term police is a psychological
> thing which has to do with the perception of
> authority and self-image of the officer.
> Most people show more deference to police
> than security. You command more respect as
> a policeman. Therefore, you are better able
> to protect yourself in the streets.

It is somewhat ironic that university police seek to identify with other police because of the respect police command when, in fact, research has shown that urban policemen usually perceive the public as granting them very little respect (Banton, 1964; Skolnick, 1966; McNamara, 1967; Niederhoffer, 1967; Bayley and Mendelsohn, 1969; Westley, 1970; Johnson and Gregory, 1971).

Despite the fact that university officers are legally police and identify with police, a majority of the officers indicated that in their daily work they function more as a security guard than a police-man.[11] Each officer was asked the following question: "Do you consider yourself to be more of a security guard or more of a policeman in your actual work?" Fifty-five percent of the officers responded that they see themselves as security guards in their work. Comments such as the following were typical among officers:

> Though we have the authority to be police,
> in our actual job performance we are more
> security. Mainly we do building security
> type work rather than investigate crimes or
> chase and arrest criminals. Realistically
> our job is about 10 percent police work and
> 90 percent security. What it all boils down
> to is that we are certified police officers
> doing security work. I guess you could say
> that we are the best paid security in the
> state.

This finding indicates an apparent dissonance between what officers know and believe they are (police) and the behavioral tasks they perform on a routine every-

day basis (security). Most officers see this discrepancy between what they believe they were hired to
be or do and what they actually do as a source of
discontentment with their job. The following
comments are representative of officer sentiments:

> Much of the frustration in this job stems
> from the fact that while we are supposed to
> be police we perform more security-like
> functions. Routinely we have to man
> stationary posts, lock and unlock doors,
> baby sit students at parking decks, and so
> on. Police don't do this kind of work.

> Functionally we are security, yet we are
> told we are police. We are hired as police,
> called public safety officers and trained as
> police. The fact that the department claims
> you are police raises expectations too much
> and causes dissatisfaction when you get into
> the field and realize your job is more
> security. It is frustrating cause you never
> get to use your training...all you do is
> shake door knobs.

Several officers suggested that a great deal of
the dissatisfaction and confusion over their role
could be alleviated by reducing the security functions officers are required to perform, by simply
hiring security personnel to supplement police
personnel. Comments such as the following were typical:

> The non-police type chores we are required
> to perform like shaking door knobs, sitting
> around buildings and standing in entrance-
> ways take away from our police duties like
> patrol. For example, our responsibility for
> securing the premises precludes having time
> to take aggressive action in other areas.
> We need security to perform security work
> and police to perform police work.

> We need to make a full change to police and
> get rid of the security holdover from other
> days. For example, door openings and
> closings could be transferred to key control
> and student assistants or security guards
> could be hired to cover the art exhibit desk
> and other stationary posts. A full change

to police would certainly clarify our role
and enhance our self-image and our image
within the campus community.

In terms of their everyday work most university
police see themselves as something more than a
security guard but something less than a policeman.
Moreover, in terms of occupational prestige most
officers see their job as a "cut above regular
security and a cut below regular police." One
officer's comments are illustrative of these perceptions:

> Our system is more complex than plain
> security. Here we are a mixture of security
> and police. We pull the authority of a
> police officer so we are legally police.
> But most of what we do is security. Yet
> sometimes we do police work. What we really
> are is glorified security guards in our
> daily work. The best title for this job is
> "security police." Prestige-wise we fall
> between security and police.

In short, realistically speaking university
police work is neither simply security work nor
simply police work--it is a mixture of both (although
a lopsided mixture). In their everyday work university police combine both security functions and
police functions into a unique profession--campus
policing.

Conception of Proper Police Work

The foregoing analysis suggests that legally and
structurally university officers are police, but
functionally they are more security. The role of the
university line officer is not a strict legalistic
one. Research has shown this to be true of municipal
officers also (Banton, 1964; Cumming et al., 1965;
Skolnick, 1966; Bittner, 1967b; Petersen, 1968;
Wilson, 1968; Bercal, 1970; Webster, 1970 and 1973;
Reiss, 1971). Like his municipal counterpart the
university patrolman is routinely involved in tasks
(e.g., giving directions, administering first aid,
and so forth) that have little relation to police
work in terms of controlling crime. In other words,
he is often called upon to perform extra-legal duties
beyond his mandate. As a measure of the extent to

which uniformed officers accept extra-legal duties to be part of what they consider to be their job as university policemen, each officer was presentd with 32 types of situations s/he may have encountered in his or her everyday work. S/he was then asked how obligated s/he feels to do each of those things. A summary of the responses of uniformed officers regarding their expectations is presented in Table 4.

If consensus is operationally defined as the situation in which at least 75 percent of the officers gave the same response to an item, only eight of the items elicited this level of consensus. Items 1, 8, 9, 13, 21, 22, 24 and 26 were perceived by officers as situations in which they absolutely must act. These items were legalistic in orientation, that is, some violation of the law or potential violation of the law was indicated. Interestingly, the highest consensus (over 93 percent of the officers in each case indicated they absolutely must act) was reached on items 8, 9, 24 and 26 which indicated some definite violation of the law. Items 1, 13, 21 and 22 indicated an immediate potential for law violation and suggest consensus on the prevention aspect of the law enforcement function. Given the high consensus on all eight items, the data suggest consensus among university officers on a law enforcement function.

No extra-legal item reached the same high level of consensus as those items which were legalistic in orientation. However, the findings in Table 4 imply that university officers do accept extra-legal functions as part of their role. In all but nine items12 75 percent or more of the officers stated at least that they should do something, that is, they indicated that either they absolutely must or preferably should act. Many of these items were service oriented such as giving directions (item 4) and assisting persons who are ill or disabled (items 5 and 20). Other of the items were prevention oriented such as keeping unauthorized persons off campus (item 12) and awakening a sleeping student in the library whose purse or briefcase is open prey (item 30). Still other of the items were security oriented such as escorting female students to their cars (item 3), investigating a door that has been propped open (item 19), and opening a secured area for faculty and staff (item 28). The strong agreement on these items suggests that university officers perceive service functions, prevention

TABLE 4

UNIVERSITY OFFICERS' CONCEPTION OF PROPER POLICE WORK (PERCENTAGES)

Item	Absolutely Must Do	Preferably Should Do	May or May not Do	Preferably Should Not Do	Absolutely Must Not do
1. Request an ID from a suspicious acting person	80	20			
2. Patrol areas where criminals acts are likely to occur in order to prevent crime	56	34	10		
3. Escort a female student to a car upon request	60	38	2		
4. Answer requests for information	32	54	12	2	
5. Assist persons who are ill-- nonemergency cases	54	34	8	2	2
6. Investigate a complaint of loud noise on fraternity or sorority row	30	38	26	6	2
7. Enforce traffic laws on streets adjacent to campus	32	34	22	10	2
8. Investigate an assault	100				
9. Investigate an auto accident on university property	100				
10. Assist a cafeteria worker who asks for help closing up so that there will be no problem	20	38	18	18	6

TABLE 4--Continued

Item	Absolutely Must Do	Preferably Should Do	May or May not Do	Preferably Should Not Do	Absolutely Must Not do
11. Investigate all unsecured areas during your tour of duty	68	30	2		
12. Keep people off campus who are unauthorized to be there	62	22	14	2	
13. Investigate a complaint that a man has been following a woman around the library	80	14	6		
14. Enforce jay walking laws	6	10	30	38	16
15. Ticket a motorist who fails to comply with an officer's order	56	22	20	2	
16. Assist a student or faculty member in jump starting their car	6	32	42	10	10
17. Turn off lights found unnecessarily burning in academic buildings after hours	8	44	42	2	4
18. Investigate someone fooling around a vending machine	52	38	6	4	
19. Investigate a door that has been propped open	60	30	8	2	
20. Assist a disabled person	64	26	8		
21. Direct traffic in time of congestion	80	16	4		2

TABLE 4--Continued

Item	Absolutely Must Do	Preferably Should Do	May or May not Do	Preferably Should Not Do	Absolutely Must Not do
22. Investigate someone fooling around a car	80	18		2	
23. Report a car with lights left on in a faculty or staff parking lot	18	54	26	2	
24. Investigate a sounding alarm	96	2	2		
25. Move a car along that is blocking traffic while waiting to get into a parking lot	62	34	4		
26. Investigate a theft of personal belongings	94	6			
27. Move men along who are making cat calls at females on university property	56	34	8	2	
28. Open a secured area for faculty or staff	48	38	12		2
29. Check empty classrooms and restrooms while on interior patrol	32	34	30	4	
30. Awaken a sleeping student in the library whose purse or briefcase is open prey	38	40	18	4	
31. Report a defective street or hall light to Operations while on patrol	32	40	26	2	
32. Investigate a loud verbal argument between two persons in the student center	66	24	8	2	

functions and security functions to be part of their role on campus.

In short, the data show that university officers accept a conception of their role that includes functions other than law enforcement. The role of the uniformed officer is not sharply defined--it includes a mixture of enforcement, service, prevention and security functions.

Support of Role Perceptions

The university officer's conception of his or her everyday role is supported and reinforced by a departmental ideology stressing a philosophy of service and prevention. According to this ideology the foremost duty of university officers is to serve by assisting members of the campus community. The essence of the service ideology is perhaps best summed up in the following comment of one line officer:

> Campus policemen are public servants. As such they serve and assist. Our purpose here is not to push people around but to help them. We are here to serve the community in any way we can...to make it safe and keep people happy.

To this end of service there is a strong emphasis within the department on public relations. University officers believe they are selling an intangible item--service. In this role courtesy and ethics are the keys. Comments such as the following were typical among officers:

> Our role on campus is basically service and PR (public relations). To fulfill our function we must smile and show a sincere interest in assisting others. Good PR makes the officer's job easier and shields the department from criticism.

The pervasiveness of the service ideology is illustrated by the fact that internal rewards within the department are based upon service not law enforcement. All officers are aware that one way to gain recognition within the department is through the performance of service tasks. On several occasions officers were observed receiving lavish public praise during roll call from fellow officers and supervisors because they had simply stopped to inquire if they could help someone who, in turn, brought their "service" to the attention of a superior. The service ideology is so strong among university officers that oftentimes they do things against their better judgment just to keep people happy and make them think they are being served. The following incident relayed by a uniformed officer is illustrative:

> One afternoon a guy came up to me and claimed that his wallet with lots of money in it and his expensive watch were stolen from his car in the parking decks. I went to the scene to investigate, even though he didn't look like he had a lot of money or could afford an expensive watch. When we got to his car I didn't find his story any easier to believe. It was a filthy old beat up job that looked like it wouldn't even turn over. I proceeded to examine the car. After about half an hour the complainant pointed out a place at the rear window which appeared that it might have been jimmied. It looked more to me like the molding had rotted out. The complainant got all excited thinking that this must be the way the thief got in. Since there were smudges on the back window (incidently there were smudges all over the car from wheel to visor), we took fingerprints. Of course they were in no way useful, but the complainant was satisfied. The moral of this story is that we are here to serve and sometimes this requires that we do things to keep people happy and make them feel like we are doing something. In other words, make them feel like they have been served.

Moreover the service ideology is so strong among university officers that they often go beyond the call of duty. The following examples taken from field observation are illustrative:

> One evening a man approached an officer requesting bus money to get home. Without hesitating, the officer pulled a dollar out of his pocket and handed it to the stranger. The officer did not ask for any identifi-

cation and merely informed the man when he would be back on duty. The next day the man returned the dollar.

One evening about 7:30 P.M. while on routine patrol an officer was stopped by a distraught man who claimed he had just mailed a financial aid request in the university post office with the wrong postage on it. Since the man was desperate to meet a mailing deadline he was fearful that the letter would not be delivered because it contained less postage than was required. Being after hours the university post office was closed and the man was unable to retrieve the letter. The officer escorted the man to Operations. Upon hearing the man's predicament the officer on desk duty phoned the Postmaster at home informing him of the situation and guaranteeing him that he (officer) would personally see to it that the post office got the additional three cents due if the letter was mailed without delay. The man was greatly relieved. The patrolman stated, "It really makes you feel good when you are able to help someone even in a small way."

University officers are aware that they provide a number of indirect services to the community on a routine basis and are proud of it. However, many officers expressed disappointment in the fact that they are not generally recognized by the community for providing them. The following comment of a line officer is representative:

Most community members are unaware of the services we provide on a daily basis such as escorts and first aid. They think all we do is walk around, lock and unlock doors and direct traffic. We're just not recognized for what we do. It's disappointing. If they could somehow be made aware of all the little things we routinely do to help them, they would think better of us.

The fact that a service ideology is deeply ingrained in the university officer is reflected in his attitude toward service work. In contrast to municipal police (see, for example, Cummins, 1971; Rubin-

148

stein, 1973; Van Maanen, 1978b), university officers do not see service work as "knit shit work." Each uniformed patrolman was presented with five tasks (patrol, traffic direction and control, investigation, assisting people, and security) which they routinely perform and asked to rank them in terms of preference. While no universal agreement on task preference was discernable among campus patrolmen, about 45 percent (44.7%) of the officers ranked "assisting people" as the task they most like to perform in their daily work; an additional 13.2 percent of the sample ranked it second. Thus, it would appear that nearly half of the university officers prefer the assistance aspects of their job more than other tasks they perform on a daily basis. Thus, not only do university policemen accept service functions as part of their role but they actually enjoy the assistance aspects of their job.

The prevention function suggested by officers' conception of their role is reinforced by a department ideology emphasizing the deterrent effect of a highly visible patrol force. Most university officers feel the university police force is a real deterrent to crime. Comments such as the following were typical among officers:

> There is a lot of crime around the outskirts
> of the university but there is little on
> campus because there are a lot of officers
> in the field who are visible. We have a lot
> of manpower here. We are probably the
> biggest force in the state for only four
> acres of land. It is like a fortress here.
> It may be overkill but probably we have the
> safest area in the whole metropolitan area
> simply because of our presence.

> Any campus with a weak, low-level operation
> is a haven for "easy-pickings" in an urban
> jungle. We can't eliminate crime, but we
> can effectively reduce it through our visi-
> bility. We deter because of our visibility.
> You can see officers all over campus all the
> time. Therefore, the opportunity to commit
> crime is not great here.

While there is no way to assess accurately the over-all deterrent impact of the policeman's work, there is a strong belief among officers in the preventative

effect of their presence. When asked to account for
the low crime rate at the university despite its
location in a downtown urban area, slightly over 94
percent (94.3%) mentioned the high visibility of uniformed officers on campus. Moreover, 94 percent of
the officers agreed with the statement: "The high
visibility of uniformed officers on campus contri-
butes significantly to the reduction of crime." In
short, the overwhelming feeling among officers is
that their presence and visibility leads to a reduction in crime and a low crime rate on campus.

The prevention ideology is so strong among university policemen that the effectiveness of both the
department and officers are qualitatively measured by
the absence of crime and disorder rather than quantitatively measured by the number of arrests as in most
municipal departments (Misner, 1967; Niederhoffer,
1967; Rubinstein, 1973; Manning and Van Maanen, 1978;
Lundman, 1980). Comments such as the following were
typical among officers:

> The basic mission of police is to prevent
> crime and disorder. Therefore, the ultimate
> test of police efficiency has to be the
> absence of crime and disorder. When campus
> police do their job well nothing happens.
> If we average over three incident reports
> daily we are not being effective. If the
> number of reports is high we are not doing a
> good job.

> A good policeman is one who has no crime in
> his area. The more crime the worse you are.
> Not making an arrest is a better measure of
> effectiveness than lots of arrests. If you
> never make an arrest and nothing ever
> happens in your area then you have been
> effective.

These comments suggest that campus police are less
oriented toward convictions than municipal police;
that is, they are more concerned with prevention than
apprehension.

In short, the university officer's conception of
his or her role to include service and prevention
functions is supported and reinforced by departmental
ideology. With respect to this ideology, campus
police appear to place less emphasis than municipal

police on definition of function in terms of law enforcement and more on service and prevention.

Notes

¹In most municipal departments mobile patrol replaced foot patrol because increasing crime demanded fast and often multiple response, and because the growth of cities and the necessity for increased coverage in virtually all areas made it economically impossible to staff walking or beat districts.

²Administratively it is believed that zonal rotation reduces officer boredom.

³Obviously in order to be able to recognize the "out of ordinary" the university officer has to be totally familiar with the campus, in particular, and the campus community, in general.

⁴It should be noted that almost all of the cases for which there are no follow-ups are for minor crimes, either not requiring follow-up or for which there is no particular justification for follow-up because the probability of success is quite small. Hence, it may be a waste of manpower and time to follow through on many cases. In other words, the nature of crime at the university and probability of success in follow-up serve to limit the investigation functions of the department.

⁵"One-way Street" is a pseudonym used to protect the anonymity of the university at which data collection was conducted.

⁶Occasionally members of the mobile patrol unit will issue a parking citation "if someone appears to be abusing the privilege." However, on the whole it is rare for a parking ticket to be issued for this reason or for any other by a university officer.

⁷Those officers assigned to mobile patrol usually carry a citation book with them, but they rarely use it.

[8]Although it is not a specific task performed in the course of DTU officers' daily work, a prominent theme reflected in the campus police literature is that campus police fulfill an important educational function (McDaniel, 1971; Holloman, 1972; Kassinger, 1972; Shanahan, 1974; Powell, 1981). The basic idea is that the attitudes that students form through contact with school police are attitudes they will take with them into society. Hence, university law enforcement can teach by example what good effective law enforcement is and have a major positive impact on the image of police officers students take with them into the community. The educational function was never mentioned by any officer during the course of data collection.

[9]Salaries at DTU at the time of the study ranged from $11,481 to $18,500, which although comparable to regular police far exceeded that of private security in the area.

[10]Theoretically and practically the principle distinction between security officers and police officers lies in the realm of the legal bases for enforcement actions. In contrast to police, security officers usually possess no more arrest powers than that of a citizen (Braun and Lee, 1971; Scott and McPherson, 1971; Steinberg, 1972; Calder, 1974; Kakalik and Wildhorn, 1977; Post and Kinsbury, 1977; Draper, 1978; O'Toole, 1978). In other words, they have no more power to control the behavior of others than the ordinary citizen.
Uniquely the state legislation from which the DTU officer derives his or her authority gives him or her police authority no matter what s/he is officially called internally, be it policeman or security guard. Thus, according to existing state law the use of the term security or police is merely a matter of terminology--the title has nothing to do with authority, jurisdiction or powers of arrest. Most DTU policemen are unaware of this unique feature of the law and consequently see law as providing a major distinction between themselves and security officers.

[11]It is worthy of note that the desire to identify with police is so strong among university officers that many of the officers who stated that their actual work was more security related added that if the researcher should divulge their answer to any co-worker they would deny it.

¹²Interestingly for all nine items (items 6, 7, 10, 14, 16, 17, 23, 29 and 31) in which a consensus of at least "preferably should do" was not reached, there exists a formal or informal norm mitigating action. For example, there is a department policy against assisting students and faculty in jump starting their cars (item 16); the officers' mandate includes enforcement of state law only and jay walking is a violation of city ordinance (item 14); fraternity and sorority row, parking areas and the cafeteria are privately leased areas which fall outside the university policeman's responsibility unless a definite complaint involving law violation is lodged (items 6 and 10); turning off lights in academic buildings (item 17) irritates custodial clean-up crews and hence does not enhance good community relations; and so on.

CHAPTER V

NATURE OF EVERYDAY POLICE WORK

Every occupation has certain general features or characteristics that pervade the day-to-day work of role incumbents. In the present chapter the characteristics of university police work are explored. Attention is focused on variety in tasks, danger, unpredictability, routine and boredom, scrutiny level, walking and stress. Additionally, patterns of solidarity among university officers are discussed.

Characteristics of Police Work

Variety of Tasks

Like all police, university police perform a variety of tasks on a routine basis. As noted above, they perform a number of law enforcement activities including directing traffic, patrolling buildings and grounds, searching people for library materials, issuing tickets, investigating suspicious people, making arrests, and so forth. In addition, they perform a number of non-police duties or service functions including lost and found, lockups and openings, paramedical services, safety services, bank escorts, car escorts, information provision, and so forth. In reality, much of university police work on an everyday basis involves duties of a perfunctory, low level, clerical, security and service nature. Stated differently, most of what university police do is not related to criminal behavior. Like their municipal counterparts, in many ways university police are more of a service organization than a law enforcement organization (see, for example, Cumming et al., 1965; Wilson, 1968; Bercal, 1970; Reiss, 1971; Webster, 1973).

Despite the fact that university officers routinely perform a variety of tasks on an everyday basis, many officers do not perceive variety to be a feature of their work. Each officer was asked his or her opinion on the following statement: "There is a lot of variety in my work." A majority (58%) of the

155

uniformed officers disagreed. This lack of perception of variety in work is probably due to the fact that while officers perform a number of different tasks daily they essentially perform the same tasks everyday. As tasks become routine they lose their "variety value." Hence, the more routine the job becomes to the officer the less likely s/he is to perceive variety in his or her work. The following officer comment is illustrative:

> After you have been here awhile every task becomes about the same...they all sort of blend in. You may do a lot of different things when you come to work each day but it doesn't seem that way. Everything becomes routine and it seems like you don't ever get to do anything new or have any variety.

Within most occupations some tasks and activities are regarded as more essential, worthy, fundamental or rewarding than other tasks and activities. Of all the tasks university officers are required to perform, security-related tasks are the most disliked among officers. While no clear task preference was discernable among officers a clear non-preference did emerge. Each uniformed patrolman was presented with five tasks (patrol, traffic direction and control, investigation, assisting people, security) which s/he routinely performs on a daily basis and asked to rank them in terms of personal preference. Sixty-three percent of the patrolmen ranked security activites (e.g., lockups and openings, safety and fire checks, stationary posts, and so forth) last and an additional 24 percent ranked them next to last. In other words, 87 percent of the patrolmen indicated that security activities were among the tasks they least like to perform. Perhaps the reason officers prefer other duties to security duties is the low prestige and lack of challenge associated with security work. Unlike their municipal counterparts who view service work (e.g., dealing with the dead, insane, ill and vice-ridden) as "dirty work" (see, for example, Westley, 1970; Rubinstein, 1973; Van Maanen, 1978b; Davis, 1979), university police see security work as the dirty part of their trade. To most officers security work is menial, inglorious, degrading and generally beneath one's dignity. It is "knit shit work" that should not have to be performed by "policemen" because it is not real police work. The most disliked of all security tasks are stationary posts. While officers recognize that the major purpose of these posts is deterrence, most feel that they waste their skills standing, for example, in front of the art gallery, the computer center or the DTU president's office. Like his or her municipal counterpart, the university officer's reward for doing work s/he considers dirty is little more than the renewal of his or her right to continue his or her job.

Despite the fact that university officers disdain security tasks and are required to perform them on a daily basis, most officers recognize their general value. Each officer of the uniformed patrol was asked the following question: "Are there any tasks you perform on a daily basis which you consider to be unnecessary?" Over 73 percent (73.8%) of the officers responded in the negative. Thus, it would appear that while security tasks are the most disliked they are apparently also considered necessary.[1] Security tasks as well as other tasks officers perform are of value.

Danger

Of the major writers on urban police all agree that police work in the field is frightening because danger lurks unpredictably in every encounter (Banton, 1964; Skolnick, 1966; Niederhoffer, 1967; Wilson, 1968; Whittemore, 1969). Municipal officers need to be alert constantly to the possibility of danger (e.g., assault by a citizen) and oftentimes they are required to become involved in real situations of danger in their work. While municipal officers are preoccupied with the possibility of danger, in their everyday work danger rarely bcomes an objective reality. Nevertheless, relative to many other occupations police work is dangerous work (Tauber, 1967; Cardarelli, 1968).

University police work at DTU is even less dangerous than municipal police work. University officers do not work in a setting characterized by a high degree of crime of a violent or personal nature or a "hostile public out to do in cops." Rarely are they called upon to become involved in situations of danger such as arrests, traffic stops, disputes, and so on. During the three months of data collection no incident was observed that posed a threat to any

157

officer. That there is little danger in university police work is supported by the fact that no officer has ever been killed on duty and only a handful have been injured.2 In short, in their everyday work university officers are not routinely subjected to imminent possibilities of personal injury, death or taking another's life. Officers are aware of this fact and consequently most do not perceive their everyday work as dangerous work. Comments such as "here you don't have to put your life on the line every minute" or "let's put it this way...I don't have to say my prayers before I go to work everyday" were typical among officers.

Despite the fact that university officers rarely encounter danger in their work, most officers believe that there is always a potential for danger. Each uniformed officer was asked his or her opinion on the following statement: "When I am on duty, there is always a potential for danger lurking around every corner." Seventy-six percent of the officers agreed. Comments such as the following were typical among officers:

> You rarely encounter danger here but there is always a potential for danger. There could always be someone out there to take a pot shot at you. It's not likely, but you never know.

> There is always a potential for danger in this work. Like the wrenchman (informal name given by officers to an unknown person suspected of committing many burglaries on campus), if he gets caught he is going to try to get away and that could be dangerous. Nevertheless, you rarely get the adrenalin flowing here.

In short, like their municipal counterparts, most officers feel that a potential for danger is ever-present in their work but it is rarely realized.

In general, among university officers uneasiness with respect to potential danger derives from the contingencies associated with the tasks they are required to perform. Patrol routes are carefully laid out and take officers through danger areas such as boiler rooms, paint rooms, stairways, military arms storage areas, and kiln oven rooms. Searches of

158

buildings are conducted in enclosed spaces where con-
cealment is possible. There is always the possibility of being struck by a car while on traffic duty.
Searches of suspects involve an element of danger
because the human factor renders them unpredictable.
While theoretically there are numerous contingencies
of work that result in a sense of potential danger
among university officers, in reality these contingencies rarely materialize into actual danger in university police work.   In short, danger is not an
everyday fact of life in university police work.

    While there are few dangers in university
policing, there is a tendency among university
officers not to become involved in those that do
exist. Though officers are occupationally expected
and required to become involved in situations of
danger that an ordinary citizen might avoid, many
university officers did not appear to be committed
enough to their organization or occupation to be
willing to share the risks of police work. An example
from field observation is illustrative:

> One day on routine patrol of a secured
> building an officer stepped off the elevator
> on the top floor and heard a loud noise
> similar to someone breaking in a door coming
> from down the hall. Immediately the officer
> got back in the elevator, rode to the ground
> floor and proceeded with patrol. At no time
> during the round did the officer return to
> the floor where the noise came from. The
> officer remarked: "It's probably a burglar
> but hell you can replace a machine...you
> can't replace me."

The comments of several other patrolmen support the
notion that there is a tendency among university
officers not to be willing to assume the risks of
university police work:

> I wouldn't risk my life to protect that junk
> we are supposed to guard in the art gallery.
> If anyone came in to rip it off, I'd tell
> them to be my guest and I'd stand aside.
> There is no reason to get yourself killed or
> hurt for the sake of this job.

> If there was a report of a physical fight
> and I was called to respond I would take the

long way around to get there...then they are
too tired to punch you out or resist you
when you arrive.

Lack of willingness to share the risks of police work
suggests that many university officers may in reality
be unaggressive in looking for work (action) while on
patrol.

One major consequence of the lack of danger in
university police work is a tendency among university
officers to not be preoccupied with danger, that is,
to accept everything as routine, relax and develop a
lackadaisical attitude.   The following officer
comments are illustrative:

Since it is not really dangerous here, an
officer can get too routine as far as
expecting something and this leads to his
not being prepared when something does
happen. One of these days someone is going
to get blown away because they take it for
granted that nothing will happen.

There is some potential for danger here but
there is little chance of it. This leads us
to be overconfident because we don't think
anything will happen. Consequently we have
a definite tendency to become lax.

As officers become lax they increase the potential
for harm to themselves. In other words, the lack of
danger in university police work might serve in the
long run to increase the potential for danger to the
university officer.

Unpredictability

Most DTU officers perceive university police work
as unpredictable work. Each patrolman was asked his
or her opinion on the following statement: "When I
begin each day on the job I can always predict what
kind of things are going to happen that day."
Seventy percent of the patrolmen disagreed. The
following comment is representative of officer attitudes:

In this business you never know what will
happen. While our work is only occasionally

160

dangerous it is definitely always
unpredictable.

To the university officer unpredictability in work
stems from three major sources. First, university
police, like all police, deal with a public which
cannot be screened prior to contact. The human
factor renders campus policework unpredictable.
Second, officers are told anew everyday where they
will work. Since assignments and zones vary daily,
officers are never sure what they will encounter
before they come to work. Finally, while officers
may understand what they are likely to be doing when
they go to work, they have little control over what
they may actually be called on to do. They may be
asked to do anything from making an arrest to
checking on an overflowing commode.

Routine and Boredom

Most jobs involve a day-in and day-out routine
that in one way or another is seen to accomplish some
end. University police work like all other police
work is no different. The university work setting
encourages repetitive, routine patterns of work
behavior. Patterned walking of patrols to detect unsecured doors, over-heated coffee pots, unauthorized
persons, and other safety and security problems requires great attention to detail and slow-paced
diligence. Much of university police work is very
routine and menial in nature. On an everyday basis
it is not action oriented, exciting nor intellect-
ually stimulating and interesting. As one officer
noted:

> Much of police work is menial no matter
> where you do it, but it is particularly
> menial here. There is just something about
> shaking door knobs and opening and closing
> doors everyday that just doesn't turn people
> on. Most anybody could do this job...even
> my two-year-old daughter.

Often officers spend long hours, sometimes even
weeks, between incidents that may break the day-in
and day-out routine of their work. As another
officer commented:

> This job is mostly a wait and see type job.

> It is kind of like being a fireman...waiting
> for something to happen...except even fire-
> men get more action than we do.

In short, the job of university police work is frequently routine, occasionally boring and noticeably
lacking in challenge, especially for the educated.

Each uniformed line officer was questioned about
his or her perception of university police work
utilizing the following question: "Do you find your
job to be routine and boring?" Thirty-six percent of
the uniformed officers said yes it is both, 30 percent indicated the job is routine but not boring and
34 percent said they find their job to be neither
routine nor boring. The data in Table 5 suggest that
officer attitudes vary with position in the organization. Examination of this table reveals that
patrolmen are far more likely to find their work
routine and boring than supervisors. Perhaps the
difference can be explained by the higher degree and
amount of control supervisors exercise over their own
everyday work. The following comments are
illustrative:

> As a lowly patrolman I have no control over
> what I do. Supervisors make the assignments
> and I do what they say. Patrolmen aren't
> given much responsibility and they follow a
> pretty definite routine.

> As a supervisor I can make my job what I
> want it to be. Therefore it is always
> interesting. If I get tired of doing one
> thing I can always do another. It's pretty
> much my choice and I can break the monotony.

The data in Table 5 also suggest that for patrolmen the job is definitely routine but not necessarily
boring. Seventy-six percent of the patrolmen implied
in one way or another that their job was routine
while at the same time 60 percent implied that it was
not boring. Comments such as the following were
typical among officers:

> Even though this job is routine there are a
> lot of little things that crop up to keep it
> from becoming boring. Besides, seeing and
> meeting people breaks the boredom.

TABLE 5

UNIVERSITY OFFICERS' JOB ATTITUDES
WITH RESPECT TO ROUTINE AND BOREDOM (PERCENTAGES)

Group	Routine and Boring	Routine but not Boring	Neither Routine or Boring
All line personnel	36	30	34
Patrolmen only	40	36	24
Supervisors only	12		88

> Here we do the same thing everyday. It is
> like working on an assembly line with a
> machine. It is the same thing everyday
> unless there is a little break in the
> machine...like a Peeping Tom. We get enough
> breaks in the machine to keep it from being
> too boring.

Most officers seem to write off daily routine as
"part of the job" and ignore it. The following
comment is representative of officer feelings:

> This tends to be a routine and mundane job.
> Patrol work is very routine in nature. But
> it's not so different from many other jobs.
> Most any job can be routine...even being
> president of a corporation. You just sort
> of accept it and forget about it. You can't
> do anything about the routine because there
> are just certain things you are required to
> do.

In contrast to their lack of control of routine in
their job, most university officers feel that they
can control to a certain degree the boredom inherent
in their work and thus render their job less boring.
There seems to be an attitude among officers that
"boredom is what you make it." Consequently officers
have devised numerous ways to cope with boredom on
the job. Basic to many boredom control techniques is
the attempt by officers to occupy their minds with

163

other thoughts, for example, girl watching, reading bulletin boards, playing games with themselves or other officers in their zones. The following comments of several officers are illustrative:

> This job is routine but not boring because I am a certified girl watcher. There are a lot of good lookers around here and I watch them to cope with boredom.

> I just try to entertain myself. I read bulletin boards and see what is going on. Sometimes I play little games when I go into a dark area. Like I'll shine my flashlight in and say "OK, you might as well come out...I know you're in there cause I can smell your breath." I know I am only joking but it's kind of fun. I'd probably die if someone did come out.

Oftentimes officers will make boredom bearable by thinking of their job as only temporary or thinking of the tasks they perform as necessary. Another technique used by officers to cope with boredom is to merely discipline one's mind that boredom is part of the job and accept it.

In addition to these techniques, the organization of work also helps to break the routine and boredom associated with university police work. Officers routinely perform a variety of tasks daily--doing different things breaks the monotony. Furthermore, officers are assigned to work different areas on different days (zonally rotated) and consequently they see different people and different things going on.

Scrutiny Level

By the nature of their job, university officers operate on duty under a microscope and in a fishbowl. Officers are highly visible and in close contact with the public on a routine basis. Further they are easily identified and set apart from the rest of the campus community by their uniforms. Stated differently, the eyes of the public are always on university officers. The fact that officers are highly visible makes it difficult for them to avoid public scrutiny and complaint. When interviewed, 74 percent of the patrolmen agreed with the statement: "On the job it is difficult to lay low and avoid getting into trouble because the eyes of the university community (students, faculty, staff) are always upon me."

Most officers believe that they work in a "tattle-tale environment"--an environment in which community members will complain to police department administrators if they feel officers are not meeting their work expectations. These work expectations of the community do not include any suggestion that an officer is avoiding work or goofing off. The following officer comment is representative:

> Complaints about goofing off come from all sources. Community members, especially faculty and staff, are constantly calling the Chief and complaining about this and that. Like they will call up and say they saw an officer sitting down or reading a book on duty. What they don't understand is that we do take breaks and eat just like normal people. They think we are goofing off when we are not.

To avoid complaints that officers are goofing off, DTU policemen are subservient to a number of departmental rules and regulations designed to manage the appearance that officers are working hard. For example, officers are prohibited from reading newspapers or other printed material on duty and they are prohibited from fraternizing with community members except in an official capacity. Perhaps the best example of the Department's attempts to avoid misperceptions by the public is found in the policy with respect to breaks. Usually no more than two or three officers are allowed to take a break in the same place at the same time. On numerous occasions officers were observed being denied a break at a requested location because two other officers were already there. Although they see the need for it, most officers dislike this policy, feeling that it is isolating and precludes the opportunity to get to know and strengthen their ties with coworkers. The following officer comment was representative:

> No more than two or three officers are allowed to eat in the same place at the same time because it would look to the public like we were sitting around having a bull

165

session. People don't realize that we are
human and have to eat too. Further they
don't realize that when we break we like to
spend time with and get to know our coworkers just like they do. But you can't do
that here. It might look like you are
goofing off. There are a lot of things we
can't do just because somebody might get the
wrong idea and complain. It's hard to be in
the public eye all the time.

Walking

Walking is the most fundamental part of university police work. As one officer noted: "Except for
forty-five minutes worth of breaks on each tour of
duty, foot patrolmen are expected to be on their feet
constantly moving." Thus, much of the physical
fatigue associated with university police work
derives from walking a beat with few breaks. While
most officers indicated that over time one eventually
gets used to the walking they also recognized that
their feet are a more fundamental tool of their job
than any of their other equipment. The following
comment was typical among officers:

You've got to have good feet to do this job.
If your feet fall down...you ain't got no
job. So I take care of my feet. I pamper
them. They are the tools of my trade. Your
feet are more important around here than
your gun. You use your feet eight hours a
day but you never use your gun.

While they do spend the majority of their work
time on their feet, in reality most university
officers do not spend all of their duty tour on their
feet. In working certain zones officers may be
formally assigned to a stationary sitting post for an
hour or so, thus enabling them to officially "get off
their feet" for a period of time during their tour of
duty. In addition to the formally prescribed sitting
posts, officers have developed certain accepted
informal ways to "beat the system" which requires
them to be on their feet.

The most common way of beating the system is to
turn the informal norms regarding time spent in a
building to one's advantage. It should take a

166

certain amount of time to patrol different buildings.
These amounts of time are informally understood by
both patrolmen and supervisors. If a patrolman
violates these norms of time, s/he leaves the
impression that s/he is not doing his or her job
properly. For example, if it takes an officer longer
to patrol a building than the norm suggests, it
appears to supervisors that s/he must be "goofing
off"; conversely, if s/he finishes a building much
earlier than expected, it appears that s/he has not
done his or her job thoroughly. In order to avoid
such impressions officers use the time norms to their
advantage. If an officer is exceeding the time norms
s/he may cease patrol and call-in claiming s/he has
completed patrol when in fact s/he has not; if s/he
finishes patrol early s/he may "hang around and rest"
before calling in and beginning his or her next
patrol. The latter use of time norms is perfectly
acceptable to the work group as a means of beating
the system and provides the officer with some time
off his or her feet if so desired. However, the
former use of time norms is unacceptable to patrolmen
and is thought to be a misuse of the system. Accept-
ability of time norm use appears to be related to the
degree to which the use implies avoidance of work.
Delay of call-in is acceptable if one has completed
his or her work. Reporting that a round has been
completed when in fact it has not is unacceptable
because one is not completing his or her work. The
following comments were typical among officers:

> If you pull your weight and do your job and
> you can still find time to relax, then it is
> okay to delay a call-in and take a rest.
> However, if you are really just avoiding
> work, then it is not okay. Then you are
> just abusing the system.

> Some days you are pretty much on the go and
> other days you can find time to relax. As
> long as you do what you are supposed to do,
> it is all right to take a little unreported
> break here and there. But it is not all
> right to say you've done something when you
> haven't. That's abuse of the system not use
> of the system.

On numerous occasions patrolmen were observed "using"
the system and on several occasions they were
observed "abusing" the system.

Most officers feel that those who continuously abuse the system will eventually get caught. At the same time, however, they believe that if one is clever enough s/he can delay getting caught and avoid being put on report if s/he is caught. To avoid potential negative sanction, patrolmen have devised a number of techniques. The following officer comments are illustrative:

> If you're smart enough you can usually find two or three hours to sit during your watch... especially on weekends and after hours when there are not as many people around to get you in trouble. There are a lot of places you can go to get away with it...for example, lounges and utility rooms.

> If you are lounging you can avoid getting in trouble by having an excuse ready. Once after hours I was sitting down and I heard a door open and someone coming. So I began huffing and puffing. Sure enough it was my sergeant. When the sergeant asked me what was wrong I said I'd been chasing a suspicious person all over and couldn't catch him. I guess the sergeant believed me because I didn't get written up. You need to have a lot of excuses on hand because if you use the same one too often supervisors become suspicious and then they don't ever believe you.

> You can always go to a utility room to sit down. If you do, you better damn well be sure you have an excuse if you get caught. Claiming you don't feel well pretty much always works. There are ways to get around the system and relax but eventually you gotta figure you are laying your ass bare, particularly if you are abusing the system just to avoid work.

It would appear from the foregoing discussion that university officers accept a certain amount of "goofing off" as long as the job gets done. The secret of the successful goof off appears to be related to the clever use of informal time norms, laying low from the public and supervisors, and having a reasonable excuse in case one gets caught.

Discretion

Police work is often described in the literature as one of the few jobs anywhere that offers as much discretionary power accompanied by so little supervision (Banton, 1964; LaFave, 1965; Skolnick, 1966; Black and Reiss, 1967; Buckner, 1967; Petersen, 1968; Wilson, 1968; Reiss, 1971; Lundman, 1980). Most police operations are portrayed as atomized with weak supervision on a routine basis, thus, enabling discretion to be greatest at the lowest levels. As noted previously, while supervision is probably greater at DTU than in most municipal departments, operations are still atomized. Hence, like their municipal counterparts, university patrolmen exercise a great deal of discretion on a routine basis.

There are, however, a number of factors at DTU which limit the discretion of the university officer. First, there are a number of formal and informal policy guidelines which have filtered down from the university administration which inhibit the exercise of discretion or set the limits within which an officer can exercise discretion. The administrative influence on discretion is found in many policies including avoidance of issuing parking tickets, sobering up a drunk faculty member, overlooking student pranks, and so forth. The fact that these policies have in effect become work norms among university officers is supported by observation. Although several situations covered by policy were observed, in no case did the officer involved act in variance with policy. (See Chapter 6 for a more detailed discussion.) Second, informal work group norms guide behavior and influence the exercise of discretion. For example, as discussed earlier, the informal norm with respect to the issuance of a ticket if a person fails to comply with an officer's order exerts a strong pressure upon the officer to issue that ticket no matter what his or her personal preference. Third, the fact that university officers are reactively mobilized renders many decisions at the discretion of the victim rather than the officer. In terms of the influence of formal and informal guidelines and reactivity on the exercise of discretion, university officers are not so different from their municipal counterparts (Black and Reiss, 1967; Buckner, 1967; Petersen, 1968; Wilson, 1968; Gardiner, 1969; Lundman, 1974; Black, 1978).

However, there is one factor present in university police work that is not present in municipal police work that in effect usurps much of the university officer's discretion: university patrolmen are given little decision-making responsibility of their own whenever an incident occurs or "something serious comes down." They are bound by department policy to inform a supervisor, who in turn appears on the scene and assumes all decision-making responsibility. Officers are not expected to take law enforcement action without checking with a supervisor. This situation is probably best illustrated by department policy with respect to arrests. At DTU there is a perceived policy against solo arrests. While officers do retain the right of individual arrest there is strong pressure from the police administration for them not to make a solo arrest unless they are absolutely sure of their action and its consequences. As noted previously, most university officers (especially those who have not been to the academy) believe they are inadequately prepared to handle such situations. Because of departmental pressures and their own uncertainties, university patrolmen virtually always check with a supervisor before making an arrest. The ultimate decision to arrest is then made at the discretion of the supervisor and not the officer. Thus, patrolmen, to a certain extent, lack discretion in arrests.

University officers are expected to check with a supervisor whenever they take action. Each uniformed patrolman was asked to agree or disagree with the following statement: "Whenever I am unsure what action to take in a situation, I always check with my supervisor." An overwhelming 86 percent of the patrolmen agreed. In reality officers are encouraged not only to check with a supervisor when they are unsure what action to take, but whenever they take any action. There is far more emphasis placed upon supervisor decision-making than officer decision-making at the university. Thus, supervisors in essence usurp much of the officers' authority on a routine basis. This results in a feeling among officers that they lack freedom of thought in their work. The following comments were typical among officers:

> They want a supervisor to direct your every move. For example, if I see a suspicious person, rather than do the wrong thing they

would rather I do nothing. As a matter of
fact you can't do anything around here
unless you check with a supervisor and by
that time it is probably too late anyway.

There is no freedom to make decisions here.
You have to check with a supervisor for
everything...for example, writing a parking
ticket, towing away a car, arresting
someone, etc. Sometimes I feel like they
expect me to ask for permission to go to the
bathroom because I'm incapable of making the
decision on my own.

The fact that they are not allowed to make
decisions on their own is a prime source of discontentment among university officers. Patrolmen view
their lack of freedom of thought as usurping their
authority, reducing their self-respect and confidence
in their ability to do their job, and decreasing
their satisfaction with their job. The following
comments were typical among officers:

We're supposed to be police officers but we
can't function as one. You are not given
any freedom to use your own judgment. You
can't make an arrest without a supervisor.
You practically need a supervisor if someone
falls down. It is degrading not to be
allowed to make decisions on your own.

Officers become dissatisfied with this job
because they feel like their hands are tied.
After the academy you know your job but you
still lack freedom of judgment in your job.
You're not allowed to do things on your own
without checking with a supervisor. Your
authority to act is taken away by supervisors because they are the only ones around
here who have any decision-making responsibility. Everyone wants to feel like they
are capable of making decisions, but you are
not given an opportunity to do that here.

Stress

Police work is generally portrayed in the literature as a high stress occupation (Kroes et al.,
1974; Kroes, 1976; Reiser, 1976; Stratton, 1978;

Wallace, 1978). This stress may be seen as deriving from many sources including lack of respect and support in the community, poor training, inadequate incentives for good performance, lack of promotional opportunities, ineffective utilization of officers' abilities, lack of communication with supervisors, shiftwork, demand for handling dangerous situations, responsibility for people, being an authority symbol and thus a target for resentment, negative effect of police work on the officer's home life, and so forth.

While DTU officers are subject to many of the same pressures as their municipal counterparts, most university police officers do not view university police work as a high stress occupation. Each uniformed officer was asked his or her opinion on the following statement: "I feel tense and under pressure during duty hours." Seventy-six percent of the officers disagreed. Moreover, 86 percent of the officers disagreed with the statement: "My home life has been made difficult by the annoyances, irritations and aggravations which are a hangover from my job." Perhaps the relative lack of stress in university policing in comparison to municipal policing is best explained by differences in the nature of work. For example, as previously noted, university police are rarely confronted with dangerous situations. Furthermore, they do not have to bear the brunt of a day-to-day grind of harrassment and insult like their municipal counterparts. Each uniformed line officer was asked to agree or disagree with the following statement: "A large percentage of my contacts with the public when I am on duty are of an unpleasant nature." An overwhelming 88 percent of the officers disagreed. In short, while university and municipal police have certain stressors in common, the nature of university police work itself is not generally stressful.

The situations which seem to bother university officers the most are those which threaten their positive self-image. Situations which threaten the officer's self-image include verbal abuse while directing traffic, questioning of police authority, demeaning treatment by supervisors, and so forth. These situations are usually sporadic and of temporary duration. Consequently, while officers may be subjected to periods of stress, stress is not an all pervasive feature of everyday university police work.

Solidarity[3]

A number of scholars have commented on the high degree of solidarity and cohesion existent in municipal police work (see, for example, Banton, 1964; Skolnick, 1966; Buckner, 1967; Petersen, 1968; Wilson, 1968; Westley, 1970). In general a high degree of solidarity among officers is not characteristic of university police work at DTU. However, there is some evidence to suggest a minimal degree of solidarity among patrolmen. Previous research on the municipal police has documented that the maintenance of secrecy is a fundamental rule of policing (Westley, 1970). To determine if a norm of secrecy had any significance for the campus police officer, each uniformed patrolman was presented with seven violations of departmental rules and regulations and was then asked the following question: "If you saw a fellow officer doing this on duty would you report him or her to your supervisor?" A summary of patrolmen responses is presented in Table 6. It would appear from examination of this table that, like their municipal counterparts (Buckner, 1967; Wilson, 1968; Bittner, 1970; Westley, 1956, 1970; Rubinstein, 1973), university officers are likely to keep their mouth shut and not inform on a fellow officer, that is, they are not likely to report their coworkers for infractions of departmental rules. In fact of all the departmental infractions asked about in interviews, the only one for which a majority of the officers indicated they would report a fellow officer was for drinking. Fifty-six percent of the officers indicated they would report a fellow officer for drinking on the job because such action would render him or her dysfunctional if s/he were needed. The following comments were typical among officers:

> I'm more concerned about drinking than the other infractions because drinking will make the officer incompetent and if I needed him I would be in trouble.

> I'd report another officer for drinking or if he was spaced out on anything because that stuff affects his senses and reduces his responses enough so he wouldn't be able to help me if I needed him. I'd report another officer if his actions might affect my safety.

173

TABLE 6

REPORTING OF COWORKERS' RULE
INFRACTIONS (PERCENTAGES)

Infraction	Yes	No
1. Sleeping	8	92
2. Drinking	56	44
3. Fraternizing	2	98
4. Reading a newspaper		100
5. Lounging in an office after normal working hours	5	95
6. Swearing on duty		100
7. Leaning against a building		100

In short, patrolmen are not likely to report their coworkers to supervisors unless the coworker's actions are in some way serious enough to affect his or her ability to perform his or her function properly when needed. However, many officers did indicate that they would report a fellow officer for less serious violations of department rules if the infractions were continued. The following comment was typical among officers:

> If I saw another officer breaking a rule I'd talk to him about it. Then if it continued and became habit forming I would report him. However, normally I would not report him if it happened only once or twice.

Informal norms against reporting fellow officers are apparently not based so much on loyalty to coworkers as they are on self-protection. Most officers do not report fellow officers out of fear that such reporting will eventually "come back on them." The following comments were representative:

> I never report anyone for anything because
> in the long run it will haunt you. If you
> rat on your fellow workers they lose your
> trust and then they are out to get you.
> Everyone violates some rule at some time.
> If you don't rat on others, they don't rat
> on you.

> It's not in my job description to report
> other officers when they break rules. It's
> the supervisors' job to catch officers
> committing offenses. It's not up to me to
> report fellow officers. We need to work
> together and that would create a bad
> atmosphere and he would try to get back at
> you. If he is a repeater he will be found
> out by a supervisor eventually.

The data suggest that what solidarity does exist
among university patrolmen may be based upon self-
protection rather than a deep bond among coworkers.

Most patrolmen do not believe that there is a
strong sense of brotherhood pervasive throughout the
force. As noted previously, officers feel that
supervisors not only fail to back them but actively
work against them; the administration of the department is perceived as always backing supervisors but
never officers. Essentially two consequences derive
from the break between supervisors and subordinates.
First, patrolmen do not subscribe to a subjective
feeling of belongingness or "weness" with the force
in the sense of "we police versus you public."
Second, patrolmen do feel a modicum of solidarity
with other patrolmen. The sense of belongingness
derives from "us officers versus you supervisors."
Most officers will go out of their way to avoid other
officers who are believed to be "supervisor stoolies"
and to support those officers who are in the same lot
as they. While officers will not help supervisors by
reporting their fellow officers, they will occasionally help each other--to cover each other's mistakes.
For example, if an officer comes across a gate that
should have been locked earlier by a coworker, s/he
may cover for his or her coworker by locking the gate
that is unlocked and not reporting it to Operations.
Or if a patrolman is assigned as dispatcher for the
day, s/he may cover for a fellow officer who forgets
to do a radio check by marking it down as if it were
done. One deciding factor in whether one patrolman

will cover for another is friendship. Officers will usually cover for their friends but not necessarily cover for other coworkers. For example, during the course of data collection the same dispatcher was observed covering for one officer and not for another though both officers had failed to make a radio check--one officer was a friend and the other was not.

In short, while officers do not report fellow officers for minor rule infractions and occasionally cover for each other, there does not appear to be a strong sense of solidarity or brotherhood among university policemen as a whole. What little sense of "weness" does exist derives more from the supervisor-subordinate rift and personal friendship than from a more general, deep loyalty to coworkers.

Research on municipal police indicates that most of their closest friends come from and leisure time is spent with other members of the force. University police are not as clannish as their municipal counterparts. When university officers were asked to indicate the occupations of their three closest friends, 86 percent of the sample said that no other university policemen were among them. In addition, 74 percent of the sample indicated that no regular police were among their closest friends. Each officer was questioned about the degree to which s/he socializes with coworkers utilizing the following question: "Approximately what proportion of your off-duty leisure time do you spend with people from work?" Seventy percent of the sample indicated they spend none of their off-duty time with other members of the force and another 26 percent said "just a little." Stated differently, 96 percent of the sample never or rarely socialize with coworkers off duty. When off-duty associations do occur they are usually associations by rank, that is, supervisors with supervisors and officers with officers. Rarely, if ever, do supervisors associate with officers. The lack of association during leisure time among university police lends further support to the idea that there is a low degree of solidarity among them.

The police literature generally identifies the high degree of solidarity among municipal police as deriving from the nature of police work--danger, perception of the public as hostile, isolation due to authority, and so forth (Banton, 1964; Skolnick;

1966; Buckner, 1967; Petersen, 1968; Alex, 1969; Rubinstein, 1973). Perhaps the reason solidarity is not strong among university officers is because these factors do not exist at the same level in university police work. University policemen do not perceive the public as hostile. University police work is not dangerous and hence it does not require trust and dependability to the same degree as municipal police work on a daily basis. Finally, the university policeman is not socially isolated from the community because of his authority. In fact, most community members are unaware of the legal authority officers do have. Furthermore, officer capacity to use force does not lead to isolation because it is rarely used. Eighty-six percent of the sample indicated that they had never pulled their weapon in the performance of their duty at the university. Of those who had pulled their weapon, 72 percent indicated that they had only pulled it once since they joined the force and 86 percent said they had never fired their weapon though they had pulled it. The data suggest that university officers do not use force very often and consequently their capacity to use force is not isolating. Moreover, university policemen are not isolated from the community in the sense that many officers are student members of the community which they are trying to police. Among patrolmen 24 percent were currently attending classes at the time of data collection and an additional 28 percent were planning to resume their studies within two quarters. In short, many university policemen are in fact students themselves.

Several other factors mitigate solidarity among university policemen. First, patrolmen work alone instead of with a partner or under a buddy system. Consequently, they do not learn to work as a team and cliques are less likely to develop. Furthermore, because they are isolated from each other there is less chance that expectations of others will influence their work. In fact 95 percent of the patrolmen indicated that their own expectations have the greatest influence on their work in carrying out their duties rather than the expectations of other members of the force, their supervisors or community members. Second, the nature of actual work activity does not call for colleague support on an everyday basis. It does not, for example, take two or more officers to lock/unlock a door, to escort a student to a car, and so on. Moreover, as noted previously, officers are rarely called upon to become involved in situations of danger (e.g., fights, arrests) and they do not work in an environment characterized by violence and personal hostility. Third, the work environment does not encourage a high degree of solidarity among university officers. There is no place where officers gather before, during or after their watch to socialize or hang out. Furthermore, there is no private lounge where officers can go on breaks to avoid public scrutiny. Consequently, officers are constantly in the public eye on their tour of duty and the emphasis on image within the department precludes getting together in public and getting to know each other. Finally, because of the high turnover of personnel most officers do not have an opportunity to get to know each other and it is difficult to build up more comradeship among them.

In short, university police do not display the same degree of solidarity as their municipal counterparts. While university officers will occasionally cover for each other, they are far less clannish and less likely to socialize with their coworkers than municipal police. The nature of the work environment at the university does not encourage a high degree of solidarity among officers.

Notes

[1]Of the approximately 27 percent of the officers who indicated they did perform unnecessary tasks on a daily basis, all indicated security related tasks (especially stationary posts) as the most unnecessary.

[2]It is noteworthy that most injuries are minor and brought on by the officer's own carelessness (e.g., getting a finger stuck in a door, burning one's arm on a coffee pot, and so on).

[3]This section does not concern corruption among campus police, although a number of students of municipal policing have examined police deviance and corruption from a subcultural perspective as a group phenomena reflecting solidarity (Skolnick, 1966; Neiderhoffer, 1967; Stoddard, 1968; Westley, 1970;

178

Barker and Roebuck, 1973; Sherman, 1974; Manning, 1977). All police officers encounter opportunities for misconduct (corruption) in the course of their work and, like their municipal counterparts, campus police do engage in some forms of misconduct that are routinely accepted by the work group. DTU officers were, for example, observed engaging in minor deviant activities such as accepting free or discount meals, transportation, and so on. During the period of study, however, we found <u>no</u> evidence of serious organizational deviance such as that identified among municipal police--extortion, bribery, shakedown practices, premeditated theft, and so on (Barker and Roebuck, 1973; Sherman, 1974; Lundman, 1980). We are not unmindful of the difficulties involved in the empirical study of corruption and recognize that it is a type of behavior that those engaged in have a vested interest in concealing from others (including researchers). Nonetheless, we would argue that while opportunities for corruption do exist in the campus environment, they are much more limited due to the structure of the community (Sherman, 1974). In other words, the nature of the campus environment directly affects the extent of corruption among university police.

CHAPTER VI

CRIME AND THE NATURE OF LAW ENFORCEMENT

The university today is a large and complex
community in and of itself, functioning within the
laws of the larger community. Conceptually the university may be viewed as a city within a city. Like
the larger city, the university is not a community of
shared values, culture or a single philosophy nor is
it composed of a single homogeneous population. Like
the larger city, the university is not a haven but a
problem-laden municipality; it is faced with "real
world problems"--economic problems, problems with
political effectiveness and problems of crime and
traffic which are often similar to and as serious as
those of the city. In fact, the problem of escalating
crime on college and university campuses has been
identified in several sources as the major challenge
to campus police departments today (Abramson, 1974;
Powell, 1981; Newsweek, 1982; U.S. News and World
Report, 1982). Like their municipal counterparts it
is a basic function of the campus police to deal with
those problems related to crime.

Crime problems on campus are universal (Bartram
and Smith, 1969; Adams and Rogers, 1971; Nielsen,
1971; Gelber, 1972; Scott, 1976). An annual summary
of reported crime at DTU from 1978 through 1981 is
presented in Table 7. A cursory examination of this
table suggests two things. First, crime does exist
on campus and it must be contended with. Crime is a
fact everywhere and the campus is no different. In
other words, the statistical data show that there is
a need for police action on campus. Second, many of
the crime problems faced by the university are common
to urban areas. The university is like a city as far
as crime is concerned; it experiences many of the
problems of the city. Stated differently, campus
police are confronted with many of the same problems
as municipal agencies.

If one assumes that the university is essentially
a microcosm of society with respect to crime, then
one would expect that the police function on campus
would be the same as that in society in general. In

181

this chapter the extent to which this assumption holds true is examined through a detailed analysis of the nature of crime at the university, basic strategies of crime control, and, finally, the nature of law enforcement on campus.

Nature of Crime

Analysis of Official Statistics

Departmental records with respect to criminal incidents are compiled monthly by the staff records officer using the categories of the FBI Uniform Crime Reports (see Table 7). Before useful interpretation of these official statistics can be made, some knowledge of the way in which the statistics are compiled is necessary. There are several unique features of the DTU records which bear on interpretation. First, like all official police statistics the DTU statistics are largely based on crimes reported to the university police or crimes known to police. Because many crimes go unreported or undetected the statistics do not represent the total volume of crime at the university. In fact since they are based on reported rather than actual crime, the figures in Table 7 are undoubtedly an underestimate of the extent of crime. Nevertheless, there is no way to know the true total volume of crime through an examination of official statistics. Second, in contrast to municipal departments that only report information for Part II offenses for crimes cleared by arrest, the DTU records reflect crimes known to the police. Like the statistics for Part I the statistics for Part II offenses in Table 7 reflect offenses reported to the university police and not just arrest information.

Third, in contrast to other police the DTU police record all incidents reported to them whether they find evidence that a crime has occurred or not. An incident becomes an official statistic as soon as a complaint is made. Stated differently, officers have little discretion in the field in deciding whether to file a report. Moreover, once a report is taken it is always classified. Hence, police-citizen interaction is a less important factor in determining what goes into the official statistics at DTU than in most municipal departments. Fourth, like all police the university police are largely reactive with res-

182

TABLE 7

ANNUAL SUMMARY OF CRIMINAL INCIDENTS BY TYPE AND NUMBER

Part I Offenses	1978	1979	1980	1981
Forcible rape	2			
Robbery	5	3	3	4
Aggravated assault	2	3	2	2
Burglary	4		1	6
Larceny (Theft by taking)				
DTU property	27	46	56	88
($ Loss)	(11,567)	(7,504)	(11,145)	(18,640)
($ Recovered)	(205)	(2,384)	(306)	(706)
Personal Property	192	156	313	239
($ Loss)	(21,225)	(16,348)	(20,276)	(26,919)
($ Recovered)	(2,872)	(2,815)	(1,577)	(3,462)
Motor vehicle theft		1	1	3
Total Part I Offenses	232	209	376	342

TABLE 7--Continued

Part II Offenses	1978	1979	1980	1981
Other assaults	20	14	13	8
Stolen property laws	1	1	1	
Weapons	1	1		
Sex offenses	10	11	13	17
Narcotic drug laws		1		
Liquor laws			1	
Drunkenness	26	15	5	2
Disorderly conduct	9	9	14	7
Vagrancy	1			
All other offenses	72	67	81	140
Total Part II Offenses	140	119	128	174
TOTAL PARTS I AND II	372	328	504	516
TOTAL NUMBER ARRESTS	10	20	24	14

pect to report taking. The official statistics in each category reflect this reactivity and, hence, are more nearly a measure of the citizen reaction to crime than the actual amount of crime. One exception to this rule is found in the DTU records under Part II Offenses "all other offenses." Detailed examination of departmental records revealed that 62 percent of the incidents in this category involved proactive discovery by officers on routine patrol of evidence that crime may have been committed. In other words, the statistics in the category of "all other offenses" are more than a measure of public reaction to crime; they are also a measure of patrol initiative.

Finally, the amount of crime included in any classification depends not only on whether crime is known but also upon what is included in the definition of the class. The figures in all categories of Table 7 reflect the Department's unique classification scheme. Given the same information, the FBI might not necessarily classify it in the same way. For example, in 1979 the FBI Annual Report showed a total of seven violent crimes at DTU--six robberies and one aggravated assault (McGovern, 1981:41). These figures are not the same as those presented in Table 7.[1] The discrepancy between Departmental records and FBI records is of little concern to university administrators. As one official noted:

> It is not really necessary for us to have
> the proper titles on our incident reports or
> to classify them according to other people's
> standards. The Crime Information Center
> will take care of that when we submit a copy
> of the incident reports. Our records
> reflect our analysis of crime. Though
> standards of classification are roughly the
> same, there are some differences. Our major
> purpose is to report what we have the way we
> see it and not to meet their arbitrary
> classification standards. We primarily keep
> records for internal purposes. Partici-
> pation in the Uniform Crime Reports is not a
> major consideration in the way we keep our
> records.

In sum, the DTU records reflect crimes reported to the police as well as possible crimes discovered by the police. Hence, they reflect more than the public and official reaction to deviance like the records of most departments; they also reflect the official reaction to suspected deviance. However, in no way do the official statistics reflect actual crime. Furthermore, while the Department uses the same categories as the FBI it does not necessarily classify crime in the same way. Hence, the Department's official statistics reflect the Department's unique perception of crime. With these cautions in mind, what can be said about crime at the university from an analysis of records?

General Features of Crime at DTU[2]

Several general features about crime on campus can be deduced from examination of Table 7. First, with respect to the extent of crime as measured by the records there appears to have been a dramatic increase in serious crime in 1980 and, hence, an increase in the overall incidence of crime on campus. Much of this increase was largely due to an increase in reported larceny. The figures for 1981 suggest that the incidence of reported crime in 1981 was also high. In short, the statistical records suggest that a serious problem facing campus police in the 1980s may be escalating crime.

Second, while the university has experienced most types of serious crime at one point or another[3] the data in Table 7 show that an overwhelming preponderance of crime committed on campus during the last several years was crime committed against property (e.g., theft, larceny, burglary). Crimes against the person were minimal. Furthermore, less than four percent of the serious crimes on campus in each year were violent in nature.[4] This suggests that in the course of their everday work university officers are not likely to encounter serious crimes of a violent or personal nature. All officers are aware that they do not work in a "high action" environment with respect to personal and violent crime. The following officer comments were typical:

> We don't have a lot of violent crime here.
> About the biggest thing that has happened in
> the last ten years has been two rapes.
> We've never had a homicide, and aggravated
> assaults and robberies are few and far
> between. Our biggest problem daily is

dealing with theft of property.

We don't have much violent crime but the
potential does exist. Nobody has ever tried
to rip off the ROTC armory or money escorts
but they could. I just can't figure out why
no one has ever tried to rip off a bank
escort, especially during registration when
we have lots of money and only one officer
and a messenger walk to the bank. We make
three or four trips a day with hundreds of
thousands of dollars at a clip. I guess
we've really been lucky that we get little
action of a serious nature on a routine
basis.

Major Types of Crime

There are essentially three major types of crime
at DTU: theft by taking, sex offenses and criminal
trespass. The former is blatantly apparent from
examination of Table 7; the latter two types are
subtly hidden within the official statistics as presented in Table 7.

Theft by taking

Many items of value that one may wish to steal
are, of course, found on any campus. DTU is no
exception. Larceny is by far the major crime on
campus. Of the total 1,720 cases reflected in
Table 7, over 64 percent (64.9%) were cases of
larceny. Essentially there are two types of larceny
on campus--thefts of university property and thefts
of personal property.5 In an average year the
reported incidence of and loss from the latter far
exceed the former. Given the amount recovered in
each type it would appear that the university police
are not very successful in solving many of these
cases.

College property

With respect to thefts of college property,
common targets appear to be audio-visual equipment
(e.g., tape recorders, radios, movie projectors, and
so forth) and other equipment (e.g., typewriters)

that are easily fenced or sold. While a number of procedures have been implemented to reduce theft of college property (e.g., serial identification of items, office machine locking devices including bolts for typewriters) the police role in controlling theft of college property is complicated by two factors. First, the university does not fix responsibility for lost items. Hence, authorized users tend to disregard storage of property in the proper place, and the university absorbs the loss without repercussion to the negligent. Second, because many items of value are not used on a daily basis, sometimes weeks or months can go by before authorized users even know the item is missing and this reduces the opportunity for recovery.

Personal property

Thefts of personal property usually involve the taking of purses, wallets, small equipment (e.g., hand calculators), textbooks and other such items which are left unattended and unsecured in the library, offices, lounges, restrooms and classrooms. Most university officers believe that many of the personal thefts could be avoided if people were more conscious about security. In fact, officers informally refer to this type of crime as "theft by opportunity" or "theft by neglect." The following comments were typical among officers:

> The principal target of any criminal is the place or person which permits the opportunity for theft. People per se make our job harder by neglect themselves. It if wasn't for their stupidity and carelessness we wouldn't have all these thefts. The best protector of any property is the owner of that property. If he leaves it lying around he is creating the opportunity to get ripped off. A secretary who leaves her purse in an open desk is just asking for trouble.

> People themselves provide the opportunity for theft by their own negligence. People leave their gear all over the place and expect it to be there when they return. You can't leave your wallet or purse on a desk and go search for a book in the library and expect it to be there when you return. We

188

can saturate the whole area but the game is still lost because people don't accept responsibility for their own belongings.

In-depth analysis of the theft by taking incident reports for 1981 supported the officers' belief in "theft by opportunity." Of 327 incidents, 215 could not have occurred except for personal negligence. In other words, 66 percent (65.7%) of the thefts by taking involved an element of blatant opportunity.

The neglect factor involved in many personal thefts has tended to make many officers skeptical of some of the reports they receive. The following comment of one officer is illustrative:

I get a big charge out of some of these reports of stolen purses. They say they had a diamond ring, a gold watch and $250 in cash in their purse when it was stolen. Well, what the hell are they doing with that here? Better yet, what the hell did they leave it lying around for so it could be lifted? We have to write it down as they tell us, but who is going to believe it? Not me.

Sex offenses

A second major type of crime found at the university is sex offenses. While only seventeen sex offenses are officially reported in Table 7 for 1981, detailed examination of incident reports suggested that a number of the crimes listed elsewhere have significant sexual overtones. For example, one of the aggravated assaults involved a man preparing to attack sexually a female in a restroom, and five of the incidents classified as "other assaults" involved men grabbing womens' buttocks. While a total of twenty-three sexually related incidents is not quantitatively overwhelming, it is substantively significant given the few incidents in most other categories.

There are essentially three kinds of sex-related offenses that occur on campus. Informally they are referred to among officers as indecent exposure, unsolicited contacts and Peeping Toms. Indecent exposure incidents include such things as a man

189

walking around in a classroom building hallway or in the library exposing his sexual organ or masturbating in front of others.6 As one officer phrased it, "we have a lot of guys shaking their wand around here." Unsolicited contacts include such things as grabbing a woman's buttocks or some other part of her anatomy and attempting to "cop a feel" as she walks by. Peeping Tom incidents usually involve a man lying on the floor, especially in the library, and attempting to look up a woman's dress. Based on their experience most officers believe that the library is the most likely place for many of these sexual incidents to occur. In fact, the library patrol is informally referred to by officers as the "pervert patrol." The following comments were typical among officers:

> The library...you never know what you will find when you go through there...people looking up dresses, playing with themselves or with someone else. There are a lot of little cubby holes there that seem to call the perverts out.

> The library is a popular place for wierdos to harrass females. Females are the targets of exhibitionists and molesters because all the shelves of books tend to isolate people. There are a lot of nooks and crannies in the library which wierdos can run to once they have performed their dastardly deeds. The library is a haven for sexual perverts.

Criminal trespass

The third major type of crime at the university is also buried in the official statistics presented in Table 7. Examination of the incident reports for 1981 revealed that out of 140 incidents classified as "other offenses," 110 or 79 percent (78.6%) were labeled "criminal trespass." There are essentially two meanings to criminal trespass reflected in the records. First, criminal trespass includes those cases in which a patrolman on his or her routine rounds discovers signs of forced entry into an office or vending machine but is unsure if something has been stolen. Second, criminal trespass includes those cases in which an unauthorized person (e.g., a derelict asleep on a loading dock, a drunk who wandered on campus, a non-student hustler in the

190

gameroom, a person living out of a locker in the gym, and so forth) is found on campus, read the criminal trespass warning and escorted off campus.7 Since 82 of the 110 reports of criminal trespass involved the former meaning, it would appear that forced entry is a formidable problem on campus. Of these 82 cases, 68 or 83 percent (82.9%) were cases involving wrench marks or broken knobs on office doors which were discovered by officers on routine patrol. If the officers had been sure that something was missing from the offices, these cases would more appropriately have been classified as burglaries. The fact that the modus operandus is the same in all these cases--wrench marks on doors causing the breaking of knobs--has led many officers to believe that their most formidable challenge is to catch a single perpetrator who is informally referred to as "the wrenchman" or "Mr. Goodwrench." Most officers further believe that the wrenchman must be an insider. The following comment was typical among officers:

> Mr. Goodwrench is our biggest problem. We
> haven't been able to catch him even though
> we have had some overtime stakeouts. His
> breakins must be an inside job. He just
> knows our routine too well...lots of times
> he hits while the shifts are changing.

The Who, When and Where of Crime

Who is committing crimes

Since few crimes are actually solved (e.g., cleared by arrest) at the university, it is impossible to know from objective review of the records exactly who is committing those crimes. As one officer noted:

> There really is no sure way to know who is
> committing crimes on campus. We have such
> an open campus that it could be anyone. If
> you don't catch them you can't know who is
> doing it.

Of those cases that have been solved, the arrest reports suggest that "off campus persons" present the most formidable problems. Of the fourteen arrests made during 1981 all involved unauthorized persons. The problem, of course, is that arrest records are

191

not a valid measure of who is committing crimes but merely a measure of who is committing that gets caught and/or who gets caught that is arrested.

There is no clear belief among officers as to who is committing crimes. Each uniformed line officer was asked his or her opinion on the following statement: "Most crimes on campus are committed by outsiders (unauthorized persons)." Forty-eight percent of the officers agreed, 24 percent remained neutral and 28 percent disagreed. This finding suggests that university officers see both unauthorized as well as authorized personnel as responsible for crime on campus. In short, they believe that the campus is not immune from criminal activities from within as well as from its surroundings.

When type of crime is taken into consideration, a clearer pattern of belief is evident among officers. Most officers believe that many of the sex crimes are committed by outsiders, but many of the thefts and burglaries are from within. The following comments are illustrative:

> Most freaky crimes are committed by outsiders, but we are beginning to realize that all these thefts, especially the burglaries and break ins are not from the outside. The wrenchman has to be an insider. He just knows too much about our operation. That's how he avoids getting caught.

> A lot of stuff that happens around here has to be an inside job. For example, in the records department by the registrar's office no one is allowed in there except those who work there. If an odd man was in they would notice. Therefore, if something is stolen it has to be an inside job.

In short, the campus is vulnerable to attack from within as well as from without. However, no one knows for sure who is committing crime on campus.

When crimes occur

The data in Table 8 suggest that most crimes on campus occur on the day and evening watches, that is, between 7 A.M. and 11 P.M. This is not surprising

192

because it is during these hours that the campus is most open and accessible to all persons. Someone walking out of an office with a briefcase or small calculator would not appear out of place, for example.

TABLE 8

CRIMINAL INCIDENTS BY WATCHES

Watch	1978	1979	1980	1981	Totals
Morning (11pm-7am)	25	10	10	17	62
Day (7am-3pm)	146	147	218	234	745
Evening (3pm-11pm)	143	130	217	216	706
Unknown*	58	41	59	49	207
TOTALS	372	328	504	516	1,720

*Time frame such that occurrence during any particular watch cannot be determined.

Officers believe that the reason fewer incidents occur on the morning watch is because there are fewer people around and the buildings are more secure. Hence, there is less opportunity to commit a crime and a perpetrator would be more easily seen. They also account for less crime over weekends and during quarter breaks in the same manner. The following comment of one line officer is representative of officer beliefs about when crime occurs on campus:

> Nothing much happens on the morning watch because it would be too obvious if someone was carrying something around. Weekends are the same on all watches and nothing much happens between quarters. Even the wrench-man lays low. Most crime happens Monday through Friday on the day and evening

watches. Most of the break ins of offices
occur on the evening watch from 6 P.M. until
about 10 P.M. During this time there are
still enough people around so the thief does
not look out of the ordinary carrying a
machine around. Also the offices are closed
and therefore they are more vulnerable.

Where crime occurs

Official departmental records indicate that crime
occurs in virtually every area of campus--offices,
classrooms, restrooms, study areas, hallways, parking
areas, the Student Center, the gameroom, and so
forth. Virtually no part of campus is immune from
possible criminal activity. However, by far the most
frequent building in which crime occurs is the
library. Of the 1,720 total criminal incidents which
took place from 1978 through 1981, 361 or
approximately 21 percent (20.9%) occurred in the
library. Given the numerous other buildings on
campus this is quite a significant figure; no other
building even approached these figures. The library
appears to be a haven for sexual offenders and a
fertile location for sneak thieves who steal hand-
bags, clothing and other personal property while
owners are studying, searching for a book or otherwise occupied. In other words, sexual offenses of
one sort or another and thefts of personal property
are common in the library.8 Most officers believe
that the library is one of the "hottest areas on
campus." The following comment was typical among
officers:

> The library is our biggest problem area. A
> lot of different things come down in
> there...people rip other people off,
> undesirables wander in and fall asleep,
> couples make out passionately, guys play
> with themselves and grab women, people try
> to steal library materials, etc. It is
> really a hot action area. If we didn't have
> all the problems in the library we could
> probably reduce our crime by 90 percent.

Arrests

Arrest procedures are the same at DTU as they are

elsewhere: a suspect is read his rights, arrested, mugged, fingerprinted, taken to jail and booked. Usually the suspect is photographed and fingerprinted at the university by a supervisor or the staff investigator and since the university has no detention facility of its own, the suspect is taken to a local county jail and booked.

The data in Table 7 indicate that few crimes at the university are cleared by arrest.9 Of the total number of criminal incidents in 1978, 1979, 1980 and 1981 only 2.7 percent, 6.1 percent, 4.8 percent and 2.7 percent, respectively, were cleared by arrest. Relative to reported criminal incidents few arrests are made.10 Moreover, the low volume of arrests is reflected in the university officers' routine work. When questioned about their arrest activity, 60 percent of the patrolmen specifically indicated that they had never made an arrest in the performance of their duty at the university. This would suggest that arrest is definitely not a feature of the university officer's everyday work. In addition, many university officers feel that it is a waste of time and money to arrest someone for a misdemeanor and, hence, they try to avoid making such an arrest. The following comment is representative:

> Most misdemeanor cases are disposed of in
> twenty seconds in court. Usually when you
> arrest someone for a misdemeanor he gets a
> slap on the wrist and the judge lets him go.
> So it really doesn't do much good to arrest
> someone. It's a waste of time. The whole
> thing costs more than it is worth (e.g.,
> court costs, officer's time). It's a lot of
> hassle for nothing. So I would try not to
> arrest someone for a misdemeanor unless they
> leave me no other choice.

Despite this feeling among officers concerning the futility of misdemeanor arrests, examination of the arrest records suggests that a substantial majority of all university police arrests are for misdemeanors. Of the fourteen arrests made during 1981, eleven or 79 percent (78.6%) were for misdemeanors (i.e., five criminal trespass, four theft by taking, one simple assault and one public indecency). Of the three felony arrests two were for aggravated assault and one was for criminal damage to property. The data not only suggest that more misdemeanors are

195

cleared by arrest than felonies, but also with respect to Part I Offenses university officers are no different than their municipal counterparts, that is, they clear by arrest more crimes against person than property (see, for example, Reid, 1982).

Volume of Crime and Performance

While there is crime on campus that needs to be controlled on an everyday routine basis, there is little call for law enforcement per se. In fact based on the figures in Table 7 the average number of criminal incidents occurring on campus per day is only 1.2. Furthermore, the chance for any given officer to be involved in that incident is miniscule. Consequently, in the performance of his or her routine patrol work there are likely to be large lulls in an officer's law enforcement activity which can extend to weeks and months at a time. Officers tend to cope with this lack of law enforcement activity in their routine work by remembering that they are there to take action should it be necessary and that their presence is important for crime prevention.

The lack of a high volume of law enforcement activity has several important consequences for the university officer in his or her routine work. First, as previously noted, during prolonged periods of order maintenance and service oriented policing the officer's ability to remain alert becomes problematic. Since little ever happens, officers tend to expect nothing to happen, they relax and develop a lackadaisical attitude. Hence, one result of this inactivity is that they may increase the potential danger to themselves. The following comment of a line patrolman is illustrative of this process:

> The first couple of times you go on a money
> escort you are really primed for something
> to happen. You know you're carrying a lot
> of money and everyone you pass on the street
> is after that money. You are really alert.
> After a couple of times out you begin to
> realize that nothing ever happens so you
> start to relax. It all becomes routine.
> You quit looking for that guy who is going
> to run you down for the money. You get
> sloppy and lay yourself open to attack.

Another consequence of the quantity of law enforcement calls being at a minimum is that officers become "rusty" and the quality of their law enforcement performance when necessary may not meet community expectations. Stated differently, in coping with crimes in progress officers may turn in incompetent performances because of a lack of routine experience. Several "performance" incidents as relayed by officers are illustrative:

One day a guy followed a woman into a restroom in the library. She screamed and he left. As he was running out of the library he was pursued by an officer who called for backup. The guy jumped into his car and was attempting to leave the parking area when an officer on a 3-wheeled scooter tried to block his exit. The suspect ran over him and totalled the scooter. By this time other officers had arrived on the scene. They unholstered and fired nine shots. None of which even hit the car. The guy got away. Fortunately one officer got his license number and we later arrested him at his home in a neighboring county. Later in court the guy acted as his own defense attorney and tore our officer apart on the stand because the officer's testimony about what the guy was wearing was different from the report. The case was thrown out.

One evening an off duty county officer saw a car in a DTU parking lot that had a bolo (formal report of theft) on it. The officer parked his car at the rear of the stolen vehicle and called Operations to check it out. We did on the CIC (Crime Information Center) machine and sure enough it was listed as stolen. My god, this was the real thing. We dispatched two officers to the scene and when they arrived one officer went to the stolen vehicle and the other went to get information from the complainant (who was standing by his car at the rear of the stolen vehicle). As they were trying to sort things out, the suspect jumped in the stolen car and drove away. We let it slip through our fingers. The Chief's only comment when he saw the report was "INEPT."

University police are not necessarily always incompetent in the performance of their duty with respect to crimes in progress. In fact examples of efficient performance could also be provided. However, the point to be made is not how efficient or how incompetent university officers are; rather it is to suggest that low-volume law enforcement activity may have some effect on quality of law enforcement performance.

Strategies of Control

Since crime exists on campus it must be controlled. The strategies of control at the university are largely oriented toward prevention rather than law enforcement. In other words, the emphasis is not placed on policing (i.e., controlling) the campus body per se but on protecting the general public of the institution from criminal activity (as well as other hazards). In the performance of their preventive role university police try to be as proactive as possible. Underlying all strategies of control is the belief that prevention is not just the responsibility of the police but of the entire community and prevention programs can only be as effective as the community wants them to be. Comments such as the following were typical among officers:

> We get blamed for everything that happens around here. Not all of it is our fault. The university community is responsible for a lot that happens because of their carelessness and neglect. Much crime on campus could be eliminated if the community would be more aware of their responsibility and quit blaming us for everything.

There are three basic crime control strategies employed at DTU: operational, crime prevention programs, and restriction of access to campus.

Operational

As previously described, the basic operational strategy used by the Department to control crime is to deploy manpower in such a way that an effective deterrent patrol is created. Beat officers are assigned to zones and expected to keep constantly moving (unless assigned to a stationary post) and highly visible at all times while patrolling both the interior and exterior of buildings. Conspicuously marked mobile units patrol the perimeter of campus, making continuous loops around campus on adjacent streets. University police view a highly visible patrol as having a significant deterrent effect on crime--being seen by those who might be contemplating criminal acts deters those acts and, hence, reduces crime. In addition to patrol, occasional special details are deployed to control crime.

Crime Prevention Programs

Given the belief that much crime at the university is a result of opportunity rather than careful and professional planning, it follows that one way to cut crime is to eliminate or reduce those opportunities. Hence, the university police offer an on-going crime prevention program largely designed to identify risks and mobilize persons to take action to minimize risks. Like all prevention programs the university program is based on the idea that protection of personal and university property must be a cooperative effort between the police and the university community. As such, much of any crime prevention program is geared toward educating the community to be security conscious. There are four aspects to the DTU formal crime prevention program: operation identification, premise surveys, provision of general information to the university community, and a self-protection program. The latter is aimed at protection from bodily injury; the former three are primarily aimed at theft control.

Operation identification is an anti-theft program designed to deter burglary on campus and, failing that, to aid police in determining ownership of recovered and stolen property. As a service to the community the DTU Police Department offers free of charge the electronic engraving equipment necessary to permanently mark the owner's movable property with an identifying number (preferably the owner's social security number). The very fact that items are marked is seen as a deterrent to the potential thief. Unfortunately as one staff officer indicated, "not many community members have availed themselves of the identification service."

Premise surveys are conducted by the staff crime prevention officer upon request by a community member. Essentially a premise survey is a security analysis of an existing facility at a specific location on campus (e.g., psychology lab, student accounts area, business offices, physical education building, and so forth). The basic purpose of the analysis is to point out existing physical and procedural security deficiencies in and around the facility and to suggest courses of action to correct problems. Like operation identification, premise surveys are wholly a function of a single staff officer; line patrolmen have no involvement with either of these two programs.

The third major aspect of the university crime prevention program is provision of general information to the university community in an attempt to make the community itself more security conscious. For example, warning signs are strategically located in the library providing information as to individual responsibility for personal belongings. It is in the provision of general information to the community that the individual line officer plays a significant role in the department's crime prevention program. If an officer on routine patrol discovers a blatant security violation (e.g., a coffee pot left on after hours, a window left open, an office left unsecured with no signs of forced entry, and so forth), s/he generally corrects the security violation (if possible) and leaves a security advisory notice in the door of the office informing the occupant of the violation. A copy of this notice is forwarded to the staff crime prevention officer. If the violations continue the staff officer writes the violators a letter informing them that they are not complying with university police security requirements. While ideally the leaving of security advisory notices would appear to be an effective means of crime prevention, in reality it is not. There are two reasons for this. First, few community members pay any attention to the security advisory notices they receive. Second, the security advisory report program does not have the full backing of line officers on a routine basis. While on numerous occasions officers were observed leaving a report in situations that warranted it, on numerous other occasions they did not, either because they did not have a report form with them or they considered leaving the report a futile effort. The following comment was typical among officers who fail to participate fully in the security advisory program:

> Leaving those reports does no good. They just pile up and nothing ever comes of it. I just correct the violation if I can and go on my merry way. If I can't correct it, I report it to Operations so the officer after me will be expecting it.

The lack of attention by community members and the lack of full cooperation of line officers in their everyday work both serve to undercut the potential utility and effectiveness of the security advisory program.

The major thrust of the Department's self-protection program is the provision of a self-protection brochure made available at student orientation and/or the dispensing of information to individuals upon request. Occasionally the staff crime prevention officer participates in lectures and seminars on self-protection and approximately ten times a year the Department (upon request) sponsors these discussions. Individual line officers are rarely involved with this program--it is largely a staff function.

In addition to the formal crime prevention program, on an informal level many university officers will sometimes on their own initiate action to reduce risk and drive home the point that "people themselves are largely responsible when they get ripped off by creating the opportunity to get ripped off." For example, on numerous occasions patrol officers were observed picking up "abandoned" books, purses, briefcases and book satchels in the library and taking them to Operations. When a student would report the loss s/he was directed to Operations and told by a supervisor, "If I had been a thief, you wouldn't be getting this back." Unfortunately, however, the many other demands made upon university officers' time preclude this type of action on a routine basis.

While crime prevention programs are supposed to be proactive, at the university they are more on the order of "we offer the service if you request it." In short, while a formal crime prevention program occasionally supplemented by informal action of line

officers does exist on campus, it is not a well
organized program. Consequently, it is not as
effective as it probably could be, particularly with
respect to enhancing community relations and warding
off potential criminals.11

Access Control

Based on the assumption that outsiders are to
some extent responsible for crime on campus, all
colleges and universities take some measures to
restrict access to campus to authorized persons only.
At DTU these measures include formal procedures such
as key control,12 the posting of signs warning of
unauthorized admittance, the use of photo IDs which
are not worn but rather carried by authorized persons
while on campus, requirements of work permits in
certain buildings after hours, and so forth. The
major responsibility for access control, however,
falls to the uniformed patrolman in the performance
of his or her everyday duty. This job is complicated
by several factors. First, because of its location
in a downtown urban area, DTU does not lead a
cloistered existence removed from the outside
community. In fact the university is so much a part
of the community that it is hard to tell where the
campus leaves off and the city begins. Access to
campus is geographically unrestricted. As a result,
the campus is virtually open to anyone who wants to
enter it.

Second, the nature of the university community
itself makes it difficult for officers to keep
unauthorized persons off campus. The university
community is composed of all types of people of
various shapes, sizes, descriptions and appearances.
On any given day dress varies from three-piece suits
or business dresses with heels to shorts with tennis
shoes and no socks or halter tops and jeans. Consequently, there are few cues on the basis of physical appearance which the university officer can use
to differentiate publics (authorized from unauthorized); in the university environment university officers are unable to routinely use an incongruity
procedure like their municipal counterparts (see
Sacks, 1971). With the exception of subteens and
drunks or derelicts who are so obviously intoxicated
and/or indigent as to make an officer automatically
question their authorization to be on campus

virtually anyone, including thieves, burglars, hustlers, drug pushers and other undesirables can blend in and wander on campus unnoticed and unquestioned.

Finally, the university officer is limited in his or her ability to control access to campus by policy. Although most crimes on campus occur on weekdays between 7 A.M. and 11 P.M., policy with respect to access to the campus is very lenient during normal working hours. The officers' main routine duty during these hours is to keep the easily identified contingent of drunks and derelicts who congregate on the periphery of the campus from wandering on campus to seek shelter or a handout. In all other cases officers are instructed against indiscriminately requesting identification from people on campus because it might appear to be harrassment. Thus, in the course of their routine work officers do not just decide to make an ID check on their own; the decision is oftentimes made by someone else (e.g., director of physical education, gameroom attendant, and so forth) and the officer merely goes along to maintain order. Such a policy allows for little initiative on the part of the individual officer in controlling access. Consequently, officers usually wait for an incident to occur before they request an ID from anyone in the performance of their routine duty during normal working hours.

Access policy is stricter after hours, on weekends and holidays. All authorized personnel are required to have a valid ID and/or work permit to enter a secured area; officers are obliged to check for proper authorization of anyone they encounter in a secured area or who requests permission to enter a secured area, particularly if they are unknown to the officer. The normal procedure for handling an "encounter case" after hours or on weekends in a secured building is to report the case's name and room number to Operations so a police log can be kept of who is in what building and where they are in the building. Most officers routinely adhere to this after-hours policy as much for their own protection as for the protection of university property. The following comment was typical among officers:

> You never know what people are doing in a
> secured building. They could be there
> working or to rip the place off. So you

really need to check them out. You can get in a lot of trouble if you don't. If the officer coming along after you checks someone out, finds he has been there a long time and reports it to Operations, it looks like you haven't done your job. It's your ass that is on the line and supervisors come down hard on you. So I check everyone out after hours except the cleaning crew whose faces I mostly know.

Given the geographic location of DTU, the nature of the university community and the lenient access policy during normal working hours, DTU is virtually an open campus. The fact that the campus is so open presents a major problem to university police--it makes it practically impossible to keep all unauthorized people off campus. Most officers feel a major problem of policing at the university is access control and, thus, keeping unauthorized people off campus. The following comments were typical among officers:

This is really an easy campus. People are here all hours of the day and night and it is hard to know who is supposed to be here. After you've been here awhile you get to know some faces but you never get to know them all. Our job would be much easier if we had a stricter policy on accessibility.

Our biggest problem here is that we have such an open campus that it is hard to keep unauthorized people off. In fact it is so open that we have found a number of people actually living on campus. We caught one guy living out of a locker in the gym. And there was a derelict who was living in a crawlspace in one of the buildings. We never caught him but we know someone was there because we found bedding, a bunch of wine bottles and cans of food in there. People pretty much come and go as they please around here. Who knows how many others are living here.

Drunks and derelicts

Patrolmen were often observed escorting drunks

204

and derelicts off campus. Such people present a
formidable problem to the DTU police largely because
on the perimeter of campus are numerous abandoned
warehouses, pawn shops and cheap bars. Furthermore,
the university is located only two blocks away from
the city jail. When the drunk tank releases detainees
every morning at eight, offenders often walk the few
blocks to the campus to look for a place to "sleep it
off" (e.g., stairwells at parking decks, warm areas
inside buildings, shaded areas beside buildings, and
so forth). University officers attempt to keep these
"undesirables" off campus more so that they will not
harrass students and faculty, as well as for esthetic
and safety reasons, rather than for the potential for
crime that they represent. The following comments
were typical among officers:

> We occasionally get a drunk sun bathing on
> an adjacent street with his member hanging
> out. Believe me it ain't no beauty to
> behold. It just doesn't look good so we run
> him off.

> These guys try to make it to a safe area on
> campus when they're let out of the city
> tank, but lots of them don't. You find them
> half sprawled in the street and half on the
> sidewalk. If you leave them there they are
> gonna get run over. Part of the reason we
> get drunks off campus is for their own
> protection.

> If you let these drunks and derelicts stay
> on campus they are going to harrass people.
> They're not going to hurt anybody or rob
> them or anything like that but they're going
> to beg for money and handouts. So we
> station men around the perimeter of campus
> to run them off so they don't bother
> students. If I see one begging for money on
> campus I tell him that I'm working this side
> of the street and for him to go work the
> other (off campus), but not to let me catch
> him back over here.

Nature of Law Enforcement

Autonomy and Authority

As previously noted, legally the DTU Police Department is a separate and autonomous police agency deriving its authority from state legislation. The city police do not exercise jurisdiction over the DTU campus within its limits. Moreover, the university police owe no allegience nor are they responsible to any other police agency.13 Thus, the DTU police are externally autonomous with respect to other agencies.

Internally, within the university the campus police retain a high degree of functional autonomy. No other component of the university organization has the same function. In contrast to earlier years under <u>in loco parentis</u>14 when the role and function of campus law enforcement and the role and function of the Office of the Dean of Student Affairs were synonymous, today campus police operate independently of most other offices and departments within the university. The following officer comments are illustrative:

> When we got rid of <u>in loco parentis</u>, some of the power of the dean was usurped and given to the police. We perform our job autonomously and advise the dean of actions taken whenever a community member is involved. We don't ask his permission to do something.

> The dean doesn't tell us what to do. We inform him of arrests and injuries. We don't ask him what to do and he doesn't tell us. We operate independently of other offices.

Because DTU police are externally and internally autonomous, in the performance of their law enforcement function they are responsible for the enforcement of state laws only, not city ordinances nor university rules and regulations. As one uniformed line officer commented:

> In our job as police we go strictly by the state criminal code. As long as there is no violation of state law, no police action is taken. We're not concerned with university rules and regulations like smoking in class-

rooms and cheating on tests. That's the
responsibility of deans and counselors. If
it ain't against state law it ain't our job
to do nothing about it.

In short, only violations of state law are within the
purview of the university police. In the performance
of the police function, the application of law is
separated from administrative concern with student
conduct and discipline.

In reality, university police are not as autonomous as they would appear. The University Police
Department is an integral, operating component of the
university organization itself. As such it cannot
function independently of the organization it serves.
Hence, the attitude of the administrators of the
organization has a strong bearing on the nature and
degree of law enforcement provided by the police department. Stated differently, since the university
police are not detached from the entity they are
working for, they must be responsive in the performance of their law enforcement function to the
discretion of university administrators. University
administrators do not interfere with the day to day
operations of the police and, thus, the Department
maintains a high degree of functional autonomy. However, the attitudes of administrators tend to become
a matter of police policy and, hence, the Department
lacks policy automony. There are two ways in which
the attitudes and policies of university administrators influence law enforcement on campus. They have
a bearing on which laws are enforced, and against
whom those laws are enforced. In other words, the
lack of policy autonomy among university police is
reflected to a certain extent in selective
enforcement and differential enforcement.

Selective enforcement

The legal system assumes a simple and clear-cut
role for the police: enforce all laws. However,
like their city counterparts, university administrators have influence over what laws are enforced; like
their municipal counterparts, university officers
respond to the desires of the administration. If the
president of DTU were to say "clean up the homo-
sexuals in the bathrooms" the university police would
attempt to do just that.[15] Because of the strong in-

fluence university administrators can exert on police, the campus police may end up enforcing university policy rather than enforcing the law as written. Perhaps the best example of this is in the area of drug violations. Many drugs and narcotics are illegal--the use, possession, supplying or selling is against the law. However, the DTU police basically do not investigate or take any action in regard to possible drug violations unless the violation is flagrant or involves a known major violator. There is a "hands-off policy" that has disseminated down to the line officers from the administration and resulted in an informal work norm stressing that drug violations be ignored, especially when community members are involved. Any type of "crack down" on drug violations would require admission that "DTU has a problem" and, hence, would not look good for the university. The following comment is representative of officers' understanding of drug policy:

> It's hard to enforce drug laws and we're
> really not supposed to. Students openly
> smoke pot around here, especially during
> morning break out on the plaza (a concrete
> courtyard bounded by several major campus
> buildings). If we see it, we ignore it. It
> would really look bad for the university if
> we started arresting a bunch of people for
> pot violations and the press got hold of it.
> It would look like the university is a drug
> center and would probably drive students
> away. We don't have as big a problem with
> drugs as some other schools because our
> population is generally older and we don't
> have any dorms. But there are a lot of drug
> violations which we see and ignore. If we
> see someone openly pushing, we'd pick them
> up. But basically we don't enforce drug
> laws, especially pot laws.

In short, as sworn police officers, university police have a responsibility to enforce all laws but in reality certain informal norms mitigate the enforcement of all laws. The strong influence of administrators on the university police may, in some cases, result in the selective enforcement of some laws.

Differential enforcement

Despite the residual effect of <u>in loco parentis</u> on many campuses today, university officers believe that they should be totally unbiased in the performance of their law enforcement duties. Most university officers firmly believe that a double standard of justice has no place on campus. In other words, they do not believe that university community members should be treated differently from members of the outside community when a law violation occurs. Each uniformed line officer was asked his or her opinion on the following statement: "Students as well as others need to accept responsibility for their actions and suffer the consequences." Almost all (94%) of the uniformed officers agreed. The following comments are representative of officer beliefs:

> With the demise of <u>in loco parentis</u> came equal rights and equal responsibility. Basically we don't treat students differently than others, that is, we do not not arrest them because they are students when they commit a serious crime. Our job is to enforce the law impartially.

> This campus is not a sanctuary. The laws of state are applicable. People can't expect just because they are a student or faculty member that they can break a law and then be excused for it. They are responsible for their actions just like anyone else and if they break a law and get caught they should suffer the consequences just like anyone else. It is our job to enforce the law equally no matter who breaks it.

In short, university officers believe it is their responsibility to ensure the equal application of the law no matter who violates it.

Another way in which administrators' attitudes affect police operations is in the area of disposition of offenders. University administrators assume a proprietary responsibility for institutional members and, thus, encourage a discretionary, non-punitive approach to policing. This attitude, as it disseminates down to the police, results in an informal policy that limits officers' authority. Stated differently, though university officers have full police authority to make arrests and are bound by oath to treat all people alike, there is an informal norm that authority should be exercised with the utmost discretion, particularly with respect to the campus community.

Policy with respect to the handling of student misconduct is illustrative of how administrators' proprietary and discretionary attitudes permeate police operations. At DTU student pranks are not considered crimes—they are handled internally by being referred to the Dean of Students office. It is left to the individual officer to use discretion in determining what a student prank is. If an officer sees a student committing a major offense against the law s/he is arrested. For minor offenses, however, the student is usually referred to the Dean, especially if the offense occurs during fraternity or sorority initiations. There are vestiges of <u>in loco parentis</u> apparent in this policy with regard to student conduct. The comment of one high-ranking official expressed the essence of the policy well:

> You can't make cities and towns out of
> college campuses. In colleges and
> universities you have to temper things. You
> need to adapt to what you are working with.
> There is a gray area as there is elsewhere.
> You have to use discretion. Many law
> infractions of students do not warrant
> arrest. I don't want my son arrested for a
> student prank during fraternity initiation.

In most cases, the officer is not on the scene when a student incident occurs, and hence the officer cannot exercise discretion. Like all police, university police are almost totally reactive with respect to law violations, and the fate of the offender lies primarily at the discretion of the victim, not the officer. If a student is not involved in the incident the victim has two options: s/he can press charges and go to court or s/he can drop charges and forget it. If a student is involved, a third option is added—the victim can inform the Dean of Students and request an internal disciplinary hearing. There is some empirical evidence to suggest that when the victim is an institutional member, there is a tendency to treat students differently from outsiders. During 1981 there were nine attempted thefts of

210

library materials. Four cases involved students and five a non-student. The only incidents for which the Director of the library decided to press charges were four of the non-student thefts. In all cases in which a student was involved, the charges were either dropped or the student was referred to the Dean. This finding is particularly surprising in light of the fact that most officers concur with the observation of one officer who noted that: "The library has been prosecuting most everyone for sometime now."

Students are not the only ones who may be "protected from the law." Faculty and staff members may also be treated differently from outsiders. The comment of one line officer is exemplary:

> There is a tendency here to sweep some campus community member violations under the rug rather than cause embarrassment to the institution or individual. I can give you a lot of examples. Take the case of the plant department employee who when he was hired was broke, but after a short while on the job had $2,000 in the bank. He was fired not arrested. Or take the case of the head of one of the academic departments who was caught embezzling from the university. He was demoted to teacher not arrested. Or like tonight we had a faculty member on campus who was falling down drunk. We gave him a cup of coffee and took him to his office to sleep it off rather than arresting him for public drunkeness even though he created quite a scene.

In short, it would appear that the proprietary attitude of administrators is, to some extent, translated into differential enforcement. A law violator who happens to be a community member may be treated differently from an outsider. This further suggests that instead of a strict law enforcement approach, university police, in certain situations, take a community services approach to policing. Campus police do not appear to be in the business of making criminals out of community members. The informal norm restricting the exercise of authority in cases involving community members may create a real problem for officers. While they are sworn to take action within their jurisdiction by the state who gave them power, they are also in effect ordered by their

211

employer (the university) not to exercise those powers in certain situations. If an officer were to act in those situations, s/he might possibly jeopardize his or her position or subject himself or herself to chastisement for being overzealous. The inconsistency between officers' ideal beliefs about equal treatment of offenders and the everyday reality of differential treatment of community members and outsiders is a major source of frustration to many officers.

Nature of Police Responses

While the campus is at once a microcosm of society in the sense that it is composed of a hetero-geneous group of people and experiences many of the same problems of the larger society, particularly in relation to crime, it is at the same time a unique community with unique requirements of policing on campus. There are essentially two features of the campus community that make it unique. First, the campus community is composed of educated people whose major purpose on campus is not to commit crime but to derive an education or impart an education to those seeking it. Consequently, community members do not expect to be treated as criminals when they come on campus. It is the fundamental responsibility of campus police to maintain a certain ambiance condu-cive to learning. The dilemma posed by this respon-sibility is that it is difficult to maintain the open academic atmosphere of the university if criminal losses and attacks are commonplace and, conversely, the development of a "police state" is equally de-structive to an open learning environment. Second, a campus community is unique because, in general, it objects to the presence of police on the campus. There is a fundamental contradiction between police and education. Universities have always been the hallowed ground of differing opinion, expression and thought. By nature educational institutions are in-terested in the unique, radical, innovative and new as well as the old, traditional and well-established. On the other hand, by nature police have always rep-resented the status quo. To many, the presence of police is an anachronism in the academic community. Police represent restriction, repression and con-trolling but education requires the opposite--openness, freedom, flexibility and an acceptance of innovation.

212

In short, the unique features of the campus environment do not call for a repressive police philosophy but rather they call for a non-repressive law enforcement approach to policing on campus. It is a sociological truism that any organization, in order to survive, must be responsive to the community it serves (see, for example, Parsons, 1951; Katz and Kahn, 1966). This is true of the university as a whole as well as its component parts. Hence, the nature of police responses cannot be divorced from the nature of the community.

In response to the call for a non-repressive approach, campus police operate under an informal policy sanctioned by the administration which emphasizes a non-aggressive, low key law enforcement approach. In other words, university police, in the performance of their everyday work, provide protective and prevention programs as well as control activities in an acceptable, unintrusive and non-repressive manner designed not to interfere with institutional activities. In short, university police are bound by informal norms to temper their authority and to keep a low profile in the performance of their law enforcement function. Several officer comments are representative:

> We try to deal with people in a low tone here. For example, we don't request IDs (identification cards) from more people because they would feel like they are being harrassed. We don't push people around. There is a conscious effort to avoid that here.

> Police work at the university is different than anywhere else because of the type of atmosphere. You can't go around pushing people around. If we approached our work the same way other police do, it would be like a police state here and that is a no no.

> Our job is to look out for the interests of university personnel and not look for more business. Therefore we rarely issue tickets, we don't report accidents unless university personnel are involved and we try to avoid making arrests. Too much of a police philosophy or too much repression

would alienate the campus community.

Officers are indoctrinated in a low key enforcement approach from the first days of employment. In fact, as noted earlier, their entry level training stresses temperance of authority, responsiveness to the community, avoidance of the use of force, and so forth. Furthermore, from the time they first hit the street they become aware that a "gung ho" approach is not likely to bring them reward.

Perhaps the best example of the low tone characteristic of university policing is found in the policy with respect to the actual conduct of making arrests. This policy in essence states that arrests should be as low key as possible. For example, if an arrest is made in the library, the service elevator rather than the customer elevator is used to remove the suspect; if a suspect is cuffed and being escorted through the halls, a coat or some other article is draped over the cuffs; if a suspect is being questioned, s/he is removed from public view before questioning begins. In the performance of their law enforcement duty, officers routinely abide by this policy. In short, officers try to promote an image of restraint in arrests (when they make them) because of the nature of the environment.

Many officers expressed concern over the low key enforcement approach characteristic of campus policing. The reasons behind this concern are essentially two-fold. First, officers suggested that this approach results in an underlying avoidance of police work at the university and, hence, limits their ability to do the job they were hired to do. Not being apprehension-oriented precludes much of the police function and the police officer's inherent responsibility. The following officer comments were typical:

> We don't do police work here...we ignore it.
> We are unable to function as police officers
> in many situations. For example, we are
> discouraged from writing tickets or
> arresting a public drunk who happens to be a
> community member.

> We're certified and sworn and there is no
> excuse for not taking action. We have to
> restrain ourselves because we're not

214

supposed to upset the community. If the
administration wants to run a nursery they
should run one but not use me to do it. The
administration should leave us alone and let
us do the job we are supposedly paid to do.

Second, the prevailing policy creates inconsistencies
for officers in the performance of their everyday
work. Officers are expected to take charge of situations but at the same time temper their authority.
These inconsistencies make it difficult for officers
to know how to act in the performance of their duty.
The following comment of one uniformed officer is
illustrative:

I don't think officers know when to be
aggressive and when not to. Because of the
university environment and the policy of
being low key, officers don't request IDs
(identification cards) or order people
around. Yet if something does happen they
are in trouble for not doing it. There is
no way you can win in this job.

Stated differently, the low key policy puts officers
in somewhat of a double bind.

Notes

[1]The discrepancy in figures is attributable to
the fact that the DTU police department forwards a
copy of the actual incident sheets to the FBI which
in turn compiles its official statistics based on the
actual content of the incident reports rather than
merely the crime classification summary provided by
the Department.

[2]It would be useful to know whether the nature
and extent of crime at DTU differs in any significant
manner from other campuses throughout the nation.
Although crime statistic information on institutions
of higher education is published yearly in the annual
report of the Federal Bureau of Investigation, any
comparison of crime statistics between campuses is
hazardous. This is because the volume and type of
crime are affected by the varying characteristics of

each educational institution, including size, location, nature of the campus community, law enforcement function, and so on. In addition, the extent of coverage of the <u>Uniformed Crime Reports</u> for campuses is relatively poor compared to the data provided by local authorities in the cities, towns, and rural areas in the various states. The annual report includes actual accounts from roughly 250 educational institutions or only about ten percent of the campuses throughout the nation (and these are almost exclusively state institutions).

3The one major exception is homicide. Throughout its history DTU has never had a single homicide.

4All Part I Offenses are considered to be serious crimes. The seven serious crimes or Part I Offenses are divided into two categories: (1) violent crimes including murder, forcible rape, robbery and aggravated assault; and (2) property crimes including burglary, larceny-theft and auto theft.

5The value of DTU property lost and recovered is an estimate based on computer printout of the cost of the item. In contrast, the value amount on personal property lost and recovered is based on estimates by the victims.

6All seventeen incidents classified as sex offenses in 1981 were of this type. They were formally labeled on the incident reports as "public indecency."

7If a person to whom the warning has been given is found on campus at a later date, s/he is usually arrested and charged with criminal trespass.

8Thefts of university property from the library (i.e., library materials) have been reduced significantly in recent years through the use of alarms on each perimeter door and an electronic book detection system at the main entrance. The former alarms limit entry and exit to one main entrance; the latter system detects potential thefts. Sensitive markers are attached to books and when they are not properly checked out or desensitized, the markers trigger locking of the exit gate as one passes through the exitway and an alarm sounds. A student assistant supplements these electronic devices by standing by the gate to prevent would-be thieves from raising

216

their arms with stolen materials to avoid triggering the alarm and to initially control the situation if an alarm does sound. Using these methods the university has significantly reduced its loss from the theft of library materials to the point that it is no longer a major problem.

[9]The lack of investigation and follow-up of cases to a great extent precludes the probability of clearing more cases by arrest.

[10]By comparison, for example, the clearance ratio for index crimes reported by all law enforcement agencies throughout the United States to the Federal Bureau of Investigation in 1980 was 19.0 percent (Federal Bureau of Investigation, 1980).

[11]There are essentially two major benefits of a well organized and determined crime prevention program. First, it spells out to the campus community that university police care, and improves community relations by breeding confidence and support for the campus law enforcement program. Second, an active campus crime prevention program has a spillover effect on off campus elements which see, in such publicized programs, that the campus law enforcement program is not a perfunctory one. Potential law violators see such emphasis as indicating a community sensitive to criminal activity and therefore crime is less likely to be attempted in such an aware community. See, for example, Johnson and Gregory (1971) and Powell (1981).

[12]In contrast to many institutions of higher education, DTU has a rather sophisticated key control program which is coordinated and operated by the university police (Gelber, 1972; Powell, 1981). The comments of one staff officer describe the essential features of this program.

> It is unusual to have key control at a
> school. Most schools have the locksmith
> under the physical plant department and keep
> no records of who gets keys and for what.
> This leads to security problems. Here the
> locksmith works out of the police department
> and we keep extensive records. Some of the
> other outstanding features of our program
> include: each person needs authorization
> for a key, people rarely get keys to

external doors, each department gets a
yearly report on who has keys and for what,
and faculty and staff must clear their keys
before they leave their job. While it is
possible for someone to get out of here
without returning a key, especially student
assistants, at least we know what locks
their keys fit and we can change them if the
situation warrants it. If keys are lost the
locks are not automatically changed. It
depends on what the key is to, where it is
lost and the circumstances of loss. For
example, normally if a key to the military
storage area is lost the lock would be automatically changed, but if it is lost in a
lake by the president of the university,
forget it.

[13]In many institutions campus law enforcement
personnel are deputized by county or city law enforcement agencies. Hence, they are responsible to
those agencies and lack autonomy.

[14]The doctrine of in loco parentis prevailed in
most institutions of higher education from about 1913
to 1961 when it was abolished by the courts in Dixon
V. Alabama State Board of Education (1961). As part
and parcel of this doctrine there was a strong tendency to "protect" students from the law (shelter and
counsel law violators rather than arrest them), pre-
serve the sanctuary concept of the academic community, and place emphasis on "dean power" in the disposition of violation of law through internal administrative measures regardless of contrary constitutional and legal prohibitions. In other words, in
the days of in loco parentis institutions assumed the
posture of a sanctuary in which the laws of the land
were aborted through the application of administrative procedures in contradiction to the laws of
society. With the demise of in loco parentis in
1961, students were granted their constitutional
rights; at the same time they assumed responsibility
for their actions. The "student ward concept" was
replaced on campus by the "student citizen concept."

[15]The university does experience some problem
with homosexuality. In fact selected bathrooms in
several buildings could be considered "tearooms" of
sorts. Homosexuality is not against the law but
sodomy is. It is very difficult to catch people in a

sodomous act and hence it would be difficult for police to "clean up the bathroom" by attempting to enforce the law. The point of argument is, however, not whether the law can be enforced but rather the important influence the administration may have on what laws police attempt to enforce.

CHAPTER VII

CAMPUS POLICING: THE TEMPERENCE OF AUTHORITY

Throughout the course of the preceding pages many comparisons were drawn between campus policing and municipal policing along several broad dimensions of organization and activity. There are numerous similarities and differences between campus and municipal policing that can be identified (an abbreviated summary of the more salient themes is presented in Figure 2). In general, there are several similarities between these two forms of police work. First, campus police share many problems in common with municipal police. By virtue of the university's size, economic importance and urban location, the university police encounter problems similar to those faced in the surrounding jurisdiction (e.g., crime). At the same time, however, campus police typically deal with issues not high on the priority list of municipal departments (e.g., parking problems). Second, the functions and responsibilities of both campus and municipal police are the same. Both campus and municipal peace officers are responsible for enforcement of laws and apprehension of violators, maintenance of order, preservation of human life, protection of property, and provision of services to the community they serve. Finally, the procedures and operations of campus and municipal police are essentially similar. Both types of police work shifts, serve irregular hours, are on call for emergencies, patrol districts, answer calls for assistance, arrest people, investigate vehicle accidents, write traffic citations and take other actions when necessary.

Despite these general similarities between campus and municipal policing, there are two unique qualities about campus policing that render it appreciably different from its municipal counterpart. First, campus police serve a clientele that is demographically different from the general populace served by municipal police. University police function in an artificial and highly structured environment which brings together a particular group of people to work or study in a geographically limited area for a short

221

period of time. This group is composed largely of middle to upper-middle class scholars and students possessing above average intelligence and idealistic motives who come to campus to work or get an education and not to commit crime. This constituent group bears little resemblance to the cross section of society to whom the local police officer is responsible. In their daily work campus police are confronted with educated and professional people, not law violators. Hence, campus police work is less dangerous and less likely to require police action. In contrast to their municipal counterparts campus police do not deal with a multitude of different publics; rather they serve a select clientele.

The second unique quality about campus policing that renders it appreciably different from municipal policing is found in the philosophical orientation to policing. A different philosophy and approach is involved on the part of the campus officer who serves an educational community--the emphasis is not on arrest but on prevention and service. The university campus is a unique place composed of unique people requiring atypical law enforcement in comparison to the usual municipality. These facts call for a non-repressive approach to policing, that is, common-sense, circumspection, gentleness, compassion and understanding. A gung ho, macho, action-oriented approach is seen as having no place on campus. Thus in contrast to their municipal counterparts who are oriented to apprehension, campus police are more oriented to service and prevention--they are more concerned with the maintenance of an atmosphere conducive to learning and the protection of the community from hazards (criminal and non-criminal) than controlling or policing the community per se.

The differences in clientele and philosophy in campus policing present several unique dilemmas for the university officer in the performance of his or her work. First, campus police are supposed to maintain a calm, serene and quiet atmosphere at the university that is conducive to learning, but they must maintain this atmosphere in a manner which is appealing to the university community and within accepted community tolerance levels. Thus, the university officer is placed in a position where s/he must at the same time be omnipresent while maintaining a low profile so as not to "disturb" the tranquil environment sought in academia. Specific-

222

FIGURE 2

COMPARISON OF CAMPUS POLICING AND MUNICIPAL POLICING

Dimension	Campus	Municipal
Organization		
internal structure:	simple bureaucratic with lack of functional specialization at patrol level	elaborate bureaucratic structure with functional specialization and status differentiation on basis of assignment at line level
operations:	work divided into shifts with maximum manpower on weekdays during the day and evening shifts	work divided into shifts with maximum manpower on nights and weekends
role incumbent relations:	neither formal impersonal nor friendly personal	intensely personal among patrolmen; personal between patrolmen and immediate supervisors; impersonal between patrolmen and higher administrative levels
basis of performance appraisal:	personal characteristics and non-law enforcement activity	law enforcement activity and involvement in dramatic aspects of policing
discipline:	formal and informal write-ups common; minor violations not ignored; formal not as strict as could be	formal rare; informal uncommon--strategic leniency is norm (minor violations ignored)

223

FIGURE 2--Continued

Dimension	Campus	Municipal
police command:	operations atomized but less precarious than municipal; greater degree of internal control and supervision because they operate in a geographically confined area and are not as mobile	precarious because operations atomized and cover wide geographic area; lack internal control
public image:	centered on security	centered on crime fighting
Socialization		
selection process:	not protracted	protracted
training:	departmental orientation and on-the-job; attend academy after minimum of 6 months	academy prior to field assignment followed by on-the-job
major theme:	temperance of authority	defensiveness, professionalism and depersonalization; emphasis on hard nosed approach and police philosophy
Role and Function		
duties:	police and non-police; much of routine work custodial, guard, service and security type duties rather than police type duties	police and non-police; much of routine work order maintenance not law enforcement

FIGURE 2--Continued

Dimension	Campus	Municipal
functions:	law enforcement, order maintenance, service and security of buildings; do everything a policeman does plus what a regular security guard has to do	law enforcement, order maintenance, and service
ideological emphasis:	prevention and service	law enforcement
Work Characteristics		
general features:	less dangerous than municipal, unpredictable, routine, and menial, very high level of public scrutiny, emphasis on foot patrol, discretion on routine basis but when an incident occurs emphasis on supervisor decision-making rather than officer, lack of stress	potential danger but not usually objective reality, unpredictable, operate in public eye, emphasis on motor patrol, high degree of discretion, high stress
solidarity:	minimal solidarity	high degree solidarity deriving from nature of work
Enforcement Responses		
nature:	non-aggressive and non-repressive, protecting	aggressive and controlling

225

ally, university officers, in the course of their everyday work, are faced with the contradictory normative expectations of exercising authority and tempering authority. Though the university police system is not geared to manufacture a "take charge guy," officers are expected to use their authority to handle situations but yet not to "throw their weight around." A second dilemma for the university officer resides in the conflict between commonweal interests and proprietary responsibility. On the one hand, as officers of the law, university policemen are ideally expected to enforce all existing rules of law and order on campus. On the other hand, they have a proprietary responsibility for institutional members and property requiring sensitivity to the community being served. The former calls for an unbiased law enforcement approach to campus policing and the latter calls for a conflicting discretionary and parental approach.

These dilemmas create problems for officers in the field in that they make it difficult for them to decide upon the appropriate action to take in varying situations. Officers are often criticized if they make the wrong decision, criticized if they make no decision and seldom praised for a correct decision. Because it is difficult to know how to respond in a university setting, officers will often withdraw from situations in which their authority is questioned and take no action in situations in which their municipal counterparts routinely take action.

Local Context and the Structuring
of Police Response

University police officers work in a unique setting which requires an atypical approach to policing. Both the nature of the academic environment and clientele served call for a non-repressive approach to police work with emphasis on protection of persons and property rather than control of human behavior. University police respond to the unique features of their environment by emphasizing service (helping) and prevention (protection) rather than law enforcement (controlling) in the performance of their everyday duties. Moreover, university police place heavy emphasis upon the temperance of authority in the academic environment. In fact, a "subculture of temperance" may be characteristic of the university police trade. That this subculture of temperance is pervasive in campus police operations and practices is reflected in many features of university policing, including entry level socialization processes, differential enforcement of laws on campus, the failure of officers to exert their authority (take action) in many situations in which their authority is challenged, the emphasis placed on definition of function in terms of service and prevention rather than law enforcement within the Department, the usurpation of officer authority by the emphasis placed on supervisor rather than officer decision-making especially in non-routine enforcement matters, the low-key enforcement approach taken in enforcement, and so on.

The type of community and citizenry served thus have a profound effect on the style of policing. The style exhibited on the DTU campus most closely resembles Wilson's (1968) service style in that emphasis is on the maintenance of order rather than law enforcement; officers are not likely to respond to requests by making arrests and imposing formal sanctions. In addition, leniency is a dominant characteristic of patrol officer work, the pace of work is leisurely, and a high emphasis is placed on public image through keeping men/women and equipment "sharp" at all times.

That policing is responsive to the structure and nature of the environment carries with it certain benefits and costs for the officers performing their work. The benefits of working in a university environment include the relative absence of danger, the rare probability of an adversary relation with the public served, and the fact that officers are not exposed to the seamier side of life. In short, when contrasted with the environment faced by a municipal police officer on a day to day basis, the university environment is a nice place to work.

The costs of working in a campus environment are essentially two-fold. First, university officers are not "real" policemen. Not only are they perceived as security guards rather than policemen by community components, but in their actual everyday work they function more as a security guard than as a policeman. Moreover, much of their training is geared toward making them security guards rather than policemen (i.e., emphasis in training of university

227

officers is placed on such things as locking up or opening doors and the layout of campus buildings rather than the law and the "how to do" of law enforcement). Second, as noted previously, the emphasis upon temperance of authority creates conflicts and uncertainties for officers in the field. As peace officers university police have the power to control the behavior of others; yet they are not supposed to project an air of repression; they are expected to take charge of situations, yet not throw their weight around. In the wake of these inconsistencies it is difficult for officers to know how to act in the performance of their duty. Since officers are expected to temper their authority in routine situations there are few means at their disposal by which they can back up their words with actions. They cannot, for example, resort to violence to establish their authority in an encounter with a citizen as is the case with their urban counterparts.

This examination of university police work suggests that future research on the police should remain sensitized to the notion that differences in police practice may be related to the local context in which the department operates. Police behavior and police administrative styles may vary from one speciality to another and from one setting to another because the social and cultural milieu in which departments are located vary as well as the conduct with which police must cope varies. Stated differently, to understand the nature of policing one must explore a variety of contexts.

Given the exploratory nature of the present investigation, the findings and their implications are bounded only by the sociological imagination of the reader. Perhaps the mark of good research is that while it answers some questions, it suggests many others. It is hoped that the present study provides a groundwork for guiding future research in an area which has only begun to be empirically investigated. Although it is no doubt a trite observation, the need for replication on the nature of campus policing in other college and university settings is paramount (e.g., a non-urban residential campus). Comparative data can only serve to enhance the understanding of campus policing, in particular, and all policing, in general.

APPENDIX A

METHODOLOGICAL NOTES

The nature of this research is exploratory, descriptive and comparative. It is exploratory in that it gains insight and familiarity with the phenomenon of university policing which heretofore has been neglected. It is descriptive in that it identifies the major components, characteristics and problems of university policing as an occupation and organization. Finally, the study is comparative in that it makes systematic and explicit comparisons between the data obtained on university police with the existing body of knowledge on municipal police.

The major thrust of the study was to gain insight into what it is like to be an urban university policeman and to understand the meaning of work and everyday activities to the person performing it, that is, to look at the world of the campus policeman as viewed by him or her. Focus was upon a systematic examination of the commonplace events of everyday behavior and routine work among uniformed patrol officers. In short, the research is a study of men and women at work in which an action perspective, intended to reveal the meaning of work to the men and women performing it, is taken.

The present study utilized a multi-method approach to the investigation of the organization and everyday activities of an urban university police force. Each data collection technique yielded a different "slice of data" (Glaser and Strauss, 1967) or a different vantage point from which to understand the problem under study. In general, it can be assumed that collectively these slices of data yield more information than any single source of data. Moreover, taken together the methods complement each other to maximize the validity of the total methodological effort.

Given the emphasis upon subjective meanings and commonsense understanding along with the exploratory nature of the present research, the major methodological technique employed was that of participant ob-

229

servation. The choice of participant observation as the major method of study was based upon several considerations. First, as a holistic qualitative method, participant observation is suitable for the building of theoretical suppositions. It enables the researcher to dispense with prejudgments about the nature of the problem, to establish specific direction in an ongoing or "in process" manner and to heighten the interplay between observation and analysis. Stated differently, participant observation is sufficiently flexible to permit discovery, exploration and exploitation of the unanticipated as well as the anticipated (see, Glaser and Strauss, 1967; McCall and Simmons, 1969; Lofland, 1971; Bogdan and Taylor, 1975; Selltiz et al., 1976). Second, participant observation as a general research technique aims at understanding human behavior from the actor's own frame of reference. Such understanding can be gained only through inquiries in and of the natural setting of daily life via direct examination of an actual group. In general, it can be assumed that one can <u>know about</u> people and things by mediated means (e.g., television, opinions of others) but one can <u>know</u> only through their direct, face-to-face association with them over time. The participant observer actually experiences the "world of the participant" and hence is able to put the subjective world together in a manner comparable to a regular participant. In addition to identifying recurrent patterns of behavior, participant observation permits the observer to see the world through the eyes of his or her subjects and to determine the meaning of action for the actor. Finally, participant observation enables the researcher to see things inaccessible to outsiders. The researcher's proximity to his or her data allow the investigator to look beyond the facades established for the public and to share the work situation of those being studied. In some instances, participant observation is the only way to obtain data. In short, participant observation was selected as the major method of study because it affords opportunities for insights that cannot be obtained by use of other techniques. In fact, participant observation is the primary means of getting at everyday policing.1

In addition to personal observation, another general technique of data collection was utilized--intensive interviewing. Informal interviews were conducted with all administrative and staff

230

personnel, and formal interviews were conducted with all uniformed line personnel. These interviews were designed to elicit the perceptions and attitudes of officers about their work and the data obtained from them was used to complement data obtained from observation.[2] Supplementing the major methods--observation of and interviews with university policemen--were several complementary methods. These supplemental methods included content analysis of the university newspaper, analysis of departmental documents (including the police manual, training materials, forms, brochures), and the analysis of departmental statistical records.

Data Collection Procedures

In this section information relevant to the collection of data is reported so the reader can understand the full methodology and can assess the validity of findings. Emphasis is placed on the procedures utilized in determining the location of the study and gaining access to it, making observations, conducting interviews, and protecting the anonymity of subjects.

Location

Site selection

The lack of substantive materials and previous research on university police made intensive case study of one department appropriate to gain an understanding of policing in a university environment. The data for the present study were gathered in an investigation of the Downtown University Police Department, which is composed of sixty-one police officers and three civilian employees. DTU is located in the downtown area of a large southeastern city of approximately two million people. Like other large urban centers, the city in which DTU is located has slum areas, a large black population, major traffic conjestion, and a high rate of crime.

The choice of Downtown University as the site for study was based upon a number of factors. First, since the University is located in the heart of a large urban area, DTU police potentially face some problems similar to those encountered by other urban

police.   Hence, comparability of data with urban
departments was enhanced.   Second, the University has
not been previously studied.   Third, DTU was selected
because of convenience for observation and the
researchers' familiarity with the area.   Fourth, the
police department at DTU was similar to other departments on campuses of a similar size in terms of composition of departmental personnel, recruitment procedures, training, type of equipment, non-policing
and policing duties.   Finally, while DTU is not representative of universities throughout the nation,
for campuses displaying similar characteristics
(e.g., size, urban location, non-residential, and so
forth) it is probably quite typical in terms of the
problems it faces and the nature of everyday
policing.[3]

Gaining entry

     The police have not been particularly receptive
to the idea of social investigators conducting
research on their organizations.   Van Maanen (1975),
for example, approached more than twenty urban police
departments before one agreed to allow his study of
academy training.   Scholars have posited a number of
reasons for the problem of gaining access to a police
department, including police distrust of the academic
outsider, fear of criticism of their administrative
and operational practices, threats to autonomy, the
nature of police work, (e.g., environmental danger),
and the nature of the occupational subculture with
its emphasis on police fraternity and occupational
secrecy (see, for example, Skolnick, 1966; Niederhoffer, 1967; Westley, 1970; Van Maanen, 1975).   In
contrast to the difficulty others have reported
regarding gaining entry into municipal departments,
gaining approval of the administration for access to
the university police department was relatively easy.
Perhaps the relative ease with which entry to the DTU
department was obtained can be largely attributed to
the absence of many of the usual obstacles to
research on municipal police.   For example, university police do not exhibit a high degree of police
fraternity and occupational secrecy nor do they work
in a dangerous environment.   Moreover, university
police are probably not as distrustful of "academic
outsiders" as other police are, because they have
contact with them on a daily basis by virtue of the
fact that they work in an academic environment.

The actual procedure for gaining entry to the DTU Police Department was formal in nature. In December 1980 a four page concept paper specifying the intent of the research was submitted via a liaison, the DTU Director of Research and Development, to the Chief of Police to see if he would be receptive to research on his organization. While the Chief was amenable to the study, he reserved judgment on final approval until such time as he would be able to assess a more detailed proposal of the purposes and procedures of the research. Again using the same go-between, at the beginning of March 1981 a full scale draft of the research proposal was submitted to the Chief and the Director of Safety and Security, who functions in the capacity of a commissioner of police at DTU. Ten days later the senior researcher met with the Chief, Director and liaison to discuss the proposal. Few questions were asked during the meeting and at its conclusion freedom of access was granted to all areas of operations. The senior researcher was told: "Whatever you need, just ask for it." Only two restrictions were placed on her by the administration: she was not to conceal her status as a researcher from members of the department and the participation of officers had to be voluntary.[4] In addition, she was required to sign a release and covenant not to sue the University in case of bodily injury or injury to her property in the course of data collection. Upon conclusion of the meeting, the Chief ordered that a memo be sent to line supervisors and staff personnel informing them of the study and its administrative sanction. Moreover, the Chief began paving the way by introducing the senior researcher to key staff personnel. His understanding of the nature of the research and general degree of cooperation are illustrated in the following statement made to the department's training officer:

> I want her to be treated just like the rest
> of the trainees when she goes through the
> training class. Make sure she gets all the
> handbooks, materials and whatever else the
> recruits are given. Treat her like one of
> them...teach her how to shoot a gun...
> fingerprint her...let her experience it all
> the same as the others.

In short, entry and approval for the study were gained easier than expected according to the literature. While a number of factors (e.g., use of a contact, personal character and openness of the Chief, nature of the university environment, personality and demeanor of the researchers, and so forth) probably influenced the decision to permit the research, one key factor seemed to be the thoroughness and sincerity of the formal proposal. The proposed study was presented in a non-critical, non-threatening manner. The proposal itself expressed a desire on the part of the researchers to seek knowledge and understand the university police occupation. Oftentimes during the course of the meeting with the Chief and Director comments such as "I can see you have really done your homework" or "I'm glad that you recognize that much of police work is menial" or "you really seem to want to truly understand this work" were made to the senior researcher in reference to statements made in the written proposal. The proposal not only demonstrated the researchers' intent but seemed to pique the interest of administrators to the point that they actually were eager for the study to be done. Thus, the formal proposal played a key role in gaining access to the DTU Police Department.

Field Work

The primary source of data was from observations of the operations of the DTU Police Department and of its patrolmen and their work in situ. Although informal observation of the university police took place over a period of several years, formal data collection was conducted early in 1981. The senior author made extensive primary observation over the three-month period of March through May.

Field work was conducted in two phases. The first phase consisted of a period of training and familiarization with the Department. The senior author formally participated in and completed the two week (80 hours) entry-level training program[5] required of incoming recruits in order to acquaint herself with the type of things officers are required to know in preparation for work in the field and to observe the initial stages of recruit socialization. In addition, during the first two weeks, numerous informal contacts and conversations with officers were initiated and departmental printed materials, forms and statistical records were reviewed.

The second phase of field work consisted primarily of observation of officers on their tours of duty. Approximately six and a half weeks (262 hours) were spent in this phase of field work. This amount of time in the field was more than sufficient to allow for numerous repetitive observations and in general to enable the researcher to reach a point of what Glaser and Strauss (1967) term saturation, or a point at which no new information is gained by continued observation. In order to provide a systematic coverage of normal police duties, observations were made of all line personnel, both supervisors and patrolmen, and on all days of the week, including both day and night shifts. The amount of time spent in observation of each shift reflected the relative amount of activity on that shift. In other words, observation time was concentrated on the most active shifts during the period of data collection. Approximately 24 percent of observation time was spent on the morning watch (11 P.M. to 7 A.M.), 34 percent on the day watch (7 A.M. to 3 P.M.) and 42 percent on the evening watch (3 P.M. to 11 P.M.). Upon beginning observations for each watch, the bulk of the first several days were spent with supervisors to gain familiarity with watch procedures and operations. The vast majority of time on each watch, however, was spent with officers in the field observing them in their daily work and task performance. At all times field work data were unobtrusively collected, and the researcher in no way interfered with the job assignments of officers. All data were systematically collected (e.g., time log of activities) and careful notes taken.

Gaining secondary access

Winning the approval and gaining the acceptance of street-level patrol officers was vital to the success of the research. Essentially the role assumed in observation was that which Gold (1958) termed observer-as-participant in that the role as researcher was made explicit to all officers from the outset. At no time during data collection was any attempt made to deceive participants about the researcher's status as a researcher. The general image presented to officers by the researcher was that of a hardworking, naive student of occupations who was genuinely interested in the welfare of the Department and the opinion and thoughts of individual officers. On the first day of observation of each watch the researcher was introduced to officers as a group during roll call and asked to say a few words. At this juncture officers were merely told that the researcher was conducting a study on what it is like to be a campus policeman, using an observational method that dictated that she spend some time with each of them in the field. Upon approaching officers in the field, the nature and purpose of the study were explained in more depth. At all times the study was justified to officers on the basis of its scientific merit and its contribution to scientific knowledge of policing in a variety of contexts. Stress was placed upon the intent of presenting the findings from the point of view of officers themselves and hence the need for their openness and cooperation. In return for their openness and cooperation, officers were offered nothing except confidentiality and the appreciation of the researcher. The combining of a sort of "fan role" (see, Van Maanen, 1978a:344) with an altruistic appeal proved effective in gaining officer participation in the study.

Gaining the confidence of officers did not prove to be especially problematic. Good rapport was established with all members of the force. Care was taken to avoid the appearance of a close alignment with any one individual or group over another. Consequently, despite some internal organizational conflicts between supervisory and patrol personnel, the researcher never perceived the rapport established with staff and supervisors in any way affected or hindered the rapport she was able to build with officers. Moreover, by maintaining a sort of "neutral" status, situations which might have resulted in the premature termination of the study were avoided.

The researcher's legitimacy derived from many sources, including the sanction of the Chief and the scholarly aims of the research. Three sources of legitimacy seemed most influential. First, officers who had already been observed were continually introducing the researcher to officers with whom she had no prior contact. During the course of these introductions comments such as "she's okay" or "she's all right" were often made. The sanction of officers with whom time had been previously spent was instrumental in gaining access to other officers. By the end of the first week in the field virtually every officer had learned via the grapevine "what the researcher was all about." Second, the researcher's willingness to listen played a key role in establishing legitimacy. Time spent with officers provided an opportunity for them to express their thoughts and opinions about their work--both positive and negative--to someone who was willing to listen in an objective, non-judgmental manner. Indeed, a few officers seemed so grateful to have the opportunity to express themselves that to them the researcher may have assumed a sort of unintended therapeutic role. The final source of legitimacy derived from the researcher's personal character. Occasionally patrolmen and supervisors would subject the researcher to a "prudence test" in which they would ask her to reveal information about what she had learned about their coworkers. On all occasions such information was refused. The meeting of this test by silence enabled the researcher to obtain data inaccessible through other means. The following officer comment is illustrative:

> I heard the supervisors tried to draw you
> into the gossip about officers and you kept
> your mouth shut. You're okay in my book.
> I'll tell you anything you want to
> know...just ask. I'll even tell you things
> you may not think to ask.

In general, the fact that the researcher was perceived as legitimate by officers and was able to gain their acceptance and confidence was demonstrated by the fact that they not only told her things which could have cost them their jobs but they openly engaged in behavior during observation which would result in trouble for them if it were revealed.

On a more general level, acceptance of the researcher's role by university policemen was enhanced by their knowledge about research per se. The very facts that officers work in an academic environment in which research is significnt and that many officers are themselves students suggest that university officers may be predisposed to understand the requirements of research and to accept it as valuable. Officer's understanding of the requirements of research was demonstrated by the unsolicited information and help they offered the researcher. For example, the training officer provided the researcher with printed materials (e.g., police manuals from

other colleges and universities) and literature citations that he believed might be helpful; several
officers directing traffic suggested the best vantage
point for observation; officers often sought out the
researcher to offer information relevant to an understanding of their work that had not been previously
discussed with the researcher; and so forth. The
officer's understanding of the value of research was
reflected in their enthusiasm about and interest in
the study from the onset. Staff officers seemed to
actually be looking forward to the study and what
they might learn from it. Comments such as the
following were typical among staff officers:

> I'm looking forward to seeing some real life
> data. It should be interesting. I'm very
> glad you are doing this study. This depart-
> ment needs to be looked at. We can learn a
> lot from your study.

Patrolmen seemed to be interested in the study
because they recognized the value of research in
effecting potential change.6 Upon completion of
formal and informal conversations with officers, on
numerous occasions they volunteered that they had
been open and candid because they felt the research
would do some good for officers "with the powers that
be" and lead to changes within the Department. The
following comment was representative:

> I was open with you because I hope your
> study will do some good for officers and the
> Department. Before changes can be made the
> facts have to be known. Your research will
> provide those facts.

In short, gaining access to patrolmen was not
problematic. Acceptance of the researcher was enhanced by the sanction of the Chief, scholarly aims,
officers who already participated, the researcher's
willingness to listen and personal character, and
officer's understanding of the requirements and value
of research. All university police personnel were
friendly, cordial and cooperative throughout the
period of data collection.

Researcher involvement

The degree of involvement of the researcher as an

observer varied somewhat thoughout the study. As already noted, the researcher was more or less a fully participating member of the recruit class but after training she took the role of a modified participant observer; that is, she observed officers on duty. Nevertheless, the researcher did become involved in matters of a routine nature on a daily basis. While on patrol, she often became somewhat of an unappointed assistant to the officer she was observing, doing little things that the officer would have had to do on his or her own if the researcher had not been along. For example, on numerous occasions the researcher would "shake knobs" on one side of the hallway during interior foot patrol while the officer would cover the other side or she would check female restrooms in lieu of the officer to make sure they were "secure" during lockup. This degree of involvement by the observer in routine tasks is an unavoidable part of the methodology utilized. Beyond this involvement in routine tasks the researcher remained strictly an observer.

Researcher effect

One problem the research approach raises is whether the observer's presence significantly altered the normal manner and behavior of the university police (see, for example, McCall and Simmons, 1969). All officers appeared to act normally and naturally around the researcher. For example, they continued to "eye foxes" (girls) in the halls, took unreported breaks and engaged in other behavior which might have resulted in their getting in trouble if viewed by a supervisor. Moreover, in many situations (e.g., suspicious person searches, assignments, lockups) officers were not free to alter their behavior. There were, however, two situations in the initial stages of observation in which the normal routine of officers was altered apparently for the benefit of the researcher. Both situations resulted from watch supervisor's desire to ensure that their watch received a favorable review in the research report. The first situation involved the extra inspection of officers during roll call. This alteration was brought to the attention of the researcher by many of the officers on the watch. The following comment was typical:

We are having all these inspections to try

239

and impress you. We really haven't had one
in four months since evaluations until you
showed up. Now we have one everyday you are
here.

The second situation involved the denial by a supervisor of normal traffic relief for an experienced
officer by a new recruit the first day the researcher
was observing traffic. The recruit, with whom the
researcher had been through entry-level training,
informed the researcher that the lack of relief was
due to the researcher's presence. His comment sums up
the intent of this alteration in normal routine:

They (supervisors) aren't letting me take
over even though I was supposed to fifteen
minutes ago because you're out here
watching. They are trying to impress you so
you will write nice things about this watch.
They're not really trying to pull the wool
over your eyes, they just want to make sure
nothing goes wrong. That's why they are
keeping the experienced guy out there.
Since I am new they figure I might screw up
and they don't want you to see that.

Both situations were handled by the researcher by
spending more time with supervisors before observations proceeded. During the course of informal conversations with supervisors, the researcher tried to
make them aware that her purpose was not to try to
rate officers or find something wrong with them but
rather to observe them in their normal activities to
understand the problems they have to contend with in
doing their job. As supervisors became familiar with
the researcher and accepted the premise of the
research, their attempts to alter the normal routine
of officers ceased entirely. This fact was repeatedly
verified by officers in the field throughout the remainder of the period of data collection.

In short, the Department operated on a normal
basis with the exception of the two situations in the
early stages of data collection. Otherwise, the
researcher's presence did not alter the normal
routine and behavior of officers.7 From the onset
rapport with officers was sufficiently good that they
informed the researcher when alterations did occur.
The more time spent with subjects the more used to
the researcher's presence they became. The cummula-

240

tive effect of familiarity weakened defenses against the researcher's presence. While there is no absolute way to assess researcher effect, it appears that the effect of the researcher's presence decreased with time. Given the overall lack of significant alterations in behavior in response to the presence of the observer, concern regarding the authenticity and representativeness of the data is greatly reduced.

Interviews

Observational data was supplemented with data obtained from in-depth personal interviews by the senior author with uniformed line officers, including both supervisory and patrol personnel. Interviews were conducted on duty after obtaining "on duty permission" from the lieutenant of each watch. They ranged in length from 45 minutes to 4 hours with the average length being 1 1/2 hours[8]. Most interviews were conducted during "quiet times" (e.g., late evening, early morning, weekends) when fewer campus community members were present and thus privacy, freedom of expression and participant anonymity were enhanced in the interview situation. Informed consent was obtained from all participants. Prior to interviewing the nature and purpose of the study was explained and each subject was required to read and sign a consent form which requested each person's cooperation in the study, but made it clear that their participation was voluntary, that they had the right of withdrawal at any time, that the information supplied would be held strictly confidential, and that no one in the Department would ever see anyone's individual responses.

Among other things the schedule was devised to obtain pertinent data about background, experience, life pattern, perception of occupational status, mobility, occupational ideology, vocational choice and working conditions.[9] Attitudinal questions concentrated upon the officers' perceptions and affective responses toward different features of their work situation. Though a more or less structured schedule was used, interviews themselves were largely informal and open-ended. Given the exploratory nature of the study, the interview schedule was used as a guide, and officers were encouraged to go beyond the questions. Moreover, they were given latitude for free and spontaneous expression of thoughts and feelings which they believed would be important to an understanding of their work lives. Occasional random probes of structured questions were employed to enhance understanding and to assess the validity of the questions themselves.

Given the relatively small size of the DTU police force, attempts were made to conduct interviews with all uniformed line officers. Of the 55 uniformed line officers at the time of data collection only two refused to be interviewed. This resulted in a response rate of 96 percent and a total sample size of 53 officers. Both of the refusals came from patrolmen who simply preferred not to participate in the in-depth interviews in order to avoid "publicly expressing their opinions on the record." However, during the course of data collection numerous informal "off the record" questions were asked of these officers and it did not appear that their opinions and attitudes differed in any significant way from officers who granted interviews. Thus, it is felt that non-participation of these officers did not in any way bias the final sample.

Given the relatively small size of the DTU police force, attempts were made to talk with all members of the force at some time or another. While the interview schedule was only administered to uniformed line personnel, many pertinent topics of investigation were broached on numerous occasions in more informal conversations with the six remaining members of the force who comprise the staff and administrative personnel. These more informal interviews enabled the researchers to gain a greater understanding of and perspective on the entire university police organization.

Protection of Subjects and Department

The confidentiality of information obtained from respondents was protected by means of a two-step procedure. First, subjects were assigned a code number for purposes of identification and to protect the anonymity of their responses. Individual data were identified only by code number. Only the researchers had access to the data base. Subjects were assured that no one else would be allowed to see their answers except in tabular form. The names of respondents and any other personal identifying information used in conducting interviews and making observations were destroyed by the researchers upon completion of the study. Second, where direct quotes were used to supplement statistical findings no reference to police officers' names were made nor were specific dates mentioned. Respondents were identified only by their structural position within the organization (e.g., recruit, patrolman, supervisor, and so forth). Where only one person occupied a given position a more nebulous title was used (e.g., a high ranking official).

The anonymity of the University and police department was maintained through the use of a pseudonym for the police force (i.e., DTU Police Department) and non-specific description of the location of the study. In addition, no reference was made to any state law or city ordinance that might aid in identification of where investigation took place. Strict adherence to these procedures virtually eliminated all potential risks (e.g., loss of job, demotion, criticism from internal or external sources) to both subjects and the University.

Description of Location of Study

In order to provide context for the findings it is necessary to provide a brief description of the location of the study. There are essentially two unique features of DTU that might bear upon policing--institutional characteristics and the campus atmosphere. Institutional characteristics include the objective qualities of the university that are important in determining the type of problems that arise on campus. The campus atmosphere includes the subjective qualities of the university that are affected by the institutional characteristics.

Institutional Characteristics

DTU is a non-residential state supported, public institution located in an urban setting in the South. It is a "high rise" university with multi-story classroom buildings. Most of the physical plant is concentrated in a four block downtown area. In addition, the University owns several properties and rents space in several buildings within a two block area surrounding the perimeter of the campus proper.

Included in this adjacent area are several parking lots and parking decks which in and of themselves do not provide adequate space for the large commuting population of the university.

Average student enrollment per quarter is approximately 20,000. Most DTU students come from a middle class background; more than three-fourths (78%) work while pursuing their studies. Approximately one third (34%) of the student body are graduate students. Also, the average DTU student is older than the average student in most American colleges and universities. Average age of undergraduate and graduate students is 25 and 31, respectively, with the average age of all students being 27.

The University offers a wide range of curricula and degree levels. Its six colleges offer 46 degree programs ranging from associates to doctorates with 197 areas of concentration. In addition to undergraduate, graduate and advanced professional programs, DTU offers expanded credit and non-credit educational opportunities in continuing education. Moreover, to serve the needs of a working and non-working commuting student population there is a very flexible academic scheduling pattern at DTU. In an average quarter over 2,000 course sections are scheduled from 8 A.M. to 10 P.M.

Essentially, DTU has two different student bodies--day and night. During the Fall quarter 1980 there were a total of 20,333 students at the University. The day students included 8,965 undergraduates and 2,216 graduate students for a total of 11,181 or 55 percent of the degree-seeking student body. The night students included 4,475 undergraduates and 4,677 graduate students for a total of 9,152 or 45 percent of the student body. Interestingly, these student enrollment statistics indicate that there are approximately twice as many undergraduate students in the day as at night and there are approximately twice as many graduate students at night as in the day. In general the young, inquiring, full-time students pursue their studies during the day and the more mature working students pursue their studies at night.

In addition to the student body, the university community is composed of numerous other people-- faculty, clerical, professional non-faculty, executive administrative managers, service, technical and

244

skilled craft personnel. In general, members of the community come from differing social, economic and ethnic backgrounds and have varied interests. Thus, the university is a heterogeneous community.

Campus Atmosphere

The University operates in an open academic atmosphere characterized by a climate of academic freedom in which creativity and innovation are encouraged. Students are exposed to a number of different ideas and a rich program of cultural events; faculty are free to express a myriad of beliefs in their classrooms, including radical beliefs. Despite the liberal character that this open academic atmosphere implies, the overall tone on campus is moderately conservative. Several possible explanations for this conservative tone exist, including DTU's location in and drawing the majority of its community members from the deep south (a region known for its conservative beliefs and attitudes), the general lack of political radicalization on the part of most students and faculty,[10] the strong historical dominance of the Business Administration faculty on campus (who set a conservative tone by training students to assume positions in the status quo), the absence of residences on campus, the fact that the average student on campus is a working adult in his mid twenties who not only already has a stake in the status quo but who enters the university to receive an education that further entrenches him in the status quo, and so forth. Given this conservative tone on campus coupled with the nature of the community (e.g., working, mature, commuting, and so forth) it is not surprising that DTU did not experience the campus disorders that plagued many other campuses during the 1960s and early 1970s.

In addition to the conservative tone on campus, another unique feature of the DTU campus atmosphere is the general lack of student life as is found on most other campuses. While there are over 100 student organizations on campus ranging from social fraternities and sororities to professional and honor societies, only a minority of the students actively participate in them. The separation of day and night students into two student bodies, the nonresidential commuter status of students, and the job and family interests of most students serve not only to reduce

245

social contacts on campus and increase student isolation but also to reduce participation in student activities and impede the development of student life.

Notes

[1]To date a number of contemporary researchers of police have employed varying degrees of the participant observation methodology in their attempts to gain an intimate understanding of the policeman and his or her world by actually riding with him or her and observing his or her activities in situ (see, Skolnick, 1966; Buckner, 1967; Petersen, 1968; Westley, 1970; Reiss, 1971; Rubinstein, 1973; Davis, 1979). All of these scholars have extolled the value of this experiential technique to the understanding of everyday policing.

[2]In the analysis of data the merging of the survey and observation approaches to field research was difficult because the two styles pulled in opposite directions, the former method being specific and the latter general. In analysis the researchers felt pressure on the one hand to tackle larger issues and on the other to ignore richness of context and concentrate solely on quantifiable aspects. Nevertheless, the two methods provide an excellent complement to each other.

[3]More limited observations and informal conversations with university police officers were undertaken at several other campuses. There was considerable variability in the sites visited by the authors in terms of pertinent campus characteristics. However, these other "slices of data" (Glaser and Strauss, 1967) did not lead us to alter our interpretation of the phenomenon of campus policing gleaned from the primary research site.

[4]It should be noted that these restrictions did not alter the researchers' plans since they had been formally incorporated in the proposal by the researchers themselves because of University requirements regarding informed consent.

[5]Entry-level training programs are conducted relatively frequently, though sporadically, throughout the year by the Department because of a high rate of personnel turnover among patrol officers. Fortunately, the start of one of these training programs coincided perfectly with the onset of data collection.

[6]Oftentimes patrolmen inquired as to whether "the report" would help officers. They were offered no guarantees except to say that the report would present their point of view and that more than likely the Chief would read it. However, as to whether it would in fact effect change was anyone's guess.

[7]Numerous observational researchers of police have implicitly stated that their presence did not significantly alter the normal behavior of their subjects. See, for example, Skolnick (1966:36), Petersen (1968:57-63), Kirkham (1974:35-52), and Sanders (1977:202-205).

[8]Since interviews were conducted on duty they were occasionally interrupted by officers' obligations. Minor interruptions (e.g., answering a brief request for information, conducting a radio check) of less than two minutes duration were calculated as part of interview time. Interruptions of more than two minutes were deleted from calculation. Thus, the figures presented reflect actual interview time not the period of time over which it took to complete an interview.

[9]A draft of the interview schedule was submitted to the Chief prior to the initiation of interviews. At this juncture he was given the opportunity to delete any items he might find objectionable. The fact that the Chief made virtually no changes in the draft further attests to the freedom with which the researchers were permitted to conduct the study.

[10]While activist groups do exist on campus their strength is minimal. Occasionally groups react to national and international issues but if a demonstration does occur it usually has few participants and is of a nonviolent and nondisruptive nature.

REFERENCES

Abramson, S. A.
  1974 "A survey of campus police departments."
        The Police Chief 41:54-56.
Adams, G. B., and P. G. Rogers
  1971 Campus Policing: The State of the Art. Los
        Angeles: University of Southern Califor-
        nia, Center for Justice Administration.
Alex, N.
  1969 Black in Blue: A Study of the Negro Police-
        man. New York: Appleton-Century-Crofts.
Balch, R. W.
  1972 "The police personality: fact or fiction."
        The Journal of Criminology, Criminal Law and
        Police Science 63:106-119.
Banton, M.
  1964 The Policeman in the Community. New York:
        Basic.
Barker, T., and J. Roebuck
  1973 An Empirical Typology of Police Corruption:
        A Study in Organizational Deviance. Spring-
        field, Ill.: Thomas.
Bartram, J. L., and L. E. Smith
  1969 "A survey of campus police forces." Journal
        of the College and University Personnel
        Association 21:34-42.
Barzun, J.
  1968 The American University: How It Runs, Where
        It Is Going. New York: Harper and Row.
Bayley, D. H., and H. Mendelsohn
  1969 Minorities and the Police: Confrontation in
        America. New York: Free Press.
Becker, H. S.
  1963 Outsiders: Studies in the Sociology of De-
        viance. London: Free Press.
Becker, H. S. (ed.)
  1970 Campus Power Struggle. Chicago: Aldine.
Bercal, T. E.
  1970 "Calls for police assistance: consumer de-
        mands for governmental service." American
        Behavioral Scientist 13:681-692.
Biddle, B. J., and E. J. Thomas (eds.)
  1966 Role Theory: Concepts and Research. New
        York: Wiley.
Bielec, J. A.
  1981 "Uniform crime report participation: mixing

249

apples and oranges." Campus Law Enforcement Journal 11:26-28.

Bittner, E.
  1967a "Police discretion in emergency apprehension of mentally ill persons." Social Problems 14:278-292.
  1967b "The police on skid-row: a study of peace keeping." American Sociological Review 32:699-715.
  1970 The Functions of Police in Modern Society. Washington, D.C.: Government Printing Office.

Black, D. J.
  1970 "Production of crime rates." American Sociological Review 35:733-748.
  1978 "The mobilization of law," in P. K. Manning and J. Van Maanen (eds.), Policing: A View from the Street. Santa Monica, Calif.: Goodyear.

Black, D. J., and A. J. Reiss, Jr.
  1967 "Patterns of behavior in police and citizen transactions," in A. J. Reiss, Studies in Crime and Law Enforcement in Major Metropolitan Areas. Volume II. Washington, D.C.: Government Printing Office.
  1970 "Police control of juveniles." American Sociological Review 35:63-77.

Bogdan, R., and S. J. Taylor
  1975 Introduction to Qualitative Research Methods. New York: Wiley.

Bordua, D. J., and A. J. Reiss
  1966 "Command, control, and charisma: reflections on police bureaucracy." American Journal of Sociology 72:68-76.

Braun, M., and D. J. Lee
  1971 "Private police forces: legal powers and limitations." University of Chicago Law Review 38:555-582.

Buckner, H. T.
  1967 The Police: The Culture of a Social Control Agency. Unpublished Ph.D. dissertation, University of California, Berkeley.

Caffrey, J. (ed.)
  1969 The Future Academic Community. Washington, D.C.: American Council on Education.

Calder, J. D.
  1974 "Policing and securing campus: the need for complimentary organizations." The Police Chief 41:60-64.

Cardarelli, A. P.
   1968 "An analysis of police killed by criminal action: 1961-1963." Journal of Criminal Law, Criminology and Police Science 59:447-453.

Chevigny, P.
   1969 Police Power: Police Abuses in New York City. New York: Vintage.

Clark, J. P.
   1965 "Isolation of the police: a comparison of the British and American situations." The Journal of Criminal Law, Criminology, and Police Science 56:307-319.

Clark, J. P., and R. E. Sykes
   1974 "Some determinants of police organization and practice in a modern industrial democracy," in D. Glaser (ed.), Handbook of Criminology. Chicago: Rand McNally.

Cohen, B., and J. M. Chaiken
   1973 Police Background Characteristics and Performances. Lexington, Mass.: D.C. Heath.

Cox, B. D.
   1977 "University police departments - are they necessary?" Campus Law Enforcement Journal 7: 43-44.

Cox, B., and D. Southerland
   1979 "A security dilemma." Campus Law Enforcement Journal 9:16-17.

Csanyi, L. H.
   1958 Parking Practices on College Campuses in the United States. Iowa Engineering Experiment Station, Bulletin 181, Vol LVII, October. Ames: Iowa State College.

Cumming, E., I. Cumming, and L. Edell
   1965 "Policeman as philosopher, guide and friend." Social Problems 12:276-86.

Cummins, M.
   1971 "Police and service work," in H. Hahn (ed.), Police in Urban Society. Beverly Hills: Sage.

Davis, P. W.
   1979 The Working Role of the Police Officer: Unofficial Police Work and Order Maintenance. Unpublished Ph.D. dissertation, University of California, Los Angeles.

Drapeau, R. F., and M. J. Cudmore
   1979 "Attitudes relating to the female officer." Campus Law Enforcement Journal 9:32-34.

Draper, H.
   1978 Private Police. Atlantic Highlands, New

Jersey: Humanities Press.

Dynes, R. R., E. L. Quarantelli, and J. L. Ross
1974 "Police perspectives and behavior in a campus disturbance," in D. E. MacNamara and M. Riedel (eds.), Police: Perspectives, Problems, Prospects. New York: Praeger.

Edwards, G.
1968 The Police on the Urban Frontier. New York: Institute of Human Relations Press.

Epstein, C.
1962 Intergroup Relations for Police Offiers. Baltimore: Williams & Wilkins.

Erikson, K. T.
1962 "Notes on the sociology of deviance." Social Problems 9:307-314.

Etheridge, R. F.
1958 A Study of Campus Protective and Enforcement Agencies at Selected Universities. Unpublished Ph.D. dissertation, Michigan State University, East Lansing.

Federal Bureau of Investigation
1980 Uniform Crime Reports for the United States. Washington, D.C.: U.S. Government Printing Office.

Flicker, B. (ed.)
1969 The Campus Crisis: Legal Problems of University Discipline, Administration and Expansion. New York: Practicing Law Institute.

Gardiner, J. P.
1969 Traffic and the Police: Variations in Law Enforcement Policy. Cambridge: Harvard University Press.

Gelber, S.
1972 The Role of Campus Security in the College Setting. Washington, D.C.: Government Printing Office.

Glaser, B. G., and A. L. Strauss
1967 The Discovery of Grounded Theory. Chicago: Aldine.

Gold, R. L.
1958 "Roles in sociological field observations." Social Forces 36:217-223.

Goldstein, H.
1963 "Police discretion: the ideal versus the real." Public Administration Review 23:140-148.
1977 Policing in a Free Society. Cambridge, Mass.: Ballinger.

Goodman, N., and G. T. Marx
    1978   Society Today. New York: CRM/Random House.
Gray, T.
    1975   "Selecting for a police subculture," in
            J. Skolnick and L. Cooper (eds.), Police in
            America. Boston: Little, Brown.
Gunson, H. P.
    1979   "Integrated function: the role of campus
            police." Campus Law Enforcement Journal
            9:40-41.
Harris, R. N.
    1973   The Police Academy: An Inside View. New
            York: Wiley.
Hollingshead, A. B., and F. C. Redlich
    1958   Social Class and Mental Illness. New York:
            Wiley.
Holloman, F. C.
    1972   "The new breed: college and university
            police." The Police Chief 39:41-45.
Holmes, G. W. (ed.)
    1969   Student Protest and the Law. Benton Harbor,
            Michigan: Patterson.
Iannarelli, A. V.
    1968   The Campus Police. Hayward, Calif.: Photo-
            Form.
Johnson, D., and R. J. Gregory
    1971   "Police-community relations in the United
            States: a review of recent literature and
            prospects." The Journal of Criminal Law,
            Criminology and Police Science 62:94-103.
Kakalik, J. S., and S. Wildhorn
    1977   The Private Police: Security and Danger.
            New York: Crane Russak.
Katz, D., and R. L. Kahn
    1966   The Social Psychology of Organizations. New
            York: Wiley.
Kassinger, E. T.
    1971   "Professional campus law enforcement: res-
            ponsibility of the academic community," in
            O.S. Sims (ed.), New Directions in Campus
            Law Enforcement: A Handbook for Adminis-
            trators. Athens, Ga: University of Georgia
            Center for Continuing Education.
    1972   "The establishment of a philosophy of law
            enforcement in the academic community, in
            O. S. Sims (ed.), The Challenge of New
            Directions in Campus Law Enforcement.
            Athens, Ga.: University of Georgia Center
            for Continuing Education.
    1980   "Campus law enforcement administration for

the 1980's." Campus Law Enforcement Journal 10:9-13.

Kimble, J. P.
1978 "Trying to be objective about our objectives." Campus Law Enforcement Journal 8:28-33.

Kirkham, G. L.
1974 "The criminologist as policeman: a participant-observation study," in D. MacNamara and M. Riedel (eds.), Police: Perspectives, Problems, Prospects. New York: Praeger.

Kirkley, J. A.
1978 "Are we private police or a security guard?" The Police Chief 45:36-38.

Kitsuse, J. I.
1962 "Societal reaction to deviant behavior: problems of theory and method." Social Problems 9:247-256.

Kobetz, R. W., and C. W. Hamm (eds.)
1970 Campus Unrest: Dialogue or Destruction? Lincoln: University of Nebraska Press.

Kornblum, A. N.
1976 The Moral Hazards. Lexington, Mass.: Heath.

Kroes, W. H.
1976 Society's Victim - the Policeman. Springfield, Ill.: Thomas.

Kroes, W. H., B. L. Margolia and J. J. Hurrell, Jr.
1974 "Job stress in policemen." Journal of Police Science and Administration 2:145-155.

LaFave, W. R.
1965 Arrest: The Decision to Take a Suspect into Custody. Boston: Little, Brown.

Lofland, J.
1971 Analyzing Social Settings: A Guide to Qualitative Observation and Analysis. Belmont, Calif.: Wadsworth.

Lundman, R. J.
1974 "Routine police arrest practices: a commonweal perspective." Social Problems 22:127-141.
1980 Police and Policing: An Introduction. New York: Holt, Rinehart and Winston.

Manning, P. K.
1974 "Police lying." Urban Life 3:283-306.
1977 Police Work: The Social Organization of Policing. Cambridge: MIT Press.

Manning, P. K., and J. Van Maanen (eds.)
1978 Policing: A View from the Street. Santa Monica, Calif.: Goodyear.

254

Mapes, G.
    1968 "Campus shoplifting." Security World 5:29-
          32.
McCall, G. J., and J. L. Simmons (eds.)
    1969 Issues in Participant Observation. Menlo
          Park, Calif.: Addison-Wesley.
McDaniel, W. E.
    1970 "Safety and security on campus." The Police
          Chief 37:68-70.
    1971 "Law enforcement: the officer as educator,"
          in O. S. Sims (ed.), New Directions in Cam-
          pus Law Enforcement: A Handbook for Admin-
          istrators.   Athens, Ga.:   University of
          Georgia Center for Continuing Education.
McGovern, J. L.
    1980 "Crime on campus 1978." Campus Law Enforce-
          ment Journal 10:34-41.
    1981 "Crime on campus 1979." Campus Law Enforce-
          ment Journal 11:40-50.
McNamara, J. H.
    1967 "Uncertainties in police work: the rele-
          vance of police recruits' backgrounds and
          training," in D. J. Bordua (ed.), The
          Police: Six Sociological Essays. New York:
          Wiley.
Merton, R. K.
    1957 Social Theory and Social Structure. New
          York: Free Press.
Misner, G.
    1967 "The urban police mission." Issues in Crim-
          inology 3:35-46.
Morgan, J. P.
    1979 "Guns on campus." Campus Law Enforcement
          Journal 9:16-18.
Muir, W. K.
    1977 Police: Streetcorner Politicians. Chicago:
          University of Chicago Press.
Myren, R. A.
    1960 "A crisis in police management." The Jour-
          nal of Criminal Law, Criminology and Police
          Science 50: 600-604.
National Advisory Commission on Criminal Justice
    Standards & Goals
    1973 Report on Police. Washington, D.C.:
          Government Printing Office.
    1976 Private Security: Report of the Task Force
          on Private Security. Washington, D.C.:
          Government Printing Office.
National Center for Educational Statistics
    1981 Digest of Educational Statistics. Washing-

ton, D.C.: Government Printing Office.

Neil, R. E.
   1980 "A history of campus security: early
         origins." Campus Law Enforcement Journal
         10:28-30.

Ness, J. J.
   1980 "Perceptions of campus law enforcement:
         security or police." Campus Law Enforcement
         Journal 10:24-27.

Newsweek
   1982 "Crime on the campus." 99:82.

Nichols, D. C., and O. Mills (eds.)
   1970 The Campus and Racial Crisis. Washington,
         D.C.: American Council on Education.

Niederhoffer, A.
   1967 Behind the Shield: The Police in Urban
         Society. New York: Doubleday.

Nielsen, R. C.
   1974 "Campus mounties UCONN style." The Police
         Chief 41:60-61.

Nielsen, S. C.
   1971 General Organizational & Administrative Con-
         cepts for University Police. Springfield,
         Ill.: Thomas.

O'Toole, G.
   1978 The Private Sector: Private Spies, Rent-a-
         cops, and the Police-industrial Complex.
         New York: Norton.

Parsons, T.
   1951 The Social System. New York: Free Press.

Peabody, R. F.
   1977 "New resource for campus police - student
         security aides." The Police Chief 44:50-51.

Peabody, R. R.
   1975 "The new thief on the campus." The Police
         Chief 42:246-247.

Petersen, D. M.
   1968 The Police, Discretion and the Decision to
         Arrest. Unpublished Ph.D. dissertation,
         University of Kentucky, Lexington.
   1971 "Informal norms and police practice: the
         traffic ticket quota system." Sociology and
         Social Research 55:354-362.
   1972 "Police disposition of the petty offender."
         Sociology and Social Research 56:320-330.
   1974 "The police officer's conception of proper
         police work." The Police Journal 47:173-
         177.

Piliavin, I., and S. Briar
   1964 "Police encounters with juveniles." Ameri-

can Journal of Sociology 70:206-214.

Post, R. S., and A. A. Kingsbury
    1977 Security Administration: An Introduction.
          Springfield, Ill.: Thomas.

Powell, J. W.
    1967 "Professionalizing campus security." Secur-
          ity World 4:23-27.
    1971a "The history and proper role of campus
          security: part one." Security World 8:18-
          22.
    1971b "The history and proper role of campus sec-
          urity: part two." Security World 8:19-25.
    1981 Campus Security and Law Enforcement. Bos-
          ton: Butterworth.

President's Commission on Campus Unrest
    1971 The Report of the Commission on Campus
          Unrest. Washington, D.C.: Government
          Printing Office.

President's Commission on Law Enforcement and the
    Administration of Justice
    1967 Task Force Report: The Police. Washington,
          D.C.: Government Printing Office.

Quinney, R.
    1964 "Crime in political perspective." The Amer-
          ican Behavioral Scientist 8:19-22.

Regoli, R. M., E. D. Poole, and J. D. Hewitt
    1979 "Refining police cynicism theory: an empir-
          ical assessment, evaluation and implica-
          tions," in D. M. Petersen (ed.), Police
          Work: Strategies and Outcomes in Law En-
          forcement. Beverly Hills: Sage.

Reid, S. T.
    1982 Crime and Criminology. New York: Holt,
          Rinehart and Winston.

Reiser, M.
    1976 "Stress, distress and adaptation in police
          work." Police Chief 43:24-27.

Reiss, A. J.
    1971 The Police and the Public. New Haven: Yale
          University Press.

Reiss, A. J., Jr., and D. J. Bordua
    1967 "Environment and organization: a perspec-
          tive on the police," in D. J. Bordua (ed.),
          The Police: Six Sociological Essays. New
          York: Wiley.

Richardson, J. F.
    1974 Urban Police in the United States. New
          York: Kennihat.

Ricks, T. A., B. G. Tillett, and C. W. Van Meter
    1981 Principles of Security. Chicago: Anderson.

Ritzer, G.
    1977 Working: Conflict and Change. Englewood
         Cliffs, N.J.: Prentice-Hall.
Rubinstein, J.
    1973 City Police. New York: Ballantine.
Sacks, H.
    1972 "Notes on police assessment of moral charac-
         ter," in D. Sudnow (ed.), Studies in Social
         Interaction. New York: Free Press.
Sanders, W. B.
    1977 Detective Work: A Study of Criminal Invest-
         igations. New York: Free Press.
Scott, E. J.
    1976 "College and university police agencies,
         police services study report 10." Workshop
         in Political Theory and Policy Analysis,
         Indiana University.
Scott, T. M., and M. McPherson
    1971 "The development of the private sector of
         the criminal justice system." Law and
         Society Review 6:267-288.
Selltiz, C., L. S. Wrightsman, and S. W. Cook
    1976 Research Methods in Social Relations. New
         York: Holt, Rinehard and Winston.
Shanahan, M.
    1974 "A criminal justice venture: the University
         of Washington Police Department." The
         Police Chief 41:72-75.
Sherman, L. W. (ed.)
    1974 Police Corruption: A Sociological Perspec-
         tive. Garden City, N.Y.: Doubleday/Anchor.
Sims, O. S. (ed.)
    1971 New Directions in Campus Law Enforcement: A
         Handbook for Administrators. Athens, Ga:
         University of Georgia Center for Continuing
         Education.
    1972 The Challenge of New Directions in Campus
         Law Enforcement. Athens, Ga.: University
         of Georgia Center for Continuing Education.
Skolnick, J. H.
    1966 Justice Without Trial: Law Enforcement in
         Democratic Society. New York: Wiley.
    1969 The Politics of Protest. New York: Simon
         and Schuster.
Skolnick, J. H., and J. R. Woodworth
    1967 "Bureaucracy, information and social con-
         trol: a study of a morals detail," in D. J.
         Bordua (ed.), The Police: Six Sociological
         Essays. New York: Wiley.

Stark, R.
1972 Police Riots: Collective Violence and Law Enforcement. Belmont, Calif.: Focus Books.

Steinberg, S. R.
1972 "Private police practices and problems." Law and the Social Order 1972:585-604.

Sterling, J. W.
1972 Changes in Role Concepts of Police Officers. Washington, D.C.: International Association of Chiefs of Police.

Stoddard, E. R.
1968 "The informal code of police deviancy: a group approach to blue-coat crime." The Journal of Criminal Law, Criminology and Police Science 59: 201-213.

Stratton, J.G.
1978 "Police stress: an overview." The Police Chief 45:58-62.

Sudnow, D.
1965 "Normal crimes: sociological features of the penal code in a public defender's office." Social Problems 12:255-276.

Tauber, R. K.
1967 "Danger and the police: a theoretical analysis." Issues in Criminology 3:69-81.

Tifft, L. L.
1970 Comparative Police Supervision Systems: An Organizational Analysis. Unpublished Ph.D. dissertation, University of Illinois, Urbana.

University Facilities Research Center
1964 Parking Problems for Universities. Madison: University of Wisconsin Monograph.

U.S. News and World Report
1982 "Colleges fight back against campus crime." 92:49.

Van Maanen, J.
1973 "Observations on the making of policemen." Human Organization 32:407-418.
1975 "Police socialization: a longitudinal examination of job attitudes in an urban police department." Administrative Science Quarterly 20:207-228.
1978a "Epilogue on watching the watchers," in P. K. Manning and J. Van Maanen (eds.), Policing: A View from the Street. Santa Monica, Calif.: Goodyear.
1978b "Kinsmen in repose: occupational perspectives of patrolmen," in P. K. Manning and J. Van Maanen (eds.), Policing: A View from

the Street. Santa Monica, Calif.:
Goodyear.

1978c "The asshole," in P. K. Manning and J. Van
Maanen (eds.), Policing: A View from the
Street. Santa Monica, Calif.: Goodyear.
Wallace, L. A.
1978 "Stress and its impact on the law enforcement officer." Campus Law Enforcement Journal 8:36-40.
Watson, N. A., and J. W. Sterling
1969 Police and Their Opinions. Washington,
D.C.: International Association of Chiefs
of Police.
Webb, J. C., Jr.
1975 "The well-trained, professional university
police officer - fact or fiction?" BBI Law
Enforcement Bulletin 44:26-31.
Weber, M.
1946 "The theory of social and economic organizations," in H. H. Gerth and C. W. Mills
(trans.), Max Weber: Essays in Sociology.
New York: Oxford University Press.
Webster, J. A.
1970 "Police task and time study." The Journal
of Criminal Law, Criminology and Police
Science 61:94-100.
1973 The Realities of Police Work. Dubuque,
Iowa: Kendall/Hunt.
Westley, W. A.
1956 "Secrecy and the police." Social Forces
34:254-257.
1970 Violence and the Police: A Sociological
Study of Law, Custom and Morality. Cambridge: MIT Press.
Whittmore, L. H.
1969 Cop! A Closeup of Violence and Tragedy.
New York: Holt, Rinehart & Winston.
Williams, R.
1979 "CMU designs officer form evaluation." Campus Law Enforcement Journal 9:42-45.
Wilson, J. Q.
1968 Varieties of Police Behavior: The Management of Law and Order in Eight Communities.
Cambridge: Harvard University Press.

CASES

Dixon v. Alabama State Board of Education, 294F.2d,
150, U.S. Court of Appeals, Fifth Circuit, August
1961.